aristophanes

FOUR PLAYS

aristophanes

FOUR PLAYS

CLOUDS

BIRDS

LYSISTRATA

WOMEN OF THE ASSEMBLY

TRANSLATED BY

aaron poochigian

Liveright Publishing Corporation

A Division of W. W. Norton & Company

Independent Publishers Since 1923

New York · London

For information about permission to reproduce selections from this book, write to
Permissions, Liveright Publishing Corporation, a division of W. W. Norton & Company, Inc.,
500 Fifth Avenue, New York, NY 10110

For information about special discounts for bulk purchases, please contact
W. W. Norton Special Sales at specialsales@wwnorton.com or 800-233-4830

Manufacturing by LSC Communications, Harrisonburg
Book design by Chris Welch
Production manager: Anna Oler

Library of Congress Cataloging-in-Publication Data

Names: Aristophanes, author. | Poochigian, Aaron, 1973– translator. |
Aristophanes. Birds. English. | Aristophanes. Clouds. English. | Aristophanes. Lysistrata. English. |
Aristophanes. Ecclesiazusae. English.
Title: Four plays : Clouds, Birds, Lysistrata, Women of the Assembly /
Aristophanes ; translated by Aaron Poochigian.
Description: First edition. | New York : Liveright Publishing Corporation, 2021. |
Includes bibliographical references.
Identifiers: LCCN 2020022630 | ISBN 9781631496509 (hardcover) | ISBN 9781631496332 (epub)
Subjects: LCGFT: Drama. | Comedy plays.
Classification: LCC PA3877 .A2 2021 | DDC 882/.01—dc23
LC record available at https://lccn.loc.gov/2020022630

Liveright Publishing Corporation, 500 Fifth Avenue, New York, N.Y. 10110
www.wwnorton.com

W. W. Norton & Company Ltd., 15 Carlisle Street, London W1D 3BS

1 2 3 4 5 6 7 8 9 0

CONTENTS

INTRODUCTION

Apart from evidence in the plays themselves, we know next to nothing about Aristophanes. An anonymous *Life* informs us that he was the son of one Philippus and belonged to the deme (district) Cydathenaeum in Athens, which included the Acropolis, but we do not know, for example, whether his family was rich or poor. Lines in his play *Peace* (421 BCE) inform us that he went bald at a young age, but we know nothing more of his appearance. Even the dates of his birth and death are unclear (though circa 446–386 BCE is the general consensus).

We learn more about Aristophanes from his plays' *parabaseis*. Common in fifth-century BCE comedy, these interludes, in which the actors exit and leave the chorus alone onstage, are occasionally employed by Aristophanes to speak directly to the audience. From them we learn details about his early and middle years. A *parabasis* in *Clouds* reveals that he was a precocious playwright, having had his first two plays, *Banqueters* (427 BCE) and *Babylonians* (426 BCE), produced for him because he had not yet reached an age at which he could produce them himself. This precociousness wasn't just a matter of artistic talent; he was also preternaturally drawn to controversy from the very start of his career. In *Babylonians*, before he was even twenty, Aristophanes initiated a vehement campaign of ridicule against the famous general and demagogue Cleon, who rose to political prominence by opposing the more cautious strategy of the preeminent statesman Pericles (ca. 495–429 BCE) in the Peloponnesian War. Mockery of prominent citizens (who were likely in the audience) is a hallmark of Aristophanic comedy, but Aristophanes's insults targeting Cleon are especially virulent. After his initial attack, Cleon, in revenge, prosecuted him for "wronging the city," but the young man was acquitted. In his next play, *Acharnians* (425 BCE), Aristophanes threatens, through the chorus, to "cut [Cleon] up to make soles for the Horsemen's shoes" (lines 299–302), and this threat is fulfilled in *The Knights* (424 BCE), in which he again attacks Cleon, portraying him, onstage, as a deceitful and corrupt warmonger. Subsequently, and probably in reaction to this, Cleon prosecuted Aristophanes again, this time for *xenias*—assuming citizen rights though not the son of citizens—but this prosecution, too, came to nothing. Though these attacks were (mostly) behind Aristophanes in *Clouds* (423 BCE), he expresses pride in them, as he says in the play's *parabasis*:

It was I
who struck a blow at Cleon's paunch when he was in his pride . . . (583–584)

Cleon died a year later while serving as general in the Battle of Amphipolis in Thrace, thus depriving Aristophanes of his favorite object of ridicule. Apart from declaring his precociousness and his animus toward Cleon, however, the *parabaseis* in Aristophanes's plays give us little in the way of biographical information. By the late 410s, Aristophanes started omitting *parabaseis* from his plays (*Lysistrata*, first produced in 411, does not have one, but *Frogs*, first produced in 405, does), and we know nothing about his later years.

Despite the obscurity of the man, his work commands respect and dominates our understanding of theatrical comedy in classical antiquity. In a career that spanned forty years (427–388 BCE), Aristophanes composed at least forty plays, at least three of which won first prize at dramatic festivals. In a *parabasis* in *Clouds*, he criticizes his rival comedic playwrights for repackaging old material year after year and boasts of his own inventiveness:

I'd never try to swindle you by putting out the same play two
or three times. Furthermore, I'm good at introducing fresh ideas,
each unlike the others, all of them quite clever. (*Clouds* 581–583)

Apparently, playgoers, both in fifth-century Athens and later, agreed. Not only did Aristophanes win accolades in his time, but more than a quarter of his output—eleven plays in all—has survived. A little further along in the same *parabasis* quoted above, Aristophanes prophetically anticipates his work being read in future ages:

If you delight in me and my inventions,
however, people in the future will remember you as wise. (*Clouds* 596–597)

Given the momentous historical transitions he witnessed—the glory of Periclean Athens in his youth, the Peloponnesian War in his adulthood, and the attempted revival of Athens in his old age—and how he responded to them in his comic art, Aristophanes is a singularly important, utterly unique writer.

The Golden Age of Athens

During most of Aristophanes's lifetime, Athens was the seat of a sprawling naval empire and the great cultural center of its time. Pericles not only secured the military superiority of Athens throughout the region during his years of leadership (from 461 to 429 BCE), but he also ensured that literature, art, and architecture flourished there, extending its power and influence. In 447 (around the time Aristophanes was born), following the Persian Wars, Pericles initiated an ambitious program to rebuild the Acropolis—the spiritual center of the city. The Parthenon, perhaps now the most famous building of all of antiquity, was mostly completed by 432 BCE. Vast in size and regarded as "the most perfect Doric temple ever built," it has come to symbolize the power, wealth, and culture of Athens's Golden Age.* The other prominent buildings visible on the Acropolis today also date to this era: the Propylaea (completed 432 BCE), the Temple of Athena Nike (completed ca. 420 BCE), and the Erechtheum (completed 406 BCE).

This period also produced what have been traditionally regarded as the first works of history—systematic and serious inquiries into the past. In his *Histories*, Herodotus (ca. 484–425 BCE) investigated the origin of the conflict between Greeks and the peoples of the East and brought his account down to his own time. Thucydides (ca. 460–400 BCE), anticipating that the Peloponnesian War would be a major one, wrote a thorough and detailed account of the war from its inception. Though it originated in the sixth century BCE, tragedy also flourished in Athens, with tragedians such as Aeschylus (ca. 523–456 BCE), Sophocles (ca. 497–405 BCE), and Euripides (ca. 480–406 BCE) competing at dramatic festivals for prizes. Euripides was prominent enough to be a recurring character in Aristophanes's plays, and *Frogs* features Aeschylus as a character as well.

Fifth-century Athens was also host to some of the age's leading orators and rhetoricians. Because the path to social advancement for any Athenian was

* John Julius Norwich, *Great Architecture of the World* (Da Capo, 2001), p. 63.

through the Assembly and the law courts, there was wide demand for instruction in public speaking and persuasion. Foreign intellectuals came to Athens from throughout the region to meet that demand, sparking the so-called Sophistic Enlightenment. These men were widely sought after as tutors, but also produced bodies of work (and acolytes) that extended their influence beyond their immediate students. Protagoras of Abdera (ca. 490–420 BCE), the earliest of the sophists, is known for being a religious agnostic and a relativist regarding the truth (claiming, famously, that "man is the measure of all things"). The rhetorician Gorgias of Leontini (ca. 485–390 BCE) was famous for taking difficult, seemingly impossibly paradoxical positions and persuasively arguing for them—even asserting (in a lost work) for the nonexistence of Being. Another sophist, Prodicus of Ceos (ca. 465–395 BCE), opened a school in Athens and gave lectures on "the correctness of names," among other subjects. Associated (somewhat unjustly) with these figures by some Athenians—and especially by Aristophanes—Socrates (ca. 470–399) spent a great deal of time in the *agora* (marketplace) discussing moral philosophy, among other philosophical topics, with a group of young disciples, including Plato (429–ca. 347 BCE), who later secured the fame of his teacher by writing down recollections of some of the master's provocative dialogues. Barefoot and unkempt, and an object of curiosity and contempt among many Athenians, Socrates was prominent enough in Athens to earn an appearance as a character in Aristophanes's *Clouds*. His teachings, and especially the challenges he posed to some of the city's most eminent and reputedly wise men, eventually provoked the citizens of Athens to put Socrates to death after trying and convicting him of impiety.

This period of prosperity and intellectual ferment, unmatched even by Renaissance Florence, came to an end in 404 BCE, when Athens was compelled to give up its naval empire as a consequence of losing a protracted war with Sparta.

The Peloponnesian War

The Peloponnesian War serves as the raison d'être for *Lysistrata*, looms large in the background of *Clouds* and *Birds*, and lingers as the haunting past in *Women of the Assembly*. An overview of this conflict and its causes will be useful for appreciating, in context, the plays in this volume.

Early in the fifth century, to fend off a Persian invasion (481–479 BCE), the Greek states formed an alliance, the Delian League, to which allies contributed ships for a Panhellenic navy. After the war, the Athenians assumed leadership of this league and started to allow member states to pay tribute money in lieu of supplying ships and sailors. This policy served to consolidate naval power in the Athenians' hands. When Athens refused to allow member states to leave the league, it became clear that its aspirations were imperial, and the Spartans and their allies responded by forming a separate Peloponnesian League in opposition. The expansion of the Athenian Empire under the leadership of Pericles eventually caused enough friction with Sparta and its allies that Sparta felt it had no choice but to declare war.

For nearly thirty years, from 431 to 404 BCE (with a short-lived peace in 421 BCE), the Athenians and Spartans fought for supremacy in the Greek-speaking world. During the first decade of the conflict, known as the Archidamian War (431–421 BCE), King Archidamus of Sparta annually invaded and ravaged the Attic countryside outside Athens. These invasions caused rural residents to move inside the city walls, and the resulting overpopulation created conditions ripe for the spread of the Great Plague (430–426 BCE) there. In 425 BCE, under the generalship of Cleon, the Athenians captured Spartan soldiers off Pylos on the island of Sphacteria. They used the threat of executing these prisoners of war as leverage to stop the annual Spartan incursions. After the Battle of Amphipolis (422 BCE), in which both Cleon and the Spartan general Brasidas were killed, both sides were exhausted and ready for peace. The Athenian general Nicias and the Spartan king Pleistoanax then negotiated a treaty, the Peace of Nicias, in which each side agreed to return nearly all of the cities and territory it had taken in the war. Skirmishes soon broke out again, however, and a resumption of hostilities seemed inevitable.

In 415 BCE the Athenians launched an armada to conquer Sicily under the generals Nicias, Lamachus, and Alcibiades. Since the Spartans sent troops to support some native Sicilian states, the conflict in Sicily served, in effect, as a proxy war between the Athenians and Spartans. This invasion proved a disastrous failure for the Athenians, with two of the generals dying there, and the third, Alcibiades, defecting to the Spartan side. After the collapse of the Sicilian expedition, Sparta encouraged the subject states in the Athenian Empire to revolt. Much of Ionia (now coastal Turkey) did. As a consequence of these losses, men opposed to democracy overthrew the government in Athens and established, in 411 BCE, an oligarchy known as "the Four Hundred," which lasted only a few months.

The following years saw the Persian Empire again become influential by providing the traditionally landlocked Spartans with ships. Eventually, the Spartans, under their general Lysander, defeated the Athenian armada at the Battle of Aegospotami in 405 BCE. The following year, they compelled the Athenians to surrender, requiring them to take down the city's defensive walls, disband their fleet, and accept a pro-Spartan government under thirty oligarchs known as "the Thirty." The war was over; Athens had lost. Though a band of exiled Athenians under Thrasybulus ousted the Thirty and restored democracy in 403 BCE, Athens never regained its former prominence.

Men and Women, Citizens and Slaves

Although in the popular imagination Athens is sometimes characterized as the birthplace of democracy, we should keep important distinctions in mind. First, Athens was a radical, not a representative, democracy: any adult male citizen could propose measures and vote in the Assembly, the equivalent of the American legislative branch. Second, all this flourishing had a darker side: as with all Greek states at the time, there was the large, ever-present, and nearly voiceless population of slaves.

Although slaves occupied the lowest place in the Athenian social hierarchy, there were still distinctions among them, with the Scythian archers of the state police force, for example, possessing greater prestige than agricultural laborers. That even middle-class Athenians could afford slaves freed up a large segment of the population to cultivate the arts and participate in the political process, so a great deal of "the glory that was Greece" depended on slave labor. As a sort of symbol of slaves' intimate relationship with the Athenian economy, it was they who worked the lucrative silver mines at Laurion, roughly fifty miles south of Athens, in order to provide material for Athens's silver coinage, which in turn financed its military adventures and great civic projects. In the plays that follow, you will encounter Strepsiades in *Clouds* threatening to strike a slave, Peisthetaerus in *Birds* insulting one as stupid, and even Lysistrata in her play speaking roughly to her Scythian slave girl—and in none of those instances is the action of the slave owner implied to be questionable. While in Aristophanes's plays slaves are little more than the butt of a joke here and there, we would do well to acknowledge that the entire edifice of the glorious civilization that was fifth-century Athens, including its rich tradition of theatrical performance, was built on a foundation of forced, uncompensated labor. Athenians themselves may have been willfully blind to the injustice of reserving democratic self-determination for themselves and relegating their defeated enemies to abject servitude, but it is impossible for us now to ignore it.

Male citizens had the right to own property such as slaves and to transact business, but they were also liable to being called up for military service. They were able to operate both within the *polis* (city-state) and the *oikos* (home), whereas the wives and daughters of citizens were mostly confined to the latter. Given their confinement and the comparative scarcity of historical evidence about them, it is striking how prominently women figure in Aristophanes's plays, as in Greek drama generally. Indeed, two of the plays in this volume—*Lysistrata* and *Women of the Assembly*—enact scenarios in which women overturn the social order and seize power for themselves. A reader or playgoer might be forgiven for interpreting this fact as evidence of a rosier underlying social reality, or perhaps inferring something like proto-feminist intent on the playwright's part, but neither is true. Women in fifth-century Athens did not have suffrage, nor were they allowed to own property or represent themselves in court. A free female had to have a *kyrios* (male legal representative)—usually her father until she married, then her husband—to manage all of her social and economic relations beyond the most quotidian household duties. Respectable females only left home on special occasions, for weddings, funerals, and some religious festivals, and they are often depicted with white skin in vase paintings, because they were rarely out in the sun. There were other classes of females—*hetaerae* (courtesans), *pornoi* (prostitutes), and impoverished women, who had considerably more freedom of movement— but what they gained in mobility they paid for by being forced into more precarious, even dangerous circumstances. Respectable women were mostly limited to the roles of wife and mother, though some few could become priestesses. Their occupations were domestic, such as supervising household tasks and slaves, raising children, and making clothing. The "double standard" was even more marked in Athens than in the United States today, since, whereas husbands were free to seek sexual relations outside of the marriage, females were closely guarded.

Lysistrata and *Women of the Assembly* give a voice to Athenian women and a glimpse into their daily lives, but we should note that male actors played female characters as a travesty, and Aristophanes's portrayals perpetuated stereotypes about females, such as bibulousness and sex obsession. Furthermore, in order to carry out their programs, Lysistrata and Praxagora become "man-like women," both acting and speaking in traditionally masculine ways. For example, the Athenians Lysistrata, Calonice, and Myrrhine look with the "male gaze" on the bodies of the Spartan Lampito and the representative from Boeotia. Additionally, in the blessed state at the end of *Lysistrata* and *Women of the Assembly*, slaves, both male and female, remain in their oppressed position. Praxagora explicitly states that there will be slaves in her collectivist utopia: when her husband Blepyrus asks, "Who will till the soil?" she answers:

> The slaves will do it. All you'll have to do
> is put on scent and go to dinner when the shadow of the sundial
> grows to ten feet long. (*Women of the Assembly* 735–737)

In the end, one can accept Lysistrata and Praxagora as proto-feminist heroes
only with major reservations.

Theater in Athens

Aristophanes's plays were originally performed at competitive dramatic festivals called the Lenaea and the City Dionysia. Held in the winter month of
Gamelium (roughly equivalent to January), the Lenaea was a religious festival in honor of Dionysus Lenaeus. The audience for this festival consisted
primarily of Athenian citizens because the sea was regarded as too rough for
travel. Held during the month of Elaphebolium in the spring, the City Dionysia, in contrast, accommodated a larger cosmopolitan audience. After three
days of performances of tragedies there, three comedies were performed on
the same day. At both of these festivals, judges representative of the ten tribes
of Athens cast votes ranking the comedies in order of merit, and five of their
opinions were then chosen at random to decide first, second, and third places.
In some of the plays in this volume, you'll notice that Aristophanes, through
the chorus, often addresses these judges, subjecting them to flattery and mock
threats.

In the second half of the fifth and early fourth centuries BCE, the Theater
of Dionysus at Athens consisted simply of the south slope of the Acropolis
and a roughly circular plane at its base. Temporary seats called *ikria* (planks
for benches) were installed for performances. A temporary wooden backdrop
called a *skēnē* was set up in the playing space. The *skēnē* usually had two doors
in it for productions of comedy, and thus there were normally four ways for
actors to make their entrances—through either of the doors or down one of
the two side aisles (*eisodoi*). The *skēnē*, with its doors, often represented the
houses of neighbors in a "middle-class" Athenian neighborhood. Thus Lysistrata at the beginning of her play greets her neighbor Myrrhine, and in *Women
of the Assembly*, a character simply called "Neighbor" calls out to Blepyrus.
The *skēnē* is very versatile, however—later in *Lysistrata*, for example, it represents the hill of the Acropolis itself, and in *Birds*, one of its doors represents
the entrance to the Hoopoe Tereus's nest. All productions of ancient Greek

drama took place during the daytime, and there was no equivalent of modern stage lighting.

Ancient Greek drama used several contraptions that seem awkward and artificial to us. Comedy borrowed from tragedy a cantilevered crane called the *mēchanē* by which a god would often make his or her entrance "flying" (suspended by a rope). In productions of tragedy, gods were often set down on top of the *skēnē*, where they would speak down to other characters (and the audience) from "on high." Drawing on the association of this contraption with the loftier genre of tragedy, Aristophanes used it for travesty and burlesque. In *Clouds*, for example, Socrates, a mere mortal, enters on the *mēchanē* like a god and speaks, at first, in tragic pastiche. The irony is that he, allegedly a disbeliever in the traditional Greek gods, is said to "look / down on the gods" from on high (lines 260–261). In *Birds* the goddess Iris flies in on the *mēchanē* only to be threatened with violence by the mortal Peisthetaerus. Comedy also occasionally employed a narrow wooden platform on wheels called the *enkyklema*. This device was used to turn the setting inside out, that is, to roll out characters who would otherwise be concealed behind the *skēnē*. In *Clouds* the *enkyklema* was used for the entrance of the pale, emaciated students from the Thinkery. They are, we are told, wheeled back in because it "is forbidden to them to remain / out in the open air for very long" (lines 230–231).

Whereas in tragedy the setting almost always remains fixed once it is established at the beginning of the play, in comedy the setting regularly "refocuses" to a new location. The setting can shift from Lysistrata's and Myrrhine's houses to the Acropolis, for example, or from the Neighbor's and Blepyrus's houses to those of the First Old Woman and the Girl. Finally, whereas the events of a tragedy are represented as taking place within a single day, scenes in comedy often take place several days after preceding scenes, so that, for example, we can see the effects of the sex strike on the men of both Athens and Sparta in *Lysistrata*.

The Plays

Of the four plays in the volume, *Clouds* (423 BCE) and *Birds* (414 BCE) were produced at the City Dionysia, and *Lysistrata* (411 BCE) was most likely produced at the Lenaea. It is not known at which festival *Women of the Assembly* (391 BCE) was produced. Scholars have assigned three of these plays—*Clouds*, *Birds*, and *Lysistrata*—to the category of "Old Comedy," and one of them, *Women of the Assembly*, to "Middle Comedy." The former three share a tendency toward personal invective against particular politicians and intellectuals, whereas *Women of the Assembly* focuses more on social themes. Furthermore, in Middle Comedy, choral odes are less often integral to the plot, if they are preserved at all, and few are preserved in *Women of the Assembly*. Also, whereas in *Clouds* there is an extended and striking *parodos* (entry song for the chorus), in *Women of the Assembly* there is no *parodos* at all—the chorus members simply come walking on singly and in groups and are greeted by Praxagora. This play also exhibits the "neighborly" middle-class settings standard in Middle Comedy. Finally, the *parabasis* (in which the playwright would, at times, address the audience) vanishes in Middle Comedy. We can see a trajectory of lessening importance for *parabaseis* from *Clouds* to *Birds*, to *Lysistrata* (which lacks a proper *parabasis*), to *Women of the Assembly*, in which there is not even the hint of one.

Despite their differences, however, these four plays share the "Great Idea" plot structure characteristic of Aristophanes. In each, a character comes up with an "ingenious" plan to solve a problem: in *Clouds* Strepsiades tries to clear his debts through the use of the "Wrong Argument"; in *Birds*, Peisthetaerus escapes life in Athens to create a utopia; in her play, Lysistrata plots to end the war through a sex strike; and in *Women of the Assembly*, Praxagora replaces a male-dominated, capitalistic democracy with a female-run, communistic one. Whereas the last three schemes meet with unmitigated success in the worlds of their plays, Strepsiades is the outlier—he does indeed escape his debts, at least for a time, but must accept the moral ruin of his son Pheidippides (and a beating at his hands).

It is clear that Aristophanes, like many of his contemporaries, was anxious about the moral relativism associated with the Sophistic Enlightenment. It is also clear, however, that Aristophanes himself was partly a product of this intellectual environment. In these plays we find *agones* (formal and rhetorical debates such as are common in the plays of Euripides). The most hyped of them is the debate in *Clouds* between the traditionalist Right Argument and the sophistic Wrong Argument over the subsequent course of education. The strong female leads, however, both engage in *agones* and are triumphant in them. Lysistrata proves that females are competent to govern the city and the empire in her debate with the Commissioner, and at the end of her arguments supporting communistic versus capitalistic democracy, Praxagora leaves her husband Blepyrus with nothing to say. She, in fact, informs us that she learned to speak so persuasively by listening to her contemporary male Athenians in the Assembly (*Women of the Assembly* 277–279). In the end, as harshly as Aristophanes lampoons the "new education" in *Clouds*, many of his characters cannot escape its influence.

I chose to collect these four plays by Aristophanes in one volume primarily because they are my favorites. I find the utopian idealism of *Birds* balances well with the moral ugliness we find in *Clouds*. Furthermore, I simply couldn't resist the challenge of translating Tereus's gorgeous lyrical summons of all the avian species in *Birds*. *Lysistrata*, the most popular of Aristophanes's plays in the contemporary world, was a must, though I confess I found the challenge that the Spartan "dialect" presented in translation alluring as well. I included *Women of the Assembly* because it develops themes that are introduced in *Lysistrata* and, with its protracted threat of onstage defecation, gives us a *ne plus ultra* in terms of obscenity. Also, it is timely in that it presents female legislators who work to "socialize" democracy. Finally, in terms of theater history, these four plays plot a clear trajectory from Old Comedy to Middle Comedy in which we can see a decrease in the role of the chorus (especially in *Women of the Assembly*) and the phasing out of the *parabasis*, and together they provide a clear picture of the deepest roots of contemporary comedy.

Additionally, as a citizen of a democracy, I felt a duty to make clear, in an era in which there are calls for "civility" in political discourse, that there is such a thing as patriotic obscenity. The citizens of ancient Athens enjoyed a freedom of speech as broad as our own. This freedom, *parrhesia*, was essentially the right to say what one pleased, how and when one pleased, and to whom. I wanted to make translations that celebrate Aristophanes's *parrhesia* for the English-speaking world. Furthermore, whatever one's political leanings, one can appreciate that when a person in power behaves obscenely, obscenity is a fitting way of condemning that behavior. "Civil" discourse, in contrast, lacks the same visceral impact. Aristophanes teaches the contemporary reader that crudity is appropriate in criticizing the crude, that, in terms of discourse, one may fight fire with fire, and this struck me as a necessary lesson.

A NOTE ON THE TRANSLATIONS

I translated the texts of the most recent editions of these plays available, those of Jeffrey Henderson, though I do occasionally attribute lines to different characters than he does.* With these translations I have striven to reproduce the full musical virtuosity of Aristophanes. In Greek prosody the most common and conversational meter, iambic trimeter, consists of six feet of iambs (with substitutions allowed). I render this meter as iambic pentameter in English, best known from the plays of Shakespeare. In order to preserve the modulation from this standard meter to longer lines, I translate Aristophanes's seven- and eight-stress lines into iambic heptameter and octometer, respectively.

Aristophanes once even calls attention to his metrical choice. The chorus of *Birds* announces that there will be "anapests on the run" before the Chorus Leader delivers a part of the *parabasis* to the audience. I render the subsequent rollicking anapestic heptameters in the original meter:

Insubstantial confections of clay, frail mortals, ephemeral featherless beings,
ineffectual weaklings who live in a dream and who perish like leaves,
    evanescent
generations of shadow, obscurities, listen to us who, ethereal, ageless
and immortal, have minds that consider perennial thoughts. (699–702)

In the Greek, sung lines (both solo and choral) are in a different dialect—

---

* *Clouds*: Aristophanes, *Clouds. Wasps. Peace*, Loeb Classical Library No. 488 (Harvard University Press, 1998); *Birds* and *Lysistrata*: Aristophanes, *Birds. Lysistrata. Women at the Thesmophoria*, Loeb Classical Library No. 179 (Harvard University Press, 2000); *Women of the Assembly*: Aristophanes, *Frogs. Assemblywomen. Wealth*, Loeb Classical Library No. 180 (Harvard University Press, 2002).

Doric as opposed to Attic. To mark this change of mode, I have translated these lines into a variety of lyric meters set off by rhyme and off-rhyme. Furthermore, where choral odes break down into *Strophe* ("Turn") and *Antistrophe* ("Counter-Turn"), I preserve what is known as metrical responsion (the identity of rhythms between them), by rendering them in stanzas matching in line lengths and rhyme schemes. As this translation seeks to preserve as much of the original musical structures of the plays as possible, I have opted to provide the headings *Strophe* and *Antistrophe* in the text.

This translation, a labor of love, aspires to bring over into English not just the "words" of Aristophanes but also his various poetic forms, so that these two together, the words and the forms, may re-create his meaning. I can only hope that my versions inspire the same delight in you as his Greek originals do in me.

aristophanes

FOUR PLAYS

CLOUDS

*C*louds, Aristophanes's parody of the "new education" in rhetoric, science, and philosophy, is remarkable for many reasons, not least for its main character, Strepsiades, who is the least sympathetic of the central characters in the extant comedies. An older affluent farmer, Strepsiades is stupid and crooked and, in the end, pitiable. His "Great Idea" is to escape from the large debts he has accrued by learning the "Wrong Argument," which wins regardless of justice. When his son Pheidippides refuses to enroll in the rhetorical and philosophical school the Thinkery, Strepsiades does so himself, and there begins the travesty of sophists and Pre-Socratic philosophers, two types of intellectuals. Aristophanes casts Socrates, a prominent figure in Athens, as the headmaster of the Thinkery, a choice that would have pleased the crowd but that unfairly lumped the famous philosopher together with less scrupulous pedagogues. In fact, in the *Apology*, Plato takes pains to distinguish Socrates from contemporary intellectuals and specifically calls out the portrayal of Socrates in *Clouds* as inaccurate, even implying that the play was (part of) the reason Socrates was brought to trial.

After Strepsiades is expelled from the Thinkery, he is told to return with his son Pheidippides. When he does so, rival personified systems of education, Right Argument and Wrong Argument, emerge from the school and try to persuade Pheidippides to study with them. Like the emcee at a boxing match, the chorus builds up the debate:

> What wisdom will be in the years to come depends
> on who prevails. (1001–1002)

The conflict that ensues, between a conservative pedophile and an amoral brat, is more than just an attempt to win Pheidippides as a student—it is a conflict between two different perspectives on living. When Right Argument concedes defeat, Pheidipiddes enters the Thinkery to study with Wrong Argument. When he graduates, he is indeed able to embarrass and refute his father's creditors, but he has also been morally ruined—going so far as to argue that it is proper to beat one's father and even one's mother. Strepsiades, enraged, decides to burn the Thinkery down. Whereas the other plays in this volume end in a blessed state, *Clouds* ends with indignation and violence.

The Chorus of Clouds is exceptional for being neither human nor animal but something more abstract—they represent inspiration in thought and language.

The passages that describe the *parodos* (or entrance of the chorus) are poetically rich. Only the choral passages in *Birds* rival them in beauty. Furthermore, whereas choruses in Aristophanes tend to be either for or against a protagonist, the Clouds here take on a more ambiguous role. They at first encourage Strepsiades in his desire for education but eventually state, up front, that he will regret what he is trying to do:

> It is an awful thing
> to have a passion to do wrong.
> That's how this old man here is passionate.
> He burns to get out of repaying debt.
>
> Surely before the sun goes down today
> this "intellectual" will have met
> with a surprise reversal—he will pay
> for his unjust pursuit. (1366–1373)

After the final argument between Pheidippides and Strepsiades over father- and mother-beating, the chorus comments no further, leaving Socrates and Strepsiades to reap what they have sown.

The text of *Clouds* that has come down to us is a revised version of the play that, when it was first produced in 423 BCE, won last place. In the *parabasis* Aristophanes, through the chorus, says to the audience,

> I thought you were discerning spectators and this was my
> most clever comedy. I put a lot of work into the thing
> and let you taste it first. Though I deserved to win, I lost the contest,
> defeated by inferior men. (559–562)

We can say with confidence that this section belongs to the revision. It is possible, too, that the original production ended with the triumph of Pheidippides— a denouement the judges would not have been able to stomach.

cLouds

(Nephelai)

First produced in 423 BCE, subsequently revised

CHARACTERS IN THE PLAY

Strepsiades
Slave
Pheidippides
First Student
Students
Socrates
Chorus of Clouds
Chorus Leader

Right Argument
Wrong Argument
First Creditor
Witness
Second Creditor
Xanthias, a slave
Chaerephon

(The setting is Athens, Greece, during the Peloponnesian War. There is a backdrop with two doors in it. This first scene takes place in front of the backdrop, a space that initially represents the inside of Strepsiades's house. There is a bed in which Strepsiades and Pheidippides are sleeping. The time is just before dawn. In front of one of the doors—the door to the Thinkery—there are a statue of Hermes, a pedestal holding a jar with a "Vortex" pattern on it, and a variety of astronomical and geometric instruments. Above the door to the Thinkery there is a window. It is very late at night.)

STREPSIADES: *(tossing and turning in bed)*
Goodness, goodness.
Great Zeus, how long the night is—infinite!
Will morning never come? I swear I heard
the rooster crow a long, long time ago.
My slaves are all still snoring. In the past
they never would have dared to sleep so late.

I say goddamn this war for oh so many
reasons: I can't even beat the help!°

          (gesturing to Pheidippides)

This fine young man right here, he never wakes up
during the night but simply goes on farting,   10
five quilts deep. Oh well, since it seems
the thing to do, let's all just snore away,
wrapped up in blankets.

     (Strepsiades lies back on the bed but then continues to toss and turn.)

                    Oh, I'm miserable!
I can't sleep. I'm being eaten up
by great expenditures, by horse feed-troughs,
by all my debts,

          (gesturing to Pheidippides)

                    because of this son here!
He, with his long hair, won't stop riding horses
and driving chariots. He dreams of horses,
and I feel ruined every time I see
the moon has reached the twentieth of the month°—   20
the interest on my debts will soon tick up.

          (shouting to a Slave offstage)

Bring me a lamp, now, boy! And bring my ledger
so I can look at all my debts and reckon
the interest up.

          (A Slave brings the ledger and a lighted lamp.)

                    Alright, then, let's just see
how much I owe: To Pasias, twelve minas.°
To Pasias, twelve minas? Why did I ever

borrow that amount? Oh—when I bought
the thoroughbred. Poor me! I wish a rock had
thoroughly put my eye out first.

PHEIDIPPIDES: *(talking in his sleep)*
                              Hey there,
you're cheating, Philo. Stay in your own lane.   30

STREPSIADES:
That's just how I am being ruined: the boy
keeps riding horses even in his sleep!

PHEIDIPPIDES: *(talking in his sleep)*
How many races will the chariots run?

STREPSIADES:
You're making me, your father, run a lot
of races. Well, what debt came over me
after my debt to Pasias?

                    (looking back to the ledger)

                    To Amynias
three minas for a chariot and wheels.

PHEIDIPPIDES: *(talking in his sleep)*
Well, let the stallion roll, then bring him in.

STREPSIADES.
Kid, you've rolled me out of all I own.
Some creditors have taken me to court;   40
others insisted that I put up assets
to cover the compounding interest.

PHEIDIPPIDES: *(waking up)*
                              Dad,
why are you such a coot? Why do you toss
and turn the whole night through?

STREPSIADES:

A bailiff-bug keeps
biting me right out of all my blankets.

PHEIDIPPIDES:

Come on, now, let me just go back to sleep.

STREPSIADES:

Alright, go back to sleep.

(Pheidippides covers himself in blankets again.)

But know that someday
all my debts will end up landing squarely
on your own head. Goddamn the marriage-maker,
that hag, who introduced me to your mother.   50
Mine was a country life, a very pleasant,
if dirty and unshaven, life, a life
that lay wherever and was rich in bees
and sheep and olive cakes. Then I, a bumpkin,
took as wife the niece of Megacles
the son of Megacles,° a city girl—
as spoiled and snobby as that bitch Coesyra.°
The night I wedded her, I went to bed
smelling of fresh wine, fleeces, figs and great
affluence, and she on her side reeked of   60
lubricant, saffron seeds, tongue kisses, wealth,
gluttony and the Goddesses of Sex.°
I won't say she was lazy, since she wove.
And sometimes, as a pretext, I would show her
this bit of cloth

(lifting his cloak and exposing his strap-on penis)

and say, "Oh you weave well."

(The lamp goes out.)

SLAVE:
The lamp has died. And there is no more oil.

STREPSIADES:
Dammit, why did you bring the wasteful lamp?
Get over here.

(threatening to strike the Slave)

Prepare to scream.

SLAVE:
Why scream?

STREPSIADES:
Because you put the thick wick in the lamp.

(He swats at the Slave, who runs off through a stage door.)

Afterwards, when this son was born to me   70
and my most estimable wife, we squabbled
about his name. She kept on wanting one
with *hippos* ("horse") in it somewhere—Xanthippus,
Charippus or Callippides.° I, though,
wanted to call the boy Pheidonides,
which was my father's name. We had it out
about the name and then, in time, agreed on
Pheidippides. Then, picking up the baby,
my wife would tell him, "When you are a big boy,
you will put on a rich, soft robe and drive   80
a chariot to the Acropolis,
just like Megacles your uncle." Well,
I, on my side, was saying, "When you're grown up,
you'll put a simple leather apron on
and drive the goats down from the hills, just like
your father did." The boy ignored, of course,
all that I said to him and now has spread
his horse disease all over my estate.

That's why I spent the whole night worrying.
Now, with the gods' help, I have found a way out,   90
a great escape route. Now, if I can only
persuade my son to go along with me,
I shall be saved! First, though, I need to wake him.
How can I rouse him in the nicest way?
How? O Pheidippides. O darling little
Pheidippides.

PHEIDIPPIDES: *(waking up)*
               What is it, Dad?

STREPSIADES:
                     Come here;
give me a kiss and take me by the hand.

       (Pheidippides leans over and kisses Strepsiades.)

PHEIDIPPIDES:
Alright. What is it?

STREPSIADES:
               Tell me: do you love me?

PHEIDIPPIDES:
Yes, by Poseidon, God of Horsemanship.

STREPSIADES:
Leave out Poseidon, God of Horsemanship.   100
He is the cause of all my troubles. Listen,
if you really love me from your heart,
then, boy, obey me!

PHEIDIPPIDES:
               How should I obey you?

STREPSIADES:
Change your ways as quickly as you can
and go and learn the skill I recommend.

PHEIDIPPIDES:
What do you recommend?

STREPSIADES:
                                Will you obey me?

PHEIDIPPIDES:
By Dionysus, yes, I will obey you.

STREPSIADES: (*gesturing to the stage-right door*)
Look over this way. Do you see this door?
The little house behind it?

PHEIDIPPIDES:
                                Yes, I see them,
but Dad, what *is* this place?

STREPSIADES:
                                A Thinkery°   110
for clever souls. Behind that door dwell men
who, when they speak about the sky, persuade
others it is an oven that surrounds us,
and we are coals inside it. For a fee
they also teach a person how to win
an argument no matter whether he
is right or wrong.

PHEIDIPPIDES:
                        Who are they, though?

STREPSIADES:
                                        I can't
exactly put a name to them: they are
good, noble and exacting intellectuals.

PHEIDIPPIDES:

I know them well and, yuck, they are repulsive.   120
You mean the shysters, the anemic smarties,
the barefoot fellows in whose number are
Chaerephon° and that wretched Socrates.

STREPSIADES:

You watch your mouth. Don't you be talking nonsense.
If you care at all about your father's
finances, then you will forget your horses
and sign up as a student here.

PHEIDIPPIDES:

                            I wouldn't,
by Dionysus, even if you were
to give me all Leogoras's pheasants.°

STREPSIADES:

O dear son, I beg you. Go. Go learn.   130

PHEIDIPPIDES:

And what am I to learn?

STREPSIADES:

                        They say there are
two Arguments in there—the one called "Right,"
whatever that might be, and then the "Wrong" one.
They say that one of these two Arguments,
the Wrong, prevails, although the points it makes
are on the wrong side. If you go and learn
one of these Arguments, the Wrong, for me,
I wouldn't have to pay back even one
obol° of all the debts I have accrued
because of you.

PHEIDIPPIDES:

I won't be going there.   140
I couldn't bring myself to stand among
the Horsemen° with my face all drawn and pasty.

STREPSIADES:

Then, by Demeter,° you shall eat no food
of mine—not you yourself and not your trace horse
and not your thoroughbred. No, I shall drive you
straight out of the house to go to hell!

PHEIDIPPIDES:

Ah, but my uncle Megacles will never
leave me without a horse. I'm going in.
I won't be listening to you in this.

(Pheidippides exits through the stage-left door in the backdrop.)

STREPSIADES:

Oh well. Although I'm down, I'm still not out.   150
No, after praying to the gods, I'll go
myself and study at the Thinkery.
How, though, will I, a slow, forgetful geezer,
learn all those keen, hairsplitting arguments?
I have to do it, all the same. Why loiter?
Why not try knocking on the door?

(He knocks on the door.)

Boy! Boy!

FIRST STUDENT: *(peeking out of the door)*
Goddamn that noise! Who's knocking on the door?

STREPSIADES:

Strepsiades out of the deme Cicynna,°
the son of Pheidon.

FIRST STUDENT:
                    You are quite a moron!
You pounded on the door so oafishly   160
that you have caused me to abort
a thought that I was carrying to term.

STREPSIADES:
I'm sorry. I'm from way out in the country.
Tell me, what was this thought that was aborted?

FIRST STUDENT:
We are allowed to speak such secrets only
to fellow students.

STREPSIADES:
                    Have no fears about that;
you can tell it to me, since I've come
to be a student at the Thinkery.

FIRST STUDENT: (stepping outside the door)
I'll tell you, but you must regard these matters
as sacred secrets. Socrates just lately   170
asked Chaerephon how far a flea could jump
as measured by its own flea-feet. You see,
a flea had bitten Chaerephon's eyebrow
and then leapt onto Socrates's head.

STREPSIADES:
How did he gauge the distance of the jump?

FIRST STUDENT:
Quite cleverly. He melted wax, then took
the flea and pressed its feet into the wax.
Then, when the wax had cooled, the flea was wearing
what looked just like a pair of Persian slippers.°
Socrates gently loosened these and used them   180
to measure out the distance.

STREPSIADES:
                              Great King Zeus,
what subtlety of thought!

FIRST STUDENT:
                              What would you say, then,
about this other idea of Socrates's?

STREPSIADES:
What is it? Please, please tell me.

FIRST STUDENT:
                              Chaerephon
of Sphettus asked him if he thought the gnat
buzzed through the mouth or through the anus.

STREPSIADES:
                                        Well,
what did that wise man have to say about this?

FIRST STUDENT:
He said the entrails of the gnat are narrow,
and wind goes powerfully through that tight space
straight to the anus, and the gnat's rump, hollow   190
where it is adjacent to the pinched
intestines, through the violence of the wind,
buzzes.

STREPSIADES:
        Gnats have a trumpet for a butt!
The man is thrice blessed for his penetrating
vision. A defendant who has grasped
the entrails of the gnat will get himself
acquitted without any difficulty.

FIRST STUDENT:
A gecko lately cheated Socrates
out of a bright idea.

STREPSIADES:

      How's that? Tell me.

FIRST STUDENT:

Well, while he was doing research on   200
the routes and variations of the moon,
he gaped into the night sky, and a gecko
pooped on him from the roof.

STREPSIADES:

             A gecko pooped
on Socrates—I love it!

FIRST STUDENT:

         Yes, and last night
we had no dinner.

STREPSIADES:

        What did he contrive
for you to eat?

FIRST STUDENT:

        He started out by sprinkling
ash on the table, then he bent a skewer,
then went out to the wrestling school and used
this new device to steal somebody's cloak.°

STREPSIADES:

Why do we wonder at the famous Thales?°   210
Hurry now, open up the Thinkery
and show me Socrates quick as you can.
I want to be a student. Open up!

      (A wheeled platform is rolled out, on which there are several
       thin and pale Students. Some are standing with their heads
        close to the ground and some with their rumps in the air.)

STREPSIADES: *(astounded)*
By Heracles, what species are these beasts?

FIRST STUDENT:
Why are they shocking? What do they resemble?

STREPSIADES:
The Spartan prisoners of war from Pylos.°
What are those doing staring at the ground?

FIRST STUDENT:
They're seeking after things beneath the earth.

STREPSIADES:
Oh, they are seeking after truffles, then.
Don't bother looking for them anymore—   220
I know where there are big sweet ones. But really,
why are they all hunched over in that way?

FIRST STUDENT:
To grope about in Tartarus's darkness.

STREPSIADES:

(to the other Students)

Why do these here have butt-holes gaping skyward?

FIRST STUDENT:
Oh, they are learning on their own to do
astronomy.

(to the Students)

        All of you, go back in
so that the master doesn't find you here.

STREPSIADES:
No, let them stay outside. I want to share
a little problem of my own with them.

FIRST STUDENT:
It is forbidden to them to remain   230
out in the open air for very long.

(*The wheeled platform is rolled back inside. Strepsiades turns
to a range of instruments displayed in front of the school.*)

STREPSIADES: (*pointing to a group of instruments*)
Tell me, then, what are all these instruments?

FIRST STUDENT:
They're for astronomy.

STREPSIADES: (*pointing to another group of instruments*)
                                And what are these?

FIRST STUDENT:
They're for geometry.

STREPSIADES: (*pointing to a third group of instruments*)
                                And these ones here?

FIRST STUDENT:
They measure Earth.

STREPSIADES:
                        They mark off plots of land?

FIRST STUDENT:
No, the entire Earth.

STREPSIADES:
                        That's very clever—
a useful tool, and democratic, too.

FIRST STUDENT:
This is a map of everything on Earth.
Here's Athens. Do you see it?

STREPSIADES:
                        What, that's Athens?
I don't believe you, since I can't make out   240
the courts in session.

FIRST STUDENT:
                    No, this really is
the land of Attica.

STREPSIADES:
                Where are my fellow
residents of Cicynna?

FIRST STUDENT:
                    Here they are.
And here's Euboea, as you see, stretched out
this very long, long distance right beside it.°

STREPSIADES:
Yes, Pericles and us have stretched it out
like that. But where is Sparta?

FIRST STUDENT:
                    Sparta? Here.

STREPSIADES:
That's much too close to us. Now pay attention—
push Sparta very very far away.

FIRST STUDENT:
It simply can't be done.

STREPSIADES:
                    You will regret it.   250

(Socrates enters suspended in a basket.)

Who is this man suspended in a basket?

FIRST STUDENT:
That is the man himself.

STREPSIADES:
                    What man himself?

FIRST STUDENT:
That's Socrates.

STREPSIADES: *(calling to Socrates)*
                    O Socrates!

                    (to the First Student)

                    Come on, now;
call out to him for me.

FIRST STUDENT:
                    Call out to him
yourself, since I have no more time for this.

                    (The First Student exits into the Thinkery.)

STREPSIADES:
Socrates! O darling Socrates!

SOCRATES:
Why, creature of a day, dost thou address me?

STREPSIADES:
First what I want to know is, what are you doing?

SOCRATES:
Walking on air and pondering the sun.

STREPSIADES:

So is it from a basket that you look   260
down on the gods, not from the earth?

SOCRATES:

                                        I never

would have properly investigated
celestial affairs if I had not
lifted my intellect aloft and mixed
my cerebrations with their kindred air.
If I had stayed on earth and scanned the heavens
from below, I never would have made
discoveries. Here is the reason: earth
forcibly draws thought's moisture to itself.
Watercress operates in much the same way.   270

STREPSIADES:

What are you saying? Thought draws moisture toward
the watercresses? Dear, dear Socrates,
come down and join me so that I might learn
what I have come to learn.

            (The basket is set down, and Socrates steps out of it.)

SOCRATES:

                        Why have you come?

STREPSIADES:

I want to learn to argue. I am being
drawn and quartered by my interest payments
and all my irritable creditors,
and I am soon to have my assets seized.

SOCRATES:

How did you not perceive your mounting debt?

STREPSIADES:

An all-consuming horse disease assailed me.   280
Come, now, and teach one of your arguments
to me, the one that never pays out fines,
and I will swear by all the gods that I
will lay down any fee that you require.

SOCRATES:

Who are these "gods" that you will swear by? First off,
the gods aren't any kind of currency
among us here.

STREPSIADES:

                    What do you swear your oaths by?
Iron coins like in Byzantium?°

SOCRATES:

Do you desire to fathom, truly fathom,
celestial matters?

STREPSIADES:

                    If I can, then yes,   290
by Zeus.

SOCRATES:

          And with the Clouds, our deities,
to have a conversation?

STREPSIADES:

                    Yes, I do.

SOCRATES: (gesturing to a chair)
Seat thyself, then, upon the sacred chair.

STREPSIADES:
Alright, I'm seated.

SOCRATES: *(handing Strepsiades a garland)*
          Take this garland also.

STREPSIADES:
A garland? Why? Oh no, don't sacrifice me,
Socrates. I don't want to play Athamas.°

SOCRATES:
No, no, all of you who are inducted
into the Thinkery go through the same
initiation.

STREPSIADES:
        What will I gain by it?

SOCRATES:
You will become an ace, a real rattle,   300
the very flower of verbosity.
But hush up, now.

STREPSIADES:
        By Zeus, you won't deceive me.
When I get sprinkled on, I'll be the flour.

SOCRATES:
You now should sit, old man, in holy silence
and listen to my prayer:

        (addressing the sky)

        O King, immeasurable Air,
who hold the earth suspended, and you, ever-gleaming Aether,
and you high goddesses, the Clouds, who send the thunder and lightning,
O Queens, arise, show yourselves, floating, to your contemplator.

STREPSIADES: *(holding his cloak over his head)*
Hold off and let me wrap this cloak around my head or else
the rain will get me. Sad. I didn't think to bring a cap.   310

SOCRATES:
Come now, you venerable Clouds, appear unto this man.
Whether you now are sitting on the sacred snowcapped peaks
of Mount Olympus, or in Father Ocean's groves performing
holy dances with the Nymphs, or drawing off the flowing
streams of the Nile in golden pitchers, or inhabiting
Lake Maeotis or the snowy rock of Mimas,° hear me,
accept my sacrifice and be propitious to these rites.

(The Chorus of Clouds is heard singing offstage.)

CHORUS:
> *Strophe*
> Let us, the deathless Clouds, arise to human vision
> out of the roaring fathoms of our father Ocean
> and fly above the forest-laden mountaintops   320
> so that we may behold the towers on the peaks,
> the sacred-soil-fomented crops,
> the holy rivers' roaring flux
> and the loud-sounding sea.
> The Aether's never-sleeping eye
> glints with glittering rays.
> Come, let us shake the water drops
> off our immortal beauty and survey
> the earth with telescopic gaze.

SOCRATES:
O most holy Clouds, you clearly heard me when I called.   330

(to Strepsiades)

Did you make out their voices and the awesome roaring thunder?

STREPSIADES: *(to the Clouds, still invisible to him)*
I, too, revere you, highly honored gods, and want to thunder
in answer (that's how much they scared and shocked me). Whether
or not it be allowed, I really need to poop right now.

SOCRATES: *(to Strepsiades)*
No cracking jokes. Don't do what all those wretched comics do.
No, utter favorable words instead, because there is
a whole great hive of deities approaching with their songs.

CHORUS:

>*Antistrophe*
>Come, rainy maidens, to the fruitful country of
>Pallas and Cecrops,° to a man-rich land we love,
>where none divulge the sacred secrets, and a house   340
>welcomes initiates to holy things, where gods
>have high-roofed temples, offerings, sacred images,
>and there are many blessed and sublime parades,
>and sacrifices crowned
>with coronals go on year-round;
>in spring the Bacchic rites°
>take place, and the melodious
>choruses do their dancing, and the sound
>echoes, the trill of double flutes.

STREPSIADES:
Please tell me, Socrates, who are these females who have chanted   350
so august a song? Surely they must be demigods?

SOCRATES:
No, they are skyborne Clouds, great goddesses to layabouts.
They fill us up with thoughts and quibbles, mindfulness and nonsense,
circumlocution and deceptiveness and comprehension.

STREPSIADES:
That's why my soul began to flutter when it heard them sing.
It yearns already to be splitting hairs and quibbling over
vapor and arguing the opposite of some old saying
it skewered with a little thought. I burn to see these powers
face-to-face, if seeing them that way is possible.

(The Chorus of Clouds enter through the side aisles.)

SOCRATES:

Look that way toward Mount Parnes. That is where I now can see them   360
gently descending.

STREPSIADES:

Where, now? Show me.

SOCRATES:

Look right over there.
Yes, quite a few of them are coming through the groves and hollows,
moving sideways.

STREPSIADES:

What is wrong with me? I still can't see them.

SOCRATES:

There by the gateway.

STREPSIADES:

Now at last I almost make them out.

SOCRATES:

Now you should see them very vividly, unless your eyes
are stuffed with styes as big as pumpkins.

STREPSIADES:

Yes, by Zeus, I see them.
O most honored Clouds! They now are covering everything.

SOCRATES:

You really mean to say you never thought the Clouds were gods?

STREPSIADES:

That's news to me. I thought that they were mist and dew and smoke.

SOCRATES:

You never knew, then, that the Clouds nourish the many sophists,   370
Thurii prophets,° doctors, lazy longhairs wearing onyx rings,

song-twisters for the cyclic contests and the weather wizards.
They nourish all these kinds of reprobates because such men
write poetry about them.

STREPSIADES:
That must be the reason why
the poets sing about "the dreaded onrush of the moist,
bright-whirling Clouds" and "curls of Typhon with his hundred heads"
and "blowhard squalls" and "aerial soddenness" and "crooked-clawed,
sky-riding birds" and "showers from dewy Clouds." In compensation,
the poets get "fillet of good fine trout" and "thrush-bird cutlets,"°

SOCRATES:
Isn't it perfect that the poets get their food from Clouds?   380

STREPSIADES:
Say, now, if they are really clouds, what has gone wrong with them
that they resemble mortal women? Clouds don't look like this.

SOCRATES:
But of what nature are the clouds?

STREPSIADES:
Well, I can't say for sure.
Clouds look like spread-out fleeces, not like women. These have noses.

SOCRATES:
Answer, now, what I ask you.

STREPSIADES:
Alright, ask me anything.

SOCRATES:
When looking skyward, have you ever seen a cloud look like a centaur?
A panther? Like a wolf? A bull?

STREPSIADES:
Of course I have. So what?

SOCRATES:
Clouds can assume whatever shape they wish. Say that they see
a man with long locks, an obscene and hairy fellow like
the son of Xenophantes.° They, then, take the form of centaurs   390
to ridicule the fellow's wildness.

STREPSIADES:
                              What if they see Simon,°
a plunderer of public property? What do they do?

SOCRATES:
They turn to wolves to comment on his nature.

STREPSIADES:
                                    Oh, that's why,
just yesterday the clouds resembled deer—it was because
they saw Cleonymus,° a very cowardly sort of fellow.

SOCRATES:
Now they have turned to women, since they looked at Cleisthenes.°

          (The Chorus of Clouds have now reached the stage area.)

STREPSIADES: (to the Clouds)
Greetings, regal powers, queens of all. If you have ever
shared your lofty voice with humans, please do so with me.

CHORUS LEADER: (to Strepsiades)
Greetings to you, old man, seeker of educated words,

                      (to Socrates)

and you, high priest of subtle blather. What do you desire?   400
Know we do not pay heed to any other of the current
astral philosophers except for Prodicus° (that wise
and learned man) and you, because you swagger through the streets
and cast your eyes askance and, barefoot, suffer much discomfort
and seem so arrogant because you put such faith in us.

STREPSIADES:

Wow, what a voice—holy and venerable and awe-inspiring.

SOCRATES:

Yes, the Clouds alone are goddesses; the rest is nonsense.

STREPSIADES:

What about Zeus? Don't say Olympian Zeus is not a god.

SOCRATES:

What Zeus? Stop talking nonsense. There's no Zeus.

STREPSIADES:

                                                    What are you saying?
Who does the raining, then? Explain that to me first of all.   410

SOCRATES:

The Clouds make rain, of course. I will convince you of it thusly:
Have you ever seen your Zeus make rain when there are no clouds?
He should be capable of raining when the clouds are gone.

STREPSIADES:

That argument has won me over. Still, before today,
I really did believe Zeus pissed the rain. But tell me this:
Who is the one that makes the thunder (and that makes me tremble)?

SOCRATES:

The Clouds do also, when they roll around.

STREPSIADES:

                                        How do you mean,
you crazy-talker?

SOCRATES:

                        When they are suspended in the sky
and full of great amounts of water, they, compelled to move
and stuffed with rain, collide with one another. Then they burst   420
open and, owing to their great weight, make a thunderclap.

STREPSIADES:

Who is it, though, that makes them start to move? That must be Zeus!

SOCRATES:

No, it's ethereal Vortex.

STREPSIADES:

Vortex? No one told me Zeus is gone
and Vortex now is ruling in his place. But you have yet
to teach me of the reason for the thunderclap.

SOCRATES:

Didn't you hear me?
I said the Clouds, when stuffed with moisture, smash against each other
and, owing to their density, create a sound.

STREPSIADES:

Come on,
who would believe that?

SOCRATES:

I will teach you out of your own body:
Haven't you, say, at the Panathenaea,° eaten too much soup
and got a queasy stomach, and a sudden breath of wind
has set you rumbling down there?

430

STREPSIADES:

I have. The soup makes lots
of trouble for me, sloshes, rumbles and at last explodes
like thunder. First there is a soft *pa-pax, pa-pax*, and then
a loud *pa-pax! pa-pax!* And then the clap, *pa-pa-pa-PAX!*

SOCRATES:

Think how immense a fart then issued from your little belly.
Isn't it likely that the boundless air could make a giant
crap of thunder?

STREPSIADES:

     Oh, that's why we call a loud fart "thunderous."
Teach me this, now: Where do fiery bolts of lightning come from?
When they hit us, they can burn us up and, if they fail
to kill a man, can leave him singed. Zeus obviously hurls them   440
at perjurers as punishment.

SOCRATES:

     You stupid Dark Age relic!
If Zeus smites perjurers, why, then, has he refrained from smiting
Simon, Theorus and Cleonymus?° All that they do
is lie in court! But, no, Zeus strikes instead the shrines of Zeus
and sacred Cape Sunium,° and the tall oak trees. Why smite them?
Do oak trees lie in law courts?

STREPSIADES:

     I don't know. Your words sound good.
What makes the lightning, then?

SOCRATES:

     When dry wind rises and gets trapped
inside a cloud, it makes the cloud expand internally
like a balloon. The dry wind, then, explodes the cloud and rushes
outward with great force, owing to its density, and catches   450
fire because of all the impetus and flatulence.

STREPSIADES:

That's just what happened to me once at the Diasia.°
When I was roasting up a sausage for my relatives,
I failed to slit it, and it swelled up and exploded, spit
juice in my eyes and burned my face.

SOCRATES:

     Henceforth will you believe
in no gods other than ones that we exalt, that is,
Chaos, the Clouds and Tongue?

STREPSIADES:

                         Yep, if I met another god,
I wouldn't even stop to speak to him. He would receive
no victims, no libations and no frankincense from me.

CHORUS LEADER:

You, mortal man, who have desired to learn great wisdom from us,   460
will live in perfect happiness among the people of Athens
and all the Greeks, if you are good at memorizing things,
if you are thoughtful, if there is endurance in your soul,
if you shall not grow tired of being on your feet or seated,
if you shall not be vexed too much by cold, nor need to eat,
if you shall keep from wine and exercise and all such nonsense,
if, like a wise man, you believe that it is proper both
to win by deed and counsel and to battle with your tongue.

STREPSIADES:

As for a stubborn spirit and unsleeping aggravation
and stinginess and pinched digestion and alfalfa-dinners,   470
have no fear—I've got them all, and I am yours to beat on.

CHORUS LEADER:

Be bold, then, tell us what to do for you, and we will do it.
Just be our true adorer. Be a seeker after wisdom.

STREPSIADES:

Queens of the sky, there's one small thing I want: to be the greatest
orator in all Greece by at least a hundred miles.

CHORUS LEADER:

That blessing will be yours. From here on out there will be no one
who gets more resolutions passed in your Assembly House.

STREPSIADES:

No, not that kind of bullshit—that's not what I want, but only
to twist laws to my benefit and to escape my debt.

CHORUS LEADER:
Then you shall have what you desire, because your hopes are modest.   480
Be resolute, now, and entrust yourself to our disciples.

STREPSIADES:
Yes, I will trust in you, because I am oppressed by need,
need born of purebred steeds and an abominable marriage.

(to the audience)

From here on out my body's theirs to do with as they please—
to beat, to starve, to parch, to soil, to freeze,
even to flay into a wineskin—if only I get free
of all my debts and win celebrity
as a glib, daring, shameless maker of deceits, a nimble
coiner of words, a fox, a tinkling cymbal,
a king of legalese, a code of laws, a shyster pest,   490
a slick impostor, rogue and whipping post.
They can, so long as I am called by names like these,
do with me absolutely as they please,
like, have my body chopped up, ground up, packed into a wiener°
and served to intellectuals as dinner.

CHORUS: *(to Strepsiades)*
Your spirit is keen and brave.
Rest assured that, if I teach
the art of speech
to you, you will possess
a sky-high stature   500
among your race.

STREPSIADES:
What is my future?

CHORUS:
All your days
you shall have
an enviable life.

STREPSIADES:

> Really truly?

CHORUS:

> Yes.

CHORUS LEADER:

Many people will be sitting always at your gateway,
wanting to converse with you and ask for your advice,
a horde of people seeking your opinions on lawsuits
and liens worth lots of money, and you will deserve their praise.   510

(to Socrates)

It's time to teach this geezer all that you intend to teach him.
Go, test his intellect and make a trial of his opinions.

SOCRATES: *(to Strepsiades)*
Come on, tell me what sort of mind you have.
Once I have grasped it, I can bring the proper
newfangled weaponry to bear on you.

STREPSIADES:
Do you intend to make a siege of me?

SOCRATES:
No, I just want to learn up front how good
a memory you have.

STREPSIADES:

> Well, it depends.
If someone owes me, I remember well;
if I, unlucky man, owe someone else,   520
I tend to be forgetful.

SOCRATES:

> Were you born
to be a clever speaker?

STREPSIADES:

A speaker, no;
a swindler, yes.

SOCRATES:

How, then, will you be able
to learn the art of speaking?

STREPSIADES:

I'll manage it.

SOCRATES:

Be sure that, when I toss out clever morsels
of subtlety, you quickly snap them up.

STREPSIADES:

What, will I feed on wisdom like a dog?

SOCRATES:

You are an ignorant barbarian.
I fear, old man, that you will need a beating
if you are to learn. Come, sir, and tell me   530
what you would do if someone beat you up.

STREPSIADES:

Well, I'd get beat up and after that
I'd summon witnesses and after that
take him to court.

SOCRATES:

Come, lay your cloak aside.

STREPSIADES:

Have I done something bad?

SOCRATES:

No, nothing wrong.
The rule among us is to cross this threshold
without a cloak on.

STREPSIADES:

I don't intend to plant
some goods and then blame you for stealing them.

SOCRATES:
Lay down the cloak. Why are you talking nonsense?

(Strepsiades takes off his cloak.)

STREPSIADES:
If I work hard and learn my lessons well,   540
which of your students will I most resemble?

SOCRATES:
I think you will be just like Chaerephon.°

STREPSIADES:
Oh no, I will become the living dead!

SOCRATES:
No guff, now. Promptly follow me inside.

STREPSIADES:
Alright, but first give me a honey cake
to feed the sacred snake. I'm scared to enter
a hole that's like Trophonius's cave.°

SOCRATES:
Go on. Stop peering through the door like that.

(Socrates and Strepsiades exit into the Thinkery.)

CHORUS:

(to Strepsiades as he exits)

Brave as you are,
may you find happiness in there.   550

(to the audience)

Yes, may success attend the man
because, though he has gone
far down his lifetime's passageway,
he dares to dye his nature
in contemporary culture
and labor toward sagacity.

CHORUS LEADER:
Audience, all I tell you will be true, so help me Dionysus,
who nurtured me. So may I win the prize and be considered wise,
I thought you were discerning spectators and this was my
most clever comedy. I put a lot of work into the thing   560
and let you taste it first. Though I deserved to win, I lost the contest,°
defeated by inferior men. I blame the most astute of you—
it was for you I worked so hard on it. Believe me, I will never
deliberately betray the smartest of you. Ever since the time
when my two characters, the Nice Boy and the Faggot,° won much praise
from certain men to whom it is a pleasure to refer, yes, back when I,
a maiden author not yet due to be a mother, left my child
exposed and had another maiden take it up, and you all had it
generously raised and educated, ever since that time
I have enjoyed sworn pledges of a favorable judgment from you.   570

So now this play is like renowned Electra,° traveling in search
of a sophisticated audience, for she will recognize,
if she should see, her brother's lock of hair. Look closely: she is modest
by nature. First of all, she hasn't come here with a dangling leather
strap-on attached to her—a thick one with a red tip meant to make
the children laugh. She doesn't mock the bald or dance a sleazy cordax,°

and there's no old man in the play who lashes people with his cane
to cover up lame jokes. She doesn't dash about the stage with torches
or yammer, "Goodness! Goodness!" No, the girl has come here trusting in
herself alone and poetry.

I'm hardly an obnoxious poet.   580
I'd never try to swindle you by putting out the same play two
or three times.° Furthermore, I'm good at introducing fresh ideas,
each unlike the others, all of them quite clever. It was I
who struck a blow at Cleon's paunch° when he was in his pride but later
refused to keep on pummeling the fellow after he was down.
But other poets, once Hyperbolus° had given them a grip,
kept beating on the sorry fellow, and his mother. First of all,
Eupolis put his *Maricas* before you.° He had plagiarized
my play *The Knights* (because he is a plagiarist) to make his play
and even added in a drunken hag to dance a naughty cordax—   590
the very woman Phrynichus° had put onstage some time ago,
the one the sea beast longed to eat. Hermippus° was the next to write
verses about Hyperbolus, and all the other poets now
will not stop battering Hyperbolus, in imitation of
the similes I wrote about the eels.° Whoever laughs at *their* jokes
should not enjoy my plays. If you delight in me and my inventions,
however, people in the future will remember you as wise.

CHORUS:
> *Strophe*
> The first god I invite to join our choir
> is mighty Zeus, the king who rules on high.
> The potent trident-wielder°   600
> comes next, who shakes the land and sea,
> then Aether who bestows vitality
> on all, a father god of great repute.
> Last comes the deity who fills the plain
> of Earth with vivid rays of light,
> the charioteer° who daily proves a great
> power among the gods and mortal men.

CHORUS LEADER:

Most clever audience, give us your attention. We were wronged by you,
and we will censure you directly.
                                    We support the city of Athens
better than all the other gods, and yet to us alone you fail   610
to offer sacrifice or pour libation. We watch over you.
Whenever you begin a foolish expedition, we erupt
in rain and thunder. When you were about to choose that god-detested
Paphlagonian tanner Cleon as a general,° we wrinkled
our brows and made frightening noises; lightning struck, and thunder
    followed;
the Moon forsook her usual course; the Sun was quick to snuff his wick
and said that he would give no light to you if Cleon should be general.
You chose him anyway.
                          They say that terrible decision-making
plagues this town but that the gods transform these lapses to successes.
We will swiftly teach you how this choice as well can come to good.   620
If you convict that vulture Cleon of embezzlement and graft
and bind his neck fast in the stocks, your situation will return
to what it was before and, though you made a bad mistake in judgment,
everything, in the end, will wind up only benefiting Athens.

CHORUS:

> Antistrophe
> Delian Apollo, Phoebus, you who live
> atop Mount Cynthus, listen to my prayer,
> and you, too, blessed goddess of
> Ephesus's golden temple,° where
> the Lydian virgins bow before your power,
> and you, Athena, goddess of this town,   630
> aegis-wielder, warden of city walls,
> and Bacchus, boon companion,
> who, from a peak of Mount Parnassus, shine
> in torchlight on the Delphic bacchanals.

CHORUS LEADER:
When we were getting ready to travel here, the Moon by chance approached
    us
and told us, first, give her greeting to the Athenians and their allies.
She then said she was irritated. You had wronged her, she explained,
though she has helped you not in words but actively.
                                        First off,
you spend less money buying torches, since, on certain evenings,
everybody tells their slaves, "No need to buy a torch because   640
the moon is shining." She explained that, though she does you other favors,
you run your calendar erroneously and confuse the dates
across the board. She said the gods reprove her when they miss a dinner
and come home after having shown up for a feast too late or early.
Then, when you should be offering them sacrifices, you are busy
torturing witnesses and litigating. Often, when we gods
are sitting for a fast to mourn the loss of Sarpedon or Memnon,°
you all are pouring drinks and laughing. That is why we stripped the garland
off Hyperbolus, this year's allotted Sacred Signatory.°
Thus he will learn that he should spend his days according to the Moon.   650

(Socrates enters from the Thinkery.)

SOCRATES:
I swear by Respiration, Air and Chaos
I have never met so ignorant,
forgetful, frustrating and dumb a hick
in all my life. The man forgets the tiniest
little quibble that I teach him even
before he learns it. All the same, I'll call him
out into daylight, and we'll try again.
Strepsiades? Come out and bring your bed.

(Strepsiades enters from the Thinkery
carrying a pallet bed and blankets.)

STREPSIADES:
Ah, but the bedbugs—they don't want me to.

SOCRATES:

Be quick, now. Set it down and pay attention.   660

STREPSIADES:

Okay.

(Strepsiades puts down the bed and blankets.)

SOCRATES:

     Of all the things you've never learned,
which do you want most to be taught about?
Shall we begin with measures, words or rhythms?

STREPSIADES:

Measures.° Just the other day a grocer
cheated me out of two whole quarts of flour.

SOCRATES:

That's not my meaning. Which is the most appealing,
three-measure? Four?

STREPSIADES:

          I like the gallon best.

SOCRATES:

What are you babbling about?

STREPSIADES:

            You want
to bet four quarts don't measure out a gallon?

SOCRATES:

Oh, go to hell, you stupid hick. Let's try   670
rhythms—they might be easier to grasp.

STREPSIADES:

Will rhythms help me earn my daily bread?

SOCRATES:
You will be great at making conversation
if you know the difference between
the "battle" rhythm and the "finger" rhythm.

STREPSIADES:
"Finger"? I know about the finger.

SOCRATES:
                    What?

STREPSIADES:
What answer can I give except

(holding up his middle finger)

                this finger?
When I was young, "the finger" stood for *this*.

SOCRATES:
You clod.

STREPSIADES:
            But I don't want to learn this stuff.

SOCRATES:
What do you want to learn?

STREPSIADES:
                That, that Argument—   680
the one you intellectuals call the "Wrong."

SOCRATES:
But there are other things you must learn first:
namely, which animals are rightly male?

STREPSIADES:
If I am not insane, I know the males:
ram, billy goat, bull, dog, bird.

SOCRATES:
That's very good. Now tell me which are female?

STREPSIADES:
Ewe, nanny goat, cow, bitch, bird.

SOCRATES:
Ah, do you see what you have done? You used
the same word, "bird," for both the male and female.

STREPSIADES:
How's that?

SOCRATES:
   You called one "bird"; the other, "bird."   690

STREPSIADES:
What should I call them, then, from here on out?

SOCRATES:
Call one "birdette" and call the other "birdus."

STREPSIADES:
"Birdette"? I promise by the Holy Air
for that one bit of learning I will fill
your kneading-trough with lots and lots of flour.

SOCRATES:
See! You have made the same mistake. You made
"trough," which is feminine, be masculine.

STREPSIADES:
How did I make the word "trough" masculine?

SOCRATES:
The -*ough*, like -*us* as in "Cleonymus."

STREPSIADES:
Say what?

SOCRATES:
Their endings—they are masculine. 700

STREPSIADES:
Cleonymus possessed no kneading-trough

(*making a masturbatory gesture*)

but worked his hands through flesh meal down below.
From now on, then, what should I call the "trough"?

SOCRATES:
Call it "troughette," just as you say *Babbette*.

STREPSIADES:
"Troughette" is feminine?

SOCRATES:
That is correct.

STREPSIADES:
Good, I can say "troughette" just like *Babbette*.

SOCRATES:
Now you must learn which names are masculine
and which are feminine.

STREPSIADES:
I know some names of females.

SOCRATES:
Tell me, then.

STREPSIADES:
Clitagora, Lysilla,
Demetria, Phillinna.

SOCRATES:
And names for males?

STREPSIADES:
Thousands: Philoxenus, Melesias,
Amynias.

SOCRATES:
But these aren't masculine,
you moron.

STREPSIADES:
Aren't they masculine to you?

SOCRATES:
No, they are not. See here, how would you call for
Amynias if you met him.°

STREPSIADES:
I would say,
"Hey, Minnie, over here!"

SOCRATES:
See? You just called
Amynias a woman.

STREPSIADES:
That makes sense,
since "she" does not do military duty.
But why learn things that everybody knows?

SOCRATES:
You are incorrigible!

(gesturing to the bed)

Lie down here.   720

STREPSIADES:
And then do what?

SOCRATES:
                    Think about your own troubles.

STREPSIADES:
Not here, I beg you. If I must lie down,
just let me do my thinking on the ground.

SOCRATES:
There is no other way.

STREPSIADES:
                    Poor me, the bedbugs
will make me pay in blood for all my debts!

*(Socrates exits into the Thinkery. Strepsiades lies down
in the bed and covers himself with blankets.)*

CHORUS:
          It's time for meditation
          and close investigation.
          Throw blankets round yourself, then toss
          and turn and, if you get in trouble,
          leap to a new thought on the double.   730
          May gentle sleep be absent from your eyes.

STREPSIDES: *(scratching himself)*
          Ow! And ow again!

CHORUS:
          What's wrong with you?

STREPSIDES: *(sitting up)*

I'm almost dead!

Poor me, the critters in this bed
are crawling all over my skin,
eating me up, biting my side,
sucking my soul,
nibbling my nuts,
and plowing my hole!
They're chewing me to bits!   740

CHORUS:

Would you stop carrying on?

STREPSIADES:

Why? My money's gone,
my color gone,
my spirit gone,
and both of my slippers, gone.
What's worse, on top of all these woes,
with singing all night long like this,
I myself am lost
almost.

SOCRATES: *(peeking out of a window in the Thinkery)*
Hey you, what are you up to? Meditating?   750

STREPSIADES:
Yes, quite a bit.

SOCRATES:

What are your thoughts about?

STREPSIADES:
Whether these bugs will eat me up entirely.

SOCRATES:
Oh, go to hell.

STREPSIADES:

        I'm there already, friend.

SOCRATES:

Now, don't be such a wimp. Get all wrapped up
inside the blankets. Think, think till you discover
scams and a fraudulent cast of mind.

STREPSIADES:

                          Poor me!
I wish someone would cast a cloak of fraud
over me to replace these sheepskin blankets.

(Socrates enters from the Thinkery.)

SOCRATES:

Alright, then, let me see what he is up to.
Hey, are you sleeping?

STREPSIADES:

        No, I'm wide awake.   760

SOCRATES:

Have you had any good ideas?

STREPSIADES:

          No,
by Zeus, no good ideas.

SOCRATES:

        Nothing at all?

STREPSIADES: *(throwing his blanket off to reveal his hand on his leather
strap-on)*
Nothing except this boner in my hand.

SOCRATES:

Cover yourself and think some grand thoughts, quick.

STREPSIADES: *(covering himself with the blanket again)*
Thoughts about what? Instruct me, Socrates.

SOCRATES:
No, you yourself tell me what you would learn.

STREPSIADES:
I've told you what a thousand times already:
how not to pay the interest on my debts.

SOCRATES:
Get down beneath the blankets, spread your thoughts
outward, make them subtle, then consider   770
your personal business, making sure to draw
the right distinctions.

STREPSIADES:
                        Oh, I'm miserable!

SOCRATES:
Keep still, and when a thought will go no further,
abandon it a little while and then
start contemplating it again until
you lock it up.

                (A few "beats" pass onstage.)

STREPSIADES:
                O most sweet Socrates!

SOCRATES:
What is it, old man?

STREPSIADES:
                I have found a way
to cheat my creditors out of the interest.

SOCRATES:
Present it to me.

STREPSIADES:
                Say that . . .

SOCRATES:
                        Yes? Go on.

STREPSIADES:
. . . I were to buy a witch from Thessaly°   780
and make her drag the moon out of the sky
and lock it in a big round box, as if
it were a mirror. Say I kept it safe . . .

SOCRATES:
But how would this be useful to you?

STREPSIADES:
                                        How?
If there were no moon, I would never need
to pay the interest on my debts.

SOCRATES:
                        Why's that?

STREPSIADES:
Because the interest increases monthly.

SOCRATES:
Excellent. Let me now propose a further
test case: Let's say a certain plaintiff sues you
for thirty thousand drachmas. How would you   790
get out of it?

STREPSIADES:
                How? How? I don't know yet.
Just give me time to think the matter over.

SOCRATES:

Don't always keep your thoughts locked up within you.
Let your mind go out and ride the air,
like a pet beetle dangling from a thread.

STREPSIADES:

Aha! I've found a very clever way
of getting out of it. You'll like it, too.

SOCRATES:

How would you do it?

STREPSIADES:

               Have you ever seen
that stone that druggists sell, the pretty, see-through
one that can be used to start a fire?   800

SOCRATES:

You mean a burning-glass?

STREPSIADES:

                   That's what I mean.
Let's say that, when the clerk was entering
the suit into his tablet, I was standing
like this some distance off and holding up
the glass between the sun and him and melting
the wax right where my suit was being entered.

SOCRATES:

Genius!

STREPSIADES:

          I know! I have expunged a case
worth thirty thousand drachmas from the dock.

SOCRATES:

Consider this, now.

STREPSIADES:

What's that?

SOCRATES:

You're on trial;
you've got no witnesses; the guilty verdict   810
is all but certain—how do you contrive
to get out of it?

STREPSIADES:

That's an easy one.

SOCRATES:

What do you do?

STREPSIADES:

Alright, I'll tell you: I,
while there is time before my suit is called,
run off and hang myself.

SOCRATES:

That's stupid talk.

STREPSIADES:

That's what I'd do! No one could sentence me
if I were dead!

SOCRATES:

You're talking nonsense. Get out!
I refuse to teach you any longer.

STREPSIADES:

Socrates, please, no. Keep on teaching me.

SOCRATES:

The things I tell you slip your mind so quickly.   820
What was the first thing that I taught you? Tell me.

STREPSIADES:

Hmn, yeah. What was the first thing? What came first?
Oh, we were kneading dough in something, hmn—
what did you call the thing?

SOCRATES:

Get out of here,
you old, forgetful oaf!

STREPSIADES:

Oh no! Poor me!
What's going to happen to me now? I'm done for
if I don't learn to wrestle with my tongue.
Clouds, can you offer any good advice?

CHORUS LEADER:

Old man, we offer you the following counsel:
If you have a full-grown son at home,   830
send him here to study in your stead.

STREPSIADES:

I have a fine and handsome son indeed,
but he refused to come and study here.
What should I do?

CHORUS LEADER:

Can't you compel him?

STREPSIADES:

No.
He's big and strong and, on his mother's side,
descends from rich girls who are like Coesyra.
Still, I will pressure him. If he refuses,
I will throw him straight out of the house!

(to Socrates)

Go in and wait for me. I'll be back soon.

(Strepsiades exits into his house.)

CHORUS: *(to Socrates)*
      Do you perceive you soon will win   840
      great blessings though our aid? That man
      will do what he is told to do.
      While he is awed and giddy, you
      will do your best to take him in.
      Still, sketchy matters of this kind
      often refuse to go as planned.

(Socrates exits into the Thinkery. Strepsiades and
Pheidippides enter from their house.)

STREPSIADES: *(to Pheidippides)*
I swear by Mist you won't be living with me
any longer. Go and eat your uncle
Megacles's fancy portico.°

PHEIDIPPIDES:
Father, what's wrong with you. You're nuts, by Zeus   850
upon Olympus.

STREPSIADES: *(laughing)*
      "Zeus upon Olympus!"
What foolishness! To think that you believe
in Zeus, a grown boy.

PHEIDIPPIDES:
      What's so funny, Dad?

STREPSIADES:
That you are young and have archaic notions.
Nevertheless, come here, and I will teach you
something that will make a man of you.
But, hey now, don't share this with anyone.

PHEIDIPPIDES:
What is it?

STREPSIADES:
            Zeus—you swore by Zeus just now.

PHEIDIPPIDES:
I did.

STREPSIADES:
        See here, ain't education great?
Pheidippides, there is no Zeus.

PHEIDIPPIDES:
                        Who's up there?   860

STREPSIADES:
Vortex has ousted Zeus and claimed the throne.

PHEIDIPPIDES:
That's dumb.

STREPSIADES:
            You can be certain that it's true.

PHEIDIPPIDES:
Who told you this?

STREPSIADES:
                The Melian Socrates
and Chaerephon, who knows the feet of fleas.

PHEIDIPPIDES:
Have you become so very mad yourself
that you believe the words of madmen?

STREPSIADES:

Hush.

Refrain from idle talk. Say nothing bad
about the wise and clever. They, through thrift,
have never shaved or rubbed themselves with oil
or ever washed their grime off in a bathhouse,   870
while you are bathing all my wealth away
as if I were already dead. Quick, now,
you go and study with them in my place.

PHEIDIPPIDES:

What could a person ever learn from *those* guys?

STREPSIADES:

All the wisdom that there is on earth.
And you will learn yourself how dumb you are,
how ignorant. Wait here for me a minute.

(Strepsiades exits into his house.)

PHEIDIPPIDES: *(to the audience)*
What can I do now that my dad is crazy?
Go to court and get him certified?
Go leave a message with the undertaker?   880

(Strepsiades returns with two birds.)

STREPSIADES:
Come, now, what do you call this here?

PHEIDIPPIDES:

A bird.

STREPSIADES:
Good, and what's this?

PHEIDIPPIDES:

A bird.

STREPSIADES:

                              You called them both
"bird." How ridiculous is that! From now on
call this one "birdus" and this here "birdette."

PHEIDIPPIDES:

"Birdette." Is this some clever thing you learned
while studying with those primordial monsters?

STREPSIADES:

Yes, and a lot more, too. The problem was
that everything I learned immediately
escaped my mind—I'm just too old for school.

PHEIDIPPIDES:

Is this the reason why you lost your cloak?   890

STREPSIADES:

I didn't lose it; I paid it as tuition.

PHEIDIPPIDES:

How did you lose your slippers, you old fool.

STREPSIADES:

I spent them on "necessities," you know,
like Pericles once said.° Come on, let's go.
So long as you obey your father, you
may do the wrong thing. I remember, back
when you were just a lisping little kid,
I was obeying you. In fact I used
the first money I earned in jury pay
to buy a toy for you, a little wagon,   900
at the Diasia.°

PHEIDIPPIDES:

                              You will regret this,

STREPSIADES:

I'm glad that you are listening to me now.

(calling into the Thinkery)

Come out, come out, now, Socrates. This is
my son—I dragged him here against his will.

(Socrates enters from the Thinkery.)

SOCRATES:

He's young; he has to get the hang of things here.

PHEIDIPPIDES: *(to Socrates)*
May you, who have the hang of them, get hanged.

STREPSIADES:

You rotten boy. Do you insult your teacher?

SOCRATES:

"Get hanged"—how childishly he spoke that phrase,
and with his lips spread wide. How will he ever
learn to win acquittal from a trial,   910
compose a writ or make convincing points
in a debate? Oh well, Hyperbolus
has learned this, though it cost him quite a bit.

STREPSIADES:

No worries. He will learn. My son was born
precocious. When he was a little boy
only as tall as *this,*

(holding out his hand)

                    he used to sit
indoors and make toy houses, model warships,
little figwood carts and—just imagine—
frogs out of pomegranate rinds.

                         You just
be sure he learns both of the arguments: 920
Right, or whatever it is called, and Wrong,
the one that, while maintaining what is wrong,
defeats the Right. If both of them are too much,
just teach the Wrong one—that's the one that matters.

SOCRATES:
He will be taught by both the Arguments
in person. I have other things to do.

STREPSIADES:
Remember, though, the boy has to be able
to give the lie to all just arguments.

          (Socrates exits into the Thinkery as Right Argument
              enters through the same stage door.)

RIGHT ARGUMENT: *(to Wrong Argument inside)*
Come out and meet the audience.
You're hardly shy.

          (Wrong Argument enters from the Thinkery.)

WRONG ARGUMENT: *(to Right Argument)*
                    You go where you want.   930
I'll destroy you all the better
with all these people watching.

RIGHT ARGUMENT:
                    You—
you'll destroy *me*? Just what are *you*?

WRONG ARGUMENT:
An Argument.

RIGHT ARGUMENT:
          Yes, but a Wrong one.

WRONG ARGUMENT:
Go and claim that you are Right.
I'm going to beat you, all the same.

RIGHT ARGUMENT:
By using what clever reasoning?

WRONG ARGUMENT:
By coming up with new ideas.

RIGHT ARGUMENT:
"New ideas" are all the rage,

(gesturing to the audience)

thanks to all these morons here.   940

WRONG ARGUMENT:
No, they are intellectuals.

RIGHT ARGUMENT:
I'll utterly obliterate you.

WRONG ARGUMENT:
Come on and tell me, how will you do it?

RIGHT ARGUMENT:
By arguing for justice.

WRONG ARGUMENT:
                         I'll trash
your arguments with my rejoinders,
since I deny that justice exists.

RIGHT ARGUMENT:
You deny the existence of justice?

WRONG ARGUMENT:
Well, then, where is it?

RIGHT ARGUMENT:
                    Among the gods.

WRONG ARGUMENTS
If justice is there, why hasn't Zeus
been removed from power for chaining up   950
his father Cronus?°

RIGHT ARGUMENT:
                    Nauseating!
You, an obscenity, have gone
too far. I need a pan to puke in!

WRONG ARGUMENT:
You Dark Age windbag.

RIGHT ARGUMENT:
                    You shameless faggot.

WRONG ARGUMENT:
Your words are roses to me.

RIGHT ARGUMENT:
                    Buffoon!

WRONG ARGUMENT:
A crown of lilies.

RIGHT ARGUMENT:
                    Father-killer!

WRONG ARGUMENT:
You just don't get it, do you? You are
sprinkling me with words of gold.

RIGHT ARGUMENT:
In the past such words were lead, not gold.

WRONG ARGUMENT:
Today they are fancy ornaments.   960

RIGHT ARGUMENT:
You're pretty obnoxious.

WRONG ARGUMENT:
                        You're pretty old.

RIGHT ARGUMENT:
It's because of you that none of the young men
want to go to school. The people
of Athens will soon come to recognize
just what sort of education
you've been giving to these morons.

WRONG ARGUMENT:
You are obscenely filthy.

RIGHT ARGUMENT:
                        You,
though prosperous now, once, as a beggar,
swore you were Mysian Telephus
and lived off nibbles from the quibbles   970
of Pandeletus.° You kept them in
a little bag.

WRONG ARGUMENT:
            Oh how witty—

RIGHT ARGUMENT:
Oh how crazy—

WRONG ARGUMENT:
                        . . . your allusion was.

RIGHT ARGUMENT:
. . . you are, and the city of Athens is nuts
for paying your bills while you corrupt
the younger generation.

WRONG ARGUMENT:
                              You Cronus!°
You won't be getting this boy as a student.

RIGHT ARGUMENT:
I will if he is going to be saved
and not given lessons in nonsense.

WRONG ARGUMENT: *(to Pheidippides)*
Come over here. Let him rave to himself.   980

RIGHT ARGUMENT:
Touch him, and I will make you howl!

CHORUS LEADER:
Enough with the insults and fisticuffs.
You both should give a presentation.

(to Right Argument)

You describe what you did to teach
the men of old,

(to Wrong Argument)

            and you describe
the modern sort of education.

After hearing both sides, the boy
can make his choice and go to school.

RIGHT ARGUMENT:
Yes, I agree.

WRONG ARGUMENT:
   I do as well.

CHORUS LEADER:
Perfect. Who will be first to speak?   990

WRONG ARGUMENT:
He can go first, and then I'll use
newfangled phrases and grand conceptions
to shoot down all his arguments.
By the end of this, if he even mutters,
I'll sting his face and both his eyes
so terribly with hornet-like
debating-points that he'll just die.

CHORUS: *(to both Right and Wrong Argument)*
         You now will strive with thoughts and adages and subtle
         distinctions. Which of you has won the battle
         soon enough will become quite clear.   1000
         What wisdom will be in the years to come depends
         on who prevails, and our important friends
         await the outcome of your verbal war.

                    (to Right Argument)

First, you who crowned our senior citizens with many virtues,
deploy the voice you love to use, explain your pedagogy.

RIGHT ARGUMENT:
Thank you. I will describe the old-style kind of education,
how people did things back when I, the advocate of justice,
was in the bloom of youth, and self-restraint was all the rage.
First off, boys never made even the slightest chatter; next,
those from the same ward marched in order to their music teacher's,°   1010
naked and in a body, even when the snow was falling
thick as oatmeal. Third, the boys would never squeeze their thighs
together as they learned to sing by heart "Some Far-off Shout"
or "Queen Athena City-Leveler"° and strained to reach

the perfect harmonies our fathers handed down to us.
If any of them hammed it up or tied the melody in knots
(you know those jazzy sounds certain contemporaries make
to copy Phrynis),° well, that boy was given quite a beating
because he had disgraced the Muses.

                                      Also, when the boys
were sitting down at their gymnastics teacher's, it behooved them   1020
to keep their thighs tucked in so that they never flashed temptation
at those who watched them. Also, when the boys got up again,
they raked the sand together and were careful not to leave
impressions for the men who dote on youth. Back then no boy
was rubbing oil on himself below the belly button,
and so the down and moisture on his private parts resembled
those on peaches. Nor would he affect a woman's voice
or whore himself out with his glances when he went to see
the man who loved him. Nor was it permitted then to take up
a radish-head at supper or to steal parsley or dill   1030
from senior citizens, eat fish or laugh or sit cross-legged.

WRONG ARGUMENT:
That's all as old as the Dipolia° and riddled with
grasshoppers, Cecydes and the Buphonia festival.°

RIGHT ARGUMENT:
And yet these are the rudiments on which I reared the men
who fought at Marathon!° You teach the boys today to go out
wrapped up in layers of clothing. What's the consequence? I choke
with laughter when I see some youth at the Panathenaea
hold out his shield to hide his flabby body, disrespecting
Tritogeneia, when he should be dancing.° Therefore, young man,
be bold enough to side with me, Right Argument, and you   1040
will learn to hate the marketplace, despise the bathhouse, feel
shame over shameful things and burn with rage when someone mocks you.
Yes, when your elders come into the room, you will surrender
your chair, and you will not be scornful of your parents.
You will do nothing that is shameful since you will have cast
afresh the statue of Restraint inside your conscience. Never
will you dash into the shanty of a dancing girl

where you, while leering at the goings-on, will feel an apple,
tossed by a hussy, hit you and destroy your reputation.
Never will you speak against your father, never call him   1050
a graybeard geezer Iapetus° and never bring to mind
how old he is, because it was his life that gave you life.

WRONG ARGUMENT:
Young man, if you side with him in this, you will be like
Hippocrates's sons,° and everyone will call you "moron."

RIGHT ARGUMENT:
And yet you will be sleek and hale because you will be spending
your days at the gymnasium, not making bawdy jokes
while chattering in the marketplace, the way the young do now.
You won't be dragged into a small-claims court because of some
hairsplitting-pettifogging-barefaced-roguish lawsuit; no,
you will go down to the Academy and, with some modest   1060
companion, sprint for exercise beneath the sacred olives.
You will be garlanded with white reeds; you will smell like yew trees
and leisure-time and poplars shedding leaves; you will enjoy
the springtime and adore the plane tree whispering to the elm.

        If you do
        the things I say,
        you will enjoy,
        your whole life long,
        a narrow waist, a healthy hue,
        massive shoulders, a little tongue,   1070
        muscular buttocks and a modest dong.

        If you behave
        like the young do now,
        you will have
        a pigeon chest and ashen hue,
        low shoulders, a colossal tongue
        immense thighs, small buttocks and long
        long speeches to give.

If you do as he directs,
you soon will share his faith   1080
that what is base is glorious
and what is glorious, base.
Still worse, the guy will taint you with
Antimachus's anal sex.°

CHORUS LEADER: *(to Right Argument)*
You are a master of the craft of lofty-towered, far-famed
wisdom. Your words have their own sweetness, their own modest bloom.
Happy were they who lived among the men of olden time.

(to Wrong Argument)

In answer, you who seem to have a flashy Muse will need
to utter fresh new words, because this man has done quite well.

WRONG ARGUMENT:
I have been spoiling in my very guts; I have been burning   1090
to ravage all that he has said with my antilogies.
That's why, among deep thinkers, I am called "Wrong Argument"—
because I was the first to come up with a way of speaking
against both law and justice. It is worth ten thousand staters,°
this art of being on the losing side and yet still winning!
Just watch as I confute the sort of education *he* relies on,
who says that he will not permit a boy to take warm baths:

(to Right Argument)

Why? On what principle do you abominate warm baths?

RIGHT ARGUMENT:
Because they are the worst—they make a man a wimpy coward!

WRONG ARGUMENT:
Stop right there. I already have you gripped about the waist   1100
and helpless. Say, of Zeus's sons, which, do you think, possessed
the bravest soul and underwent the greatest number of labors?

RIGHT ARGUMENT:

I think no man was ever mightier than Heracles.

WRONG ARGUMENT:

Well, have you ever seen cold "Baths of Heracles"?° And who
was mightier than he?

RIGHT ARGUMENT:

                              That's just the guff that stuffs the bathhouse
with bratty blabbermouths and leaves the wrestling school forsaken.

WRONG ARGUMENT:

Next, you assert that spending whole days in the marketplace
is bad. I think it's good. If there were something wrong with it,
Homer would never have referred to sages, such as Nestor,
as "market orators."° Next, turning to the tongue, he claims   1110
young men ought not to exercise it, while I say they should.
He also says we should be modest—that's another evil.
If you have ever seen a person get ahead in life
through modesty, you tell me and refute me with your words.

RIGHT ARGUMENT:

Many people have done well because of modesty.
The hero Peleus acquired a knife because of it.°

WRONG ARGUMENT:

A knife? The poor wretch took in quite a haul, it seems. Ha, ha!
Hyperbolus who sells the lamps,° by being nasty, made
lots and lots of money, but he never got a knife!

RIGHT ARGUMENT:

And Peleus's virtue got him Thetis as a bride.°   1120

WRONG ARGUMENT:

Yes, and his virtue also made her leave him: he wasn't rough
enough with her in bed. That's how the lusty ladies like it,
you geezer from the Stone Age!

(to Pheidippides)

      Stop and think, young man, of all
that modesty can't do, of all that you will miss out on—
boys, women, drinking games, rich food and benders, giggles.
What would your life be worth if you could not enjoy such things?
But let that go. I want to focus now on natural urges.
Imagine you have gone astray, become obsessed, seduced
somebody's wife and up and gotten caught. You are a goner
if you do not know how to speak. But if you side with me,   1130
you can indulge your urges, dance and laugh and never shy
away from so-called "shameful" acts. If you should happen to be
caught with some man's wife, you will be able to reply
that you "have done no wrong," since even Zeus is overcome
by lust for women. How could you, a mortal man, have greater
strength than a god?

RIGHT ARGUMENT:
      What if he listens to you and endures
the hot-ash-on-the-pubes and radish-up-the-asshole treatment?°
Will he be able to debate his way out of the fact
he has a faggot's asshole?

WRONG ARGUMENT:
      Hold on, now. What's wrong with having
a faggot's asshole?

RIGHT ARGUMENT:
      What is *wrong* with that? What could be *worse*?   1140

WRONG ARGUMENT:
What would you say if I were to defeat you on this score?

RIGHT ARGUMENT:
I would concede. There would be nothing else that I could say.

WRONG ARGUMENT:
Now tell me: To what class do court professionals belong?

RIGHT ARGUMENT:
The faggots.

WRONG ARGUMENT:
                Yes, and to what class do tragic poets belong?

RIGHT ARGUMENT:
The faggots.

WRONG ARGUMENT:
                Yes, and to what class do politicians belong?

RIGHT ARGUMENT:
The faggots.

WRONG ARGUMENT:
                Don't you see that you were just now talking nonsense?
Look at the audience. Tell me: To what class do they belong?

RIGHT ARGUMENT: *(looking out at the audience)*
Alright, I'm looking.

WRONG ARGUMENT:
                Well, what do you see there?

RIGHT ARGUMENT:
                                        By the gods,
they're mostly faggots. That guy is, and that guy, and that longhair.

WRONG ARGUMENT:
What do you say?

RIGHT ARGUMENT: *(throwing his cloak away and running to join the audience)*
                I am defeated. Take my cloak, you faggots!   1150
I surrender. I am coming over to your side.

WRONG ARGUMENT: *(to Strepsiades)*
What next? Will you escort your son back home
or shall I teach him how to be an orator?

STREPSIADES:
Go, teach him, beat him, just be sure to give him
a razor edge for me. Hone half his face
for little lawsuits, and the other half
for bigger stuff.

WRONG ARGUMENT:
                    Relax. You will be taking
a clever sophist home with you in time.

PHEIDIPPIDES: *(aside)*
Yes, and a pale-faced and accursèd one.

CHORUS LEADER: *(to Wrong Argument and Pheidippides)*
You two can go.

                    (to Strepsiades)

                    And as for you, I think   1160
you will eventually regret this choice.

                    *(Worse Argument and Pheidippides exit into the
                    Thinkery. Strepsiades exits into his house.)*

CHORUS LEADER:
We want to tell you judges what you stand to gain if you
support us Clouds by voting for us, who deserve to win.° First off,
in spring, when you are plowing up your acres, we will send you rain
earlier than the others. Next we will protect your crops and vineyards
so that neither drought nor excess moisture injures them. However,
any mortal who dishonors our divinity should know
the punishments he will receive from us: he will obtain no wine,
no harvest. When his olive trees and grapevines sprout, we will assail them
so harshly that they will be ruined. If we see him making bricks,   1170

we will unleash much rain and smite his roof tiles with a volley of hailstones.
What's more, if he or any of his friends or family get married,
we will rain the whole night through so that he probably will wish
he were in Egypt even, rather than to have miscast his vote.

(Strepsiades enters from his house.)

STREPSIADES:
Five days until the month is over, four,
now three and after that it will be two
and then, most frightful, dreadful and repulsive,
the day called "Old and New"° will be at hand.
Then everyone I owe goes down to court, deposits
a fixed amount and swears he will destroy me,   1180
however much I beg for fairness, beg
for mercy: "Please don't call the loan in now";
"Give me till next month"; "Give me a reduction."
They say that they will never get their money
paid back that way. They call me villainous
and vow to sue. Now let them sue away—
it doesn't matter, since Pheidippides
has learned to be an expert orator.
By knocking on the school's door here, I soon
will know how he turned out.

(Strepsiades knocks on the door of the Thinkery.)

Hey, boy! Hey, boy!   1190

SOCRATES:
Greetings, Strepsiades.

STREPSIADES:
How good to see you.

(handing Socrates a bag of money)

Please accept this gift. One must, you know,
honor the teacher. Tell me, does my son
now know the Argument you brought out here
not long ago?

SOCRATES:

He does.

STREPSIADES:

By great Queen Fraud,
that's excellent.

SOCRATES:

Henceforth you will be able
to get out of any debt you please.

STREPSIADES:
Even if several witnesses were present?

SOCRATES:
Yes, even if a thousand men were there.

STREPSIADES:

Then I shall yawp a raucous yawp.   1200
You usurers with all
your talk of "principal"
and "interest," learn to weep!
No longer will you wear my wealth away.
A son is being reared for me
inside this house, a boy with razor-tongue,
my mighty wall, my house's guardian,
my enemies' demise,
the lifter of my woes.

(to Socrates)

Go, please, and bring   1210
my boy to me.

(shouting into the Thinkery)

Come out, O darling son!
Your loving dad is calling.

(Pheidippides enters from the Thinkery.)

SOCRATES:

Here he is.

STREPSIADES:

My darling boy!

SOCRATES:

Collect him now and go.

(Socrates exits into the Thinkery.)

STREPSIADES:

Hip, hip, hooray, my child! Hip, hip, hooray!
How pleased I am to see your pale complexion.
You seem, at first glance, contradictory
and problematic, and our native Attic
litigiousness is blooming in your face—
the what-exactly-are-you-saying? look,
the seeming to be injured when, in fact,   1220
you're giving injury and doing wrong.
Oh yes, your face now looks Athenian.
Boy, since you've ruined me, it's time to save me.

PHEIDIPPIDES:

What are you frightened of?

STREPSIADES:

The day they call
the Old and New.

PHEIDIPPIDES:
What day is "Old and New"?

STREPSIADES:
The day each month when creditors lay down
their court deposits.

PHEIDIPPIDES:
Well, all those who do so
will lose them, since it is impossible
one day be two days.

STREPSIADES:
How, "impossible"?

PHEIDIPPIDES:
It is impossible unless you think   1230
one woman can be simultaneously
old and young.

STREPSIADES:
The law says "Old and New Day."

PHEIDIPPIDES:
I think your creditors misunderstand
the meaning of the law.

STREPSIADES:
What does it mean?

PHEIDIPPIDES:
The wise man Solon° loved the people, right?

STREPSIADES:
What has that got to do with Old and New Day?

PHEIDIPPIDES:
That's why he made the summons last for two days,
Old Day and New Day, so that creditors
could lodge deposits on the second day,
the New Day, which we also call "New Moon."   1240

STREPSIADES:
What was the Old Day for?

PHEIDIPPIDES:
                    So that defendants
could appear the day before the due date
and settle the dispute. And, if they couldn't,
to give them extra time to fret before
the morning of the New Moon.

STREPSIADES:
                    Hmn, why then
do magistrates not take deposits on
the New Moon, only on the Old and New Day
a day before?

PHEIDIPPIDES:
            It seems that they are acting
like those who taste the food for festivals—
they want to get their hands on the deposits   1250
a whole day early.

STREPSIADES: *(to Pheidippides)*
            Genius!

                    (to the audience)

                    All you wretches,
why do you just sit there so stupidly,
like stones, like zeros, like a flock of sheep
or heaped ceramic jugs—the easy marks
of intellectual men like us? Because

of my good luck, I'm going to sing a song
to celebrate myself and this my son.

> "How blest you are,
> Strepsiades,
> because you are so wise   1260
> and have so excellent a son."

(to Pheidippides)

That's what my friends and neighbors, everyone,
will say in envy when you prove victorious
in every case you argue at the bar.

Let's go inside the house and have a party.

(Strepsiades and Pheidippides enter their house. The First Creditor,
who has a big belly, and a Witness enter from stage left.)

FIRST CREDITOR:
Should men just hand out portions of their wealth
to others? Never. An unblushing "no"
up front is better than contention later.
Like now, since I must drag you here as witness
all for the sake of my own money. Furthermore,   1270
I will become the enemy of a man
from my own district. Nonetheless, so long
as I am living, I will never shame my country,
and so I hereby call Strepsiades—

STREPSIADES: *(peeking out of the door)*
Who's there?

FIRST CREDITOR:
                    —to come to court on Old and New Day.

STREPSIADES: *(to the Witness)*
You be my witness: he has named two days.

(to the First Creditor)

Why do you summon me?

FIRST CREDITOR:
                              Your debt to me,
twelve minas, which I fronted you to buy
a dappled horse.

STREPSIADES:
                      A horse? You hear this man?
Everyone knows that I hate everything   1280
that has to do with horses.

FIRST CREDITOR:
                      Still, by Zeus,
you vowed by all the gods you would repay it.

STREPSIADES:
I did (because back then Pheidippides
has not yet mastered the Indomitable
Argument).

FIRST CREDITOR:
              Do you, then, deny the debt?

STREPSIADES:
What else will I get back for all that money
I paid out for tuition?

FIRST CREDITOR:
                      Are you willing
to break the oath you swore by all those gods,
wherever I set forth the summons to you?

STREPSIADES:
By all which gods?

FIRST CREDITOR:

          Zeus, Hermes and Poseidon.   1290

STREPSIADES:

By great Zeus, I would throw in three more obols
to swear by him.

FIRST CREDITOR:

              Your gall may yet come back
to haunt you.

STREPSIADES: *(patting the First Creditor's belly)*
          Aw, this chubby little fellow's
belly is begging to be soaked in brine.

FIRST CREDITOR:

Now you are making fun of me.

STREPSIADES: *(still patting the First Creditor's belly)*
               This sack
would hold ten liters.

FIRST CREDITOR:

            You won't get away
with mocking me like this, so help me Zeus
and all the gods!

STREPSIADES: *(laughing)*
          "And all the gods"—I love it!
And oaths by Zeus are very lively jokes
among philosophers.

FIRST CREDITOR:

          Believe you me,   1300
the time will come when you will pay for this.
Now give it to me straight, before I go:
Will you repay the debt you owe to me?

STREPSIADES:
Just hold tight here, and I will answer shortly.

(Strepsiades exits into the house.)

FIRST CREDITOR:
What do you think he'll do?

WITNESS:
I think he'll pay you.

(Strepsiades enters holding a trough.)

STREPSIADES:
Where is the man who claims he lent me money?
Tell me what this is.

FIRST CREDITOR:
What's that? A trough.

STREPSIADES:
And you, who don't know anything, demand
I pay you money? I would not pay even
an obol to a man who called this here   1310
"troughette" a "trough."

FIRST CREDITOR:
Then you refuse to pay me?

STREPSIADES:
As far as I know, yes. But won't you now
get off my stoop as quickly as you can?

FIRST CREDITOR:
I'm going, but be sure that, on my life,
I will deposit money with the court.

STREPSIADES:

Then you will lose it, that and all twelve minas.
Still, I wouldn't have you suffer such misfortune
just for calling a "troughette" a "trough."

> *(The First Creditor and the Witness exit stage left. The*
> *Second Creditor enters, limping, stage right.)*

SECOND CREDITOR:

Ouch! Ouch! Ow!

STREPSIADES:

        Who's carrying on like that?
Surely it wasn't some god out of Carcinus°   1320
that spoke just now.

SECOND CREDITOR:

        Why do you want to know
what man I am? I am a man accursed.

STREPSIADES:

Well, keep it to yourself.

SECOND CREDITOR:

        O cruel Fate!
O goddesses of fortune who have broken
my chariot wheels! O how you have destroyed me,
Pallas Athena!

STREPSIADES:

        What has Tlepolemus°
ever done to injure you?

SECOND CREDITOR:

        Don't mock me.
Just tell your son to pay his debt to me,
especially since I'm in bad shape now.

STREPSIADES:
What debt is that?

SECOND CREDITOR:
                        The money that he borrowed.   1330

STREPSIADES:
You truly are a sad man, then, I think.

SECOND CREDITOR:
I fell out of my chariot while racing.

STREPSIADES:
Why are you talking nonsense, like you tumbled
off an ass?

SECOND CREDITOR:
                How am I talking nonsense?
I only want to get my money back.

STREPSIADES:
Too bad there's no way you are sane.

SECOND CREDITOR:
                                Why's that?

STREPSIADES:
It seems to me your brains have gotten scrambled.

SECOND CREDITOR:
It seems to me that you will soon be summoned
to court, if you do not repay the money.

STREPSIADES:
Tell me now, do you think that, when it rains,   1340
Zeus always sends new water down or is it
water the sun has drawn back from the earth
into the sky again.

SECOND CREDITOR:
           I don't know which,
and I don't care.

STREPSIADES:
           But how can you expect
to be repaid if you know nothing of
meteorology?

SECOND CREDITOR:
           Alright, if you
are feeling pinched, just pay the interest to me.

STREPSIADES:
Tell me, what sort of creature is this "interest"?

SECOND CREDITOR:
What other than the tendency of money
to be always growing, daily, monthly,   1350
as time proceeds?

STREPSIADES:
           You have described it well.
What do you think, now? Has the sea grown larger
than it was before?

SECOND CREDITOR:
           No, it's the same.
It would be wrong if it were any larger.

STREPSIADES:
You wretch, how does the ocean grow no larger
with all those rivers flowing into it,
and yet you want your money to increase?
Get out of here. Now, go.

(to a Slave inside)

Bring me the goad!

*(A Slave enters with a goad. Strepsiades takes it
and jabs the Second Creditor with it.)*

SECOND CREDITOR: *(to the audience)*
I call you all as witnesses to this.

STREPSIADES:
Go, Mr. Fancy Horse. Why drag your hooves?   1360
Why not get galloping?

SECOND CREDITOR:
                        This is an outrage!

STREPSIADES:
Move along or else I'll shove this goad up
your equine asshole. Oh, you're running now?
I thought this goad would get you moving, you
and all your chariots and chariot wheels.

*(The Second Creditor exits, stage right.
Strepsiades exits into his house.)*

CHORUS:
        Strophe
        It is an awful thing
        to have a passion to do wrong.
        That's how this old man here is passionate.
        He burns to get out of repaying debt.

        Surely before the sun goes down today   1370
        this "intellectual" will have met
        with a surprise reversal—he will pay
        for his unjust pursuit.

Antistrophe
I think he very soon
will get what he was after. His son
will prove so skillful at presenting views
that mock what's right and uttering abuse,

that he will vanquish in debate
everyone he comes across.
Perhaps, perhaps the man will wish his brat   1380
were cursed with speechlessness.

(Strepsiades runs out of the house.)

STREPSIADES:
Help! Help me, neighbors! Help me, relatives!
Men of the deme Cicynna, help, help, help!
I'm getting beaten up! My head! My jaw!

(Pheidippides enters from the house.)

You monster, do you dare to hit your father?

PHEIDIPPIDES:
Yes, I do.

STREPSIADES:
See that? The brat admits it!

PHEIDIPPIDES:
I do.

STREPSIADES:
You wretched, parricidal thug!

PHEIDIPPIDES:
More, more insults. Don't you know I love it
when you curse me?

STREPSIADES:

O you gaping asshole.

PHEIDIPPIDES:

Roses, you are sprinkling me with roses.   1390

STREPSIADES:

You dare to beat your father?

PHEIDIPPIDES:

Yes, I do,
and I will prove that I am justified
in doing it.

STREPSIADES:

You monster! How could you
be justified in beating up your father?

PHEIDIPPIDES:

I will present my case, and you will lose
this argument.

STREPSIADES:

What, I am going to lose?

PHEIDIPPIDES:

Yes, I will win this easily. Now choose
which of the Arguments you want to take.

STREPSIADES:

Which of the Arguments?

PHEIDIPPIDES:

Yes, do you want
the Right one or the Wrong one?

STREPSIADES:

                         Pal, if you   1400
are going to convince me that it's just
for fathers to be beaten by their sons,
well, then I really did get you taught well
to speak against what's right.

PHEIDIPPIDES:

                        I'm confident
I'll win, quite confident that, once you hear me,
you'll be left without an argument.

STREPSIADES:

Alright, I guess I'll have to hear you out.

CHORUS:

        Strophe
        If he didn't have a plan,
        he wouldn't be so confident.
        You now must find a way, old man,   1410
        to win this argument.
        That boy is hot to trot. His haughtiness
        is obvious.

CHORUS LEADER:

First things first: it now behooves you to inform the Chorus
how this war got started (though you'd tell us anyway).

STREPSIADES:

I'll tell you how the fight got started. As you know, we'd feasted
and, after that, I asked if he would take his lyre and sing me
something by Simonides, "The Shearing of the Ram."°
Straight off he starts complaining that it's antiquated—strumming
the lyre and singing at a drinking party, tedious like   1420
a woman grinding grain.

PHEIDIPPIDES:

                              Just for requesting that I sing
you ought to have been kicked and beaten. Were you entertaining
cicadas?

STREPSIADES:

              That's the sort of thing he said inside. What's more,
he called Simonides a rotten poet. I could scarcely
control myself, and yet I did. And then I asked him please
to take a bough of myrtle in his hand and speak a speech
from Aeschylus.° Straight off he started saying, "Should I think
Aeschylus is the best of all the poets? Aeschylus
the windbag, the grotesque loudmouth whose words are big as mountains?"
Believe you me, my heart was thumping loudly after that,   1430
but I bit back my wrath and said, "Alright, then, please recite
some sort of clever thing by a contemporary poet."
Straight off he started speaking something by Euripides
about a brother who (I ache to utter it) was screwing
his half sister.° I could no longer keep my rage in check.
I started hurling insults at him, and—you know what happens—
we traded barb for barb. Then, all at once, he's on his feet
and wrestling with me, beating on me, throttling me good.

PHEIDIPPIDES:

And weren't you begging for it, you who scorn Euripides,
the wisest of the poets?

STREPSIADES:

                              What, the wisest? Why, you are a . . .   1440
but I will just get beaten up again.

PHEIDIPPIDES:

                              And justly, too.

STREPSIADES:

Justly? Who brought you up, you wretch? Who guessed at what you wanted
when you were a babbling baby? If you said "wa-wa,"
I'd go and get a drink for you, and if you said "ed, ed,"

I'd go and get you bread. Soon as you started saying "poo-poo,"
I'd lift you in my arms, take you outdoors and hold you out
in front of me. But when you had your hands around my neck

> just now and I was shouting that I had to poop,
> you wouldn't let me go outside,
> you boor,   1450
> but went on choking me until I up
> and dropped a load
> right there.

CHORUS:

> *Strophe*
> Now all the pulses of the young
> are racing, keen for his reply.
> If he can do a deed so wrong
> and win through subtlety,
> then I would value old men's hides henceforth
> of little worth.

CHORUS LEADER: *(to Pheidippides)*
You there, the one with leverage to move new words, must now   1460
find arguments that will convince us you were justified.

PHEIDIPPIDES:
I love consorting with the witty wisdom of today
and scorning all established laws and customs. In the past,
when all I thought about was horsemanship, I couldn't speak
three words together without making a mistake. But now
my father here has got me to forsake my vain pursuits,
and I'm an expert in the subtleties of thought
and argument and speculation. I'm quite confident
that I can demonstrate it's just to strike one's father.

STREPSIADES:
Go back to riding horses, boy! I'd rather pay to keep   1470
a team of four of them than get another thorough thrashing.

PHEIDIPPIDES:

To start again with where I was before the interruption,
I want to ask you: Did you spank me when I was a child?

STREPSIADES:

I did, because I cared for you and hoped to help you.

PHEIDIPPIDES:

Tell me,
shouldn't I show my care for you in just the same way, that is,
by striking you, since violence is, it seems, the same as caring?
Why should your body be immune from blows, and mine not be?
I wasn't born a slave, but free, as you were. "Children cry;
shouldn't their fathers cry as well?"° You will contend, of course,
that spanking children is the custom, but I would reply   1480
old men are in a second childhood. Furthermore, because
the old should certainly know better than to misbehave,
it's more appropriate that they be beaten than the young.

STREPSIADES:

Nowhere is it a custom that a child can beat a father.

PHEIDIPPIDES:

Was it not a man like you and me who first proposed
the custom barring sons from beating fathers? Did he not
persuade the men of old by speaking words? Why can't I then
propose a custom of my own—that it is just for sons
to beat their fathers in revenge? All of the injuries
we suffered from our dads before this novel rule was passed,   1490
we sons hereby forgive—though we were beaten, we will not
seek reparations. Look how roosters and the other beasts
attack their fathers, and the only difference between us
is they don't sit in the Assembly pushing resolutions.

STREPSIADES:

Well, if you want to copy everything that roosters do,
why not go eat manure and take a nap atop a perch?

PHEIDIPPIDES:
It's not the same thing. Socrates would side with me on this.

STREPSIADES:
Still, you shouldn't beat me. If you do, you will regret it.

PHEIDIPPIDES:
Why?

STREPSIADES:
    Just as I have authority to strike my child,
you, too, will have that right, if you have offspring.

PHEIDIPPIDES:
                                  If I don't,   1500
I'll never get revenge for all the times you made me cry,
and you'll be laughing in your grave. What can you say to that?

STREPSIADES: *(to the audience)*
Well, age-mates, as I see it, he has made a valid point.
We must admit the youth are right. It's fitting we should howl
when naughty.

PHEIDIPPIDES:
            Take this other point.

STREPSIADES:
                        Oh no, you're killing me!

PHEIDIPPIDES:
I'll beat on Mom, just like I beat on you.

STREPSIADES:
                      What's that? What's that?
Another even greater wickedness!

PHEIDIPPIDES:
                              What if I took
Worse Argument and used it in debate with you to prove
that it is just to beat one's mother?

STREPSIADES: *(to Pheidippides)*
            Here's what: 1510
            If you proceed to argue this,
            then nothing will prevent
            you from being sent
            tumbling into the Pit
            of Death, along with Socrates
            and your accurséd Argument.

                        (to the Chorus)

Clouds, I entrusted everything to you,
and look at what you've done to ruin me!

CHORUS LEADER:
No, sir; you are to blame for all of it,
because you turned to working wicked schemes.   1520

STREPSIADES:
Why didn't you forewarn me? Why did you
lead on a simple codger from the country?

CHORUS LEADER:
This is what we always do to people
we recognize as lovers of the wrong—
we cast them into wretchedness so that
they learn that henceforth they must fear the gods.

STREPSIADES:
Ah, that is vicious, Clouds, but only just.
I shouldn't have attempted to defraud
my creditors. Now, therefore, come with me,
my dear, dear son. Let's go and get that awful   1530

Chaerephon and Socrates because
they hoodwinked us.

PHEIDIPPIDES:

I won't attack my teachers!

STREPSIADES:
Yes, get them both. Respect Paternal Zeus.

PHEIDIPPIDES:
"Paternal Zeus." How out of date you are!
You think that Zeus exists?

STREPSIADES:

He does.

PHEIDIPPIDES:

He doesn't:
"Vortex has ousted Zeus and claimed the throne."

STREPSIADES:
No, he has not,

(pointing to the "Vortex" jar)

although this Vortex here
made me believe it. Taking a ceramic
jar for a deity—how dumb I was!

PHEIDIPPIDES:
You go on talking nonsense to yourself.   1540

(Pheidippides exits into Strepsiades's house.)

STREPSIADES:
Madness! It was insanity for me
to scorn the gods because of Socrates!

(to the statue of Hermes)

Ah, Hermes, please do not be angry with me,
do not destroy me. No, be merciful,
since someone else's blather made me crazy.
Be my advisor. Should I prosecute them?
What do you think?

(Strepsiades pauses as if to hear the statue's advice.)

You're right, of course. I shouldn't
waste time in court. Yes, I should go and burn
those babblers' house down quickly as I can.

(shouting into the house)

Xanthias, get out here and bring a ladder   1550
and pickax! Climb atop the Thinkery
and hack the roof in. If you love your master,
bring the whole damn ceiling down upon them.

(Xanthias climbs up to the roof of the Thinkery.)

Somebody, light a torch and bring it to me!
I'm going to make them pay for all they've done.
No fancy talk is going to save them this time.

*(The Slave brings Strepsiades a lit torch.
A Student emerges from the Thinkery.)*

STUDENT:
Oh no!

STREPSIADES:
Get to it, torch! Set things ablaze!

(Strepsiades climbs onto the roof of the Thinkery.)

STUDENT: *(to Strepsiades)*
You there, what are you doing?

STREPSIADES:

What am I doing?
I'm going to split your roof beams just like you
split hairs.

CHAEREPHON: *(opening a window in the wooden backdrop)*
Oh no! Who's set our house on fire?   1560

STREPSIADES:
Who? It's the man whose cloak you stole. That's who.

CHAEREPHON:
You'll kill us all! You'll kill us!

STREPSIADES:

So I will,
unless that pickax cheats my hopes or I
slip for some reason, fall and break my neck.

(Socrates opens another window in the wooden backdrop.)

SOCRATES: *(to Strepsiades)*
Hey you, what are you doing on the roof?

STREPSIADES:
"Walking on air and pondering the sun."

SOCRATES:
Oh no! I'm going to cough myself to death!

CHAEREPHON:
What about me? I will be burned alive!

STREPSIADES:
What were you thinking when you insolently
mocked the gods and scoped the Moon's behind?   1570

> *(to Xanthias and the other Slave)*

Remember—all these men have wronged the gods!
Hunt them, stone them, hit them for their crimes!

> *(Strepsiades and Xanthias climb down from the roof of
> the wooden platform and, with the other Slave, chase
> Socrates, Chaerephon, and the Student off stage right.)*

CHORUS: *(to the Chorus Leader)*
It's time to lead us off. We have performed
sufficient choral business for today.

> *(The Chorus Leader leads the Chorus off, stage left.)*

BIRDS

Whereas *Clouds, Lysistrata,* and *Women of the Assembly* all take as their setting Athens at their dates of production, *Birds,* Aristophanes's great play of escape, is exceptional in that it is set outside of Athens and focuses on a non-human world. Considering life in Athens litigious and stressful, two Athenians, Peisthetaerus and Euelpides, head into the wilderness to find Tereus the Hoopoe, leader of the birds, and to make their home there. After meeting Tereus, Peisthetaerus asks him to summon the birds for a conference, and Tereus's monodic song to summon the chorus for the *parodos* contains some of the most beautiful poetry Aristophanes composed:

Epopopoi popopopoi popoi,
ee-you, ee-you, ee-to, ee-to,
come here, all you endowed with wings,
all you who flutter over acres
of fertile land, you myriad throngs
who feed on grain, you swift seed-pickers
who warble such delightful songs.
Come all that over furrowed ground
twitter, *molto espressivo,*
this pleasant sound—
tio, tio, tio, tio, tio, tio, tio, tio. (256–266)

After recovering from their initial hostility to these human beings, the birds learn of their primacy and regality from Peisthetaerus and accept his "Great Idea" to establish a city in the sky—Cloudcuckooland, from which they will usurp the prerogatives of the Olympian gods. This city is simultaneously a utopian dream and a reflection of the Athenian Empire itself. It takes an Athenian, Peisthetaerus, to give the birds imperial ambitions.

The *parabasis* of *Birds* is exceptional in that the various sections of it are all spoken by the Chorus Leader in bird-character. Furthermore, unlike in *Clouds,* the Chorus Leader continues to develop the argument of the play, taking the case directly to the audience (of mortal men):

If you regard us birds as gods,
we shall be seers for you and Muses,
and winds, and winter, and mild summer,

and hot summer. We shall never
run off and sit snobbily in the clouds
like Zeus but, ever present among you,
shall give to you yourselves, to your children
and your children's children, wealth-healthiness,
prosperity, happiness, peace, youth,
good humor, choral dances and festivals
and bird's milk. You'll all be so well off
you could knock yourselves out with your blessings! (732–743)

Peisthetaerus and Euelpides emerge from the *skēnē* adorned with wings and feathers to mark the beginning of the second half of the play. The reprobates and annoying characters who then flock to Cloudcuckooland—the Oracle Collector, the Decree Seller, the Father-Beater, and others—represent all that makes life in Athens unbearable, and each must be rejected in order for the fledgling city to remain a utopia. In a play famous for its poetry, it is striking that we also encounter parodies of poets (in the character of the Poet) and of dithyrambic poets in particular (in the character of Cinesias). Though they are not treated as harshly as other undesirable visitors, they, too, must be hurried out of Cloudcuckooland as swiftly as possible.

After the walls of the city are built and the gods are excluded from the birds' airspace, the birds refuse to allow the smoke of sacrifice to ascend to the gods—an embargo of sorts. On the advice of the sympathetic god Prometheus, Peisthetaerus demands Princess, the keeper of Zeus's lightning bolt, from the divine ambassadors, Poseidon, Heracles, and the Triballian, as a condition of peace. He receives her, and the play ends with a blessed marriage scene that unites man, bird, and god. Whereas *Lysistrata* and *Women of the Assembly*, the other plays in this volume that end in mirth, present the resolution of some particular problem—the Peloponnesian War and political mismanagement, respectively—*Birds* gives us the solution of all problems, a complete escape from the things that make human life unpleasant.

BIRDS

(Ornithes)

First produced in 414 BCE

CHARACTERS IN THE PLAY

Euelpides

Peisthetaerus

Xanthias

Manodorus (Manes)

Slave Bird

Tereus

Piper

Flamingo

Attendant Birds

Persian Bird

Hoopoe

Gobbler

Chorus of Birds

Chorus Leader

Procne

Priest

Poet

Oracle Collector

Meton

Inspector

Decree Seller

First Messenger

Second Messenger

Iris

First Herald

Father-Beater

Cinesias

Informer

Prometheus

Poseidon

Heracles

Triballian

Second Herald

Princess

(The setting: 414 BCE, a remote locale in mainland Greece. There is a backdrop that represents a thicket, and a door in it leads to Tereus's nest. Peisthetaerus and Euelpides enter from stage left. Their slaves, Xanthias and Manodorus, follow, carrying baggage consisting of kettles, bowls, and skewers. Peisthetaerus has a crow perched on his arm, and Euelpides has a jay.)

EUELPIDES: *(to his jay)*
What, is it straight ahead you're pointing to,
toward where that tree is over there?

PEISTHETAERUS: *(to his crow)*
                                    Damn bird,
what are you croaking at me, "Back that way"?

EUELPIDES: *(to Peisthetaerus)*
Hey, screwup, what good's walking round in circles?
We're lost out here and taking routes at random.

PEISTHETAERUS:
To think that I should trust a crow that's made me,
poor wretch, hike a hundred miles and more!

EUELPIDES:
To think that I should trust a jay that's made me,
poor sucker, pound the toenails off my toes.

PEISTHETAERUS:
Heck, I don't even know where in the world   10
we've wound up. Do you think that you could find
your way back to our native land from here?

EUELPIDES:
Not even Execestides° could find
his way back home from here.

PEISTHETAERUS: *(tripping and stumbling into Euelpides)*
                    Goddammit!

EUELPIDES:
                                    Hey there,
keep off my path!

PEISTHETAERUS:
                    The mad Philocrates,°
that guy who sells birds by the tray, has really
screwed us good. He said that these two birds
would show us how to get to Tereus,
the hoopoe who was once a human being
but turned into a bird. That jay right there,   20
a son of Tharrelides,° cost an obol,
and this crow here cost three. What are they good for?
Nothing but nipping at us.

                    (to the crow)

                    Hey you there,
where are you staring with your beak wide open?
Do you want to make us climb those cliffs?
There's no way through them here.

EUELPIDES:
                    Not even a path.

PEISTHETAERUS:
This crow of mine here must be saying something
about the passage through the cliffs. Ah yes,
he's croaking something different.

EUELPIDES:
                    What's he saying
about the passage?

PEISTHETAERUS:
                    Oh, no, nothing other   30
than that he wants to bite my finger off.

EUELPIDES: *(to the audience)*
What terrible frustration! Though we want to
go to the birds, and though we've brought along
ample provisions, we can't find the way!

Yes, members of the audience, we're sick
with just the opposite of the disease
that Sacas has:° he's not a citizen
but tries to bung in access. We, in contrast,
true-blue Athenians, though we were born
into a noble tribe and family,   40
though no one wants to drive us out, are running
with both feet flying to escape our country.
It's not that we hate Athens. No, it's not
as if it weren't a great and prosperous place
for everyone to go broke paying fines in.
It's just that, though the crickets only chirp
a month or two beneath the fig-tree boughs,
the men of Athens spend their whole lives chirping
over their lawsuits.
                  So we've started walking
with baskets, cooking pots and myrtle boughs   50
in search of some relaxing land to settle
and spend our lives in. Tereus the Hoopoe—
he's what we're after, so that he can tell us
if he's ever seen this sort of place
while flying through the sky.

PEISTHETAERUS:
                  Hey, there.

EUELPIDES:
                    What is it?

PEISTHETAERUS:
The crow's been pointing me to something up there
for quite a while now.

EUELPIDES:
              And the jay keeps gaping
upward as if he wants to show me something.
There must be birds about. We'll soon find out
if we start making noise.

PEISTHETAERUS:

Know what to do?

Go kick that rock.

EUELPIDES:

You hit it with your head,
so that the noise is twice as loud.

PEISTHETAERUS:

No, you
go get a stone and knock.

EUELPIDES:

Alright.

(knocking on a rock with a smaller stone)

Boy! Boy!°

PEISTHETAERUS:
Why are you shouting "Boy!" to call a hoopoe?
You should be shouting "Hoopoe!" not "Boy! Boy!"

EUELPIDES: *(knocking and shouting)*
Hoopoe! Hoopoe!

(to Peisthetaerus)

Should I just try again?

(again knocking and shouting)

Hoopoe!

*(The Slave Bird enters through the stage door. He
is wearing a bird mask with a long beak.)*

SLAVE BIRD:

       Who's there? Who's calling for my master?

EUELPIDES:

Goodness, what a gigantic beak he has!

       (Euelpides and Peisthetaerus are so frightened that
          they let go of the birds they are holding.)

SLAVE BIRD: *(frightened)*

Help, help! We have a pair of bird-thieves here.

EUELPIDES:

Why be so rude? Why not be more polite?   70

SLAVE BIRD:

You guys are dead.

EUELPIDES:

       But we're not mortal men.

SLAVE BIRD:

What are you, then?

EUELPIDES: *(with his knees knocking in fear)*

       Me, I'm a scaredy-bird,

native to Libya.°

SLAVE BIRD:

       What a bunch of nonsense!

EUELPIDES:

"Nonsense"—really? See what's on my legs?

SLAVE BIRD:

And this one here, what bird is he?

(to Peisthetaerus)

Speak up!

PEISTHETAERUS:
Me, I'm a shit-bird from the Land of Pheasants.°

EUELPIDES: *(to the Slave Bird)*
In the name of all the gods, what sort
of creature might you be?

SLAVE BIRD:

Me, I'm a slave bird.

EUELPIDES:
What, did some fighting cock make you a slave?

SLAVE BIRD:
No. When my master turned into a hoopoe,   80
he begged me to become a bird as well,
to follow and attend him.

EUELPIDES:

Does a bird
really need a servant?

SLAVE BIRD:

This bird does,
no doubt because he used to be a man.
Sometimes he gets a hankering for sardines
from Phalerum,° and I get out my pail
and run to fetch him some. Sometimes pea soup
is what he wants and, since he needs a ladle
and soup tureen, I run and get them for him.

EUELPIDES: *(to Peisthetaerus, pointing at the Slave Bird)*
So he's a runner bird.

(to the Slave Bird)

Hey, Runner Bird,   90
you know what you should do? Run for your master.

SLAVE BIRD:
No, he has just lain down to take a nap
after a lunch of grubs and myrtle berries.

EUELPIDES:
Wake him up all the same.

SLAVE BIRD:
                    I know for certain
he'll be angry. Still, I'll wake him up;
I'll do this special favor for you.

(The Slave Bird exits through the stage door.)

PEISTHETAERUS: *(to the departing Slave Bird)*
                          Damn you.
Why, you nearly frightened me to death!

EUELPIDES:
I was so frightened that I lost my jay!

PEISTHETAERUS:
You got so scared you let him go, you coward!

EUELPIDES:
Say, didn't you collapse and lose your crow?   100

PEISTHETAERUS:
Not me.

EUELPIDES:
        Where is it, then?

PEISTHETAERUS:
                              It flew away.

EUELPIDES:
You sure you didn't let it go? Oh no,
not you, you're far too brave for that, I guess.

TEREUS: *(from behind the backdrop)*
Open the forest, that I may emerge!

> *(Tereus enters through the stage door. He has few feathers and
> is wearing a bird mask with a crest on top and a beak.)*

EUELPIDES:
My goodness, what a fowl this is! What plumage!
What a crest!

TEREUS:
                      Who is inquiring for me?

EUELPIDES: *(looking at Tereus)*
The twelve great gods° have done you wrong, it seems.

TEREUS:
What, are you taunting me about my feathers?
Strangers, I once was human.

EUELPIDES:
                              We're not laughing
at you.

TEREUS:
          At what, then?

EUELPIDES:
                      It's your beak. It looks   110
ridiculous.

TEREUS:

   It's Sophocles that makes me,
Tereus, shameful in his tragedies.°

EUELPIDES:

You're Tereus? Are you a fowl? A peacock?

TEREUS:

I am a fowl.

EUELPIDES:

   Where are your feathers, then?

TEREUS:

They fell off mostly.

EUELPIDES:

    Due to some disease?

TEREUS:

No, but in winter all birds molt their feathers,
then grow them back again. And who are you?

EUELPIDES:

Who, us? We're men.

TEREUS:

    What country have you come from?

EUELPIDES:

From the country of attractive warships.°

TEREUS:

What, are you jurors?°

EUELPIDES:

    No, if anything,   120
we're anti-jurors.

TEREUS:

                What, does non-litigious
seed still sprout among you?

EUELPIDES:

                    If you squinted,
you'd find a smidgen of it in the country.

TEREUS:

What business brings you here?

EUELPIDES:

                     We've come to see you.

TEREUS:

What for?

EUELPIDES:

           Because you used to be a man
like us, because, like us, you once had debts
and didn't want to pay them. Furthermore,
when you became a bird, you, in your journeys,
surveyed both land and sea, so that you now
have all the knowledge both of men and birds.   130
We've come, therefore, to ask you please to point us
toward some relaxing town, some place where life's
like lying on a comfortable blanket.

TEREUS:

You want to find a greater place than Athens?

EUELPIDES:

Not greater, no, just easier to live in.

TEREUS:

Then you are obviously looking for
an aristocracy.°

EUELPIDES:
                    Not me. No way.
Even the son of Scellias—you know,
the guy named Aristocrates°—disgusts me.

TEREUS:
What sort of city would you most enjoy   140
residing in?

EUELPIDES:
                    The sort of city where
my greatest troubles would be just like this:
A good friend pays a visit in the morning
and tells me, "By Olympian Zeus, make sure
you and the kiddies come around to *my* place
early, just after you have bathed. I'm giving
a wedding feast. Now don't you disappoint me
or else you needn't bother stopping by
to help when I'm in trouble."

TEREUS: *(ironically)*
                    Yes, by Zeus,
those would indeed be serious, serious troubles.   150

                    (to Peisthetaerus)

And you?

PEISTHETAERUS:
                    I'm after much the same as him.

TEREUS:
Such as?

PEISTHETAERUS:
                    I want the kind of city where
a sweet boy's dad will stop me in the street
and say reproachfully, as if I'd wronged him,

"You smooth-talker, when you saw my son
at the gymnasium, fresh from his bath,
you didn't chat him up or give him kisses
or lead him off somewhere or grope his balls,
so how are you an old friend of the family?"

TEREUS: *(ironically)*
O you poor man, what troubles you are after!   160

(sincerely, to both Euelpides and Peisthetaerus)

There really is a happy city like
the one you have described—it's on the Red Sea.°

EUELPIDES:
No, nothing with a harbor, nothing where
that ship the *Salaminia*° can show up
one morning with a bailiff on its deck.
Is there no town in Greece you could suggest?

TEREUS:
Why not go try out Lepreus, in Elis?°

EUELPIDES:
No, by the gods, the city of Lepreus
disgusts me (though I've never seen the place)
because Melanthius is a leper.°

TEREUS:
                             Well,   170
there are, in Locris, the Opuntians°—
you could go live with them.

EUELPIDES:
                             Opuntians?
I wouldn't be Opuntian if you paid me.

PEISTHETAERUS:
But what is life like here among the birds?
No doubt you know it well.

TEREUS:

                It's very pleasant.
First off, you never need to carry money.

EUELPIDES:
That would eliminate a fair amount
of thievery right there.

TEREUS:

            The gardens give us
white sesame seeds, myrtle berries, poppies
and water mint to eat.°

EUELPIDES:

             You birds are living   180
like newlyweds!

PEISTHETAERUS:

          Oh yes! Oh yes! I'm starting
to come up with a plan for all birdkind.
Heed my advice, and you'll be powerful.

TEREUS:
Heed what advice?

PEISTHETAERUS:

          "Heed what advice?" For starters,
don't fly all over with your beaks agape—
it isn't dignified. Among us humans,
when we meet someone fickle, we inquire,
"Who is that man that's flighty as a bird?"
And Teleas° responds, "The man's a goose—
brainless and baffling, unreliable,   190
he never stays in any one place long."

TEREUS:
By Dionysus, that's a fair assessment.
What should we do about it?

PEISTHETAERUS:
                              You should found
a single city.

TEREUS:
                   Aw, what sort of city
could birds like us establish?

PEISTHETAERUS:
                              Really? Really?
What a stupid thing to say! Look down.

TEREUS: *(looking down)*
Alright, I'm looking.

PEISTHETAERUS:
                        Now look up.

TEREUS: *(looking up)*
                                 I'm looking.

PEISTHETAERUS:
Now turn your head around.

TEREUS: *(rotating his head)*
                              Twisting my head off
is such great fun.

PEISTHETAERUS:
                        What did you see out there?

TEREUS:
The sky and clouds.

PEISTHETAERUS:
              Well, isn't that the proper   200
sphere for you birds?

TEREUS:
              Our "sphere"? How do you mean?

PEISTHETAERUS:
Your "place," if you prefer. Because it covers
the flat round earth, it's called a "hemisphere."
Now if you build it up and fortify it,
this "sphere" of sky will soon become your city.
Then you will all rule over humankind
in just the way you now rule over locusts.
Furthermore, you will devastate the gods
with Melian famine.°

TEREUS:
              How will we do that?

PEISTHETAERUS:
Air is what stands between the sky and earth.   210
In the same way that, when we want to go
to Delphi, we Athenians must ask
the people of Boeotia for a visa,°
you birds, when men burn offerings to the gods,
should stop the smoke from passing through the air
unless the gods agree to pay you tribute.

TEREUS:
Well, well! By earth, by snares, by nets and cages,
I've never heard a cleverer idea!
I'd love to join you in establishing
this city, if my fellow birds agree.   220

PEISTHETAERUS:
Who will explain the business to them?

TEREUS:

                              You will.
You see, they're not barbaric like they were
before I moved here. Now that I have lived
with them a long time, they have learned to speak.

PEISTHETAERUS:

How will you summon them?

TEREUS:

                            It will be easy.
I will retire into this little thicket
and wake my nightingale, my darling Procne.°
Soon as they hear our voices, they'll come flying.

PEISTHETAERUS:

My dear, dear hoopoe, don't just stand there waiting.
Come on, I beg you, go into the thicket   230
as quickly as you can and wake up Procne.

(Tereus exits through the stage door and
sings from behind the backdrop.)

TEREUS:

        Rouse yourself, my companion.
        Come, let the sacred music surge
        out of your godlike lips. Bemoan
        Itys, your son and mine.
        He is the cause
        of many tears for us.
        Come, let your gorgeous throat
        emit
        a holy dirge.   240

        (The Piper starts playing from behind the backdrop.)

        Pure is the melody
        that rises from the green-leafed bryony

    to Zeus's house,
    where Phoebus, with his golden hair,
    listening to your elegies,°
    strumming his ivory lyre
    in musical response,
    stirs all the gods to dance.
    Then from immortal mouths ascend
    divine laments—   250
    a pleasing sound.

EUELPIDES:
Great Zeus in heaven, what a voice he has!
It's like he's turned the whole grove into honey.

PEISTHETAERUS: *(to Euelpides)*
Hey there.

EUELPIDES:
    What's the matter?

PEISTHETAERUS:
          Quiet.

EUELPIDES:
            Why?

PEISTHETAERUS:
Because the Hoopoe's going to sing again.

TEREUS:
    Epopopoi popopopoi popoi,
    ee-you, ee-you, ee-to, ee-to,°
    come here, all you endowed with wings,
    all you who flutter over acres
    of fertile land, you myriad throngs   260
    who feed on grain, you swift seed-pickers

who warble such delightful songs.
Come all that over furrowed ground
twitter, *molto espressivo,*
this pleasant sound—
tio, tio, tio, tio, tio, tio, tio, tio.

You garden birds who feed on ivy boughs,
you mountain birds who eat wild strawberries
and oleaster, hasten toward my voice—
trioto, trioto, totobrix.   270

Come all who in the swampy lowlands feast
on sharp-mouthed gnats, all you who dwell
in lands of much rainfall
and on the luscious plain of Marathon,
and you, too, bird with dappled breast,
O francolin, O francolin.

All you who, like the halcyons, fly
over the salt swell of the sea,
come hear the news. I'm calling in
every breed of long-necked bird.   280
A clever old man has appeared,
a man of ingenuity,
an active man who gets things done.
All of you come to the assembly now!
Torotorotorotorotix!
Kikkabau! Kikkabau!
Torotorotorolililix!

PEISTHETAERUS: *(to Euelpides, who is looking upward)*
See any birds?

EUELPIDES:
                I sure don't, though I'm straining
my eyes to scan the sky.

PEISTHETAERUS:
                        It seems the Hoopoe
went into the grove and started clucking   290
to no avail.

TEREUS:
            Torotix, torotix!

PEISTHETAERUS:
Hey, check it out, my friend: a bird is coming!

            (Flamingo enters, dancing, from stage left.)

EUELPIDES:
                                    That's a bird alright.
What kind of bird, though? Possibly a peacock?

            (Tereus reenters from the stage door,
            flanked by two Attendant Birds.)

PEISTHETAERUS:
                            Tereus will tell us.

            (to Tereus)

What kind of bird is that?

TEREUS:
                Not one of those you men are used to watching:
he's a marsh-bird.

EUELPIDES:
            Oh my goodness, but he's flamingly attractive.

TEREUS:
And that's appropriate—his name's Flamingo.

EUELPIDES: *(to Peisthetaerus)*

Hey there! Hey! Yeah, you.

PEISTHETAERUS:

What are you shouting for?

EUELPIDES:

Another bird is coming.

(The Persian Bird [a rooster] enters, dancing, from stage right.)

PEISTHETAERUS:

Yes, there is:

a foreign looking bird.

(to Tereus)

What in the world's this musical diviner,
this exotic mountain-traveler?

TEREUS:

His name is Persian.°

PEISTHETAERUS:

Persian?

Why, if he's one of those, how did he fly in here without a camel?°   300

(The Hoopoe enters, dancing, from stage left.)

EUELPIDES: *(to Tereus)*
Here's a bird who has a crest like yours.

PEISTHETAERUS:

How fascinating! So
you aren't the only hoopoe hereabouts but there's this other one?

TEREUS:

This Hoopoe is the son of Philocles° the Hoopoe's son,
so I'm his grandpa. Just as you might say, "Here's Callias's son
Hipponicus" and "Callias Hipponicus's son."

PEISTHETAERUS:

This bird
is Callias! He sure has lost a lot of feathers.°

EUELPIDES:

That's because
he's pedigreed. He gets them plucked by the informers, and his women,
too, keep plucking at them.

(Gobbler enters, dancing, from stage right.)

PEISTHETAERUS:

Here's another brightly colored bird.
What do you call him?

TEREUS:

This one? Gobbler.

PEISTHETAERUS:

Wait, you mean Cleonymus°
is not the only gobbler?

EUELPIDES:

If this really were Cleonymus,   310
he surely would have thrown his crest away.

PEISTHETAERUS:

Hey, for what reason do
so many of the birds have crests? Do they intend to march like soldiers?

TEREUS:

No, no, my friend. They are like Carians:° they roost on crests for safety.

PEISTHETAERUS:

Holy—look at what an awful lot of birds are gathering here!

EUELPIDES:

My goodness, what a cloud! You can't make out the aisles for all the wings!

> (Other birds now enter. They will constitute the
> Chorus of Birds. Flamingo, Persian Bird, Hoopoe, and
> Gobbler exit, dancing, down the side aisles.)

TEREUS:

That one's a partridge.

EUELPIDES:

That one there a francolin.

PEISTHETAERUS:

And there's a widgeon.

EUELPIDES:

This here's a halcyon.

PEISTHETAERUS:

And what's that one behind the halcyon?

TEREUS:

Right there—the barber.

PEISTHETAERUS:

What? a barber bird?

TEREUS:

Sure Sporgilus° is one.

Here comes an owl.

EUELPIDES:

What are you saying? Who has brought an owl to Athens?°

TEREUS:

Turtledove, Magpie, Horned Owl, Swallow. Buzzard and Pigeon, Ring Dove,
    Falcon.   320
Purple-Cap, Red-Cap, Red-Foot, Cuckoo. Woodpecker, Kestrel, Dabchick,
    Bunting
and Lammergeier.

PEISTHETAERUS:

                        Look at all those birds! Those big beaks! How they scold
and strut around trying to screech the loudest. Are they angry with us?
Are they ogling us with beaks agape?

EUELPIDES:

                            That's how it seems to me.

CHORUS:

Whe-whe-whe-whe-where's the man who called me? Where's he come to
    roost?

TEREUS:

Here I am. I've been waiting for you. I don't disappoint my friends.

CHORUS:

Wha-wha-wha-wha-what message do you have for me, your friend?

TEREUS:

One that applies to all, promotes our safety, and is right and sweet
and valuable. Two men have come to us, a pair of intellectuals.

CHORUS:

Where? How?

TEREUS:

                    Just what I said: diplomats from the world of men have come. 330
They've brought a monumental plan along with them to prop us up.

CHORUS:

What are you saying to us? You have done the worst thing to be done
since I was fledged!

TEREUS:

           Hold on a moment. Now don't let my words upset you.

CHORUS:

What have you done to us?

TEREUS:

               All that I've done is welcome in two men
who love our ways.

CHORUS:

        You've really gone and done this?

TEREUS:

                        Yes. I'm glad of it.

CHORUS:

And they're already here somewhere among us?

TEREUS:

                      Just as much as I am.

CHORUS:

    Strophe
    We have been cheated! We have been abused!
    Our friend, who fed on the same fields with us,
    has violated our long-standing trust,
    broken the oaths that link the avian race.   340
    This so-called friend has lured us into snares,
    betrayed us to the violent tribe of men
    who, from their start, have been
    our murderers.

CHORUS:
We'll settle our account with this bird later.

(turning to Peisthetaerus and Euelpides)

                                    Right now we'll attend,
I think, to these two geezers: they'll be torn apart.

PEISTHETAERUS:
                                    We're done for, then.

EUELPIDES: *(to Peisthetaerus)*
You are the one I blame for this. Why did you lead me way up here?

PEISTHETAERUS:
To have you with me.

EUELPIDES:
                    No, more like to make me weep big tears.

PEISTHETAERUS:
                                                Come on,
that makes no sense at all: How will you weep with both your eyes pecked
    out?

CHORUS: *(moving aggressively toward Peisthetaerus and Euelpides in military
formation)*
        Antistrophe
        Start marching! Launch an onslaught! Batter them   350
        with wingbeats! Hem them in! Attack! Attack!
        Oh yes, the two of them will learn to scream.
        They both will feed fresh gobbets to my beak.
        There is no shady mountain, no gray sea,
        no bank of clouds above us anywhere
        that can conceal this pair
        of men from me.

CHORUS LEADER:
Quick, peck them, nip them. Where's the sergeant? Have him lead the right
   wing in.

EUELPIDES:
Oh no! Oh no! Where can I run and hide? I'm done for!

PEISTHETAERUS:
                                                    Stand your ground!

EUELPIDES:
So they can tear me limb from limb?

PEISTHETAERUS:
                              How do you think you'll get away?   360

EUELPIDES:
I couldn't tell you.

PEISTHETAERUS:
                     Well, I'll tell you: we should stand and fight it out.
Take up those kettles.

EUELPIDES:
                     How will kettles help?

PEISTHETAERUS:
                                        The owl won't get us then.°

   (Peisthetaerus, Euelpides, Xanthias, and Manodorus
       pick up the kettles and hold them like shields.)

EUELPIDES:
Just look at those hooked claws!

PEISTHETAERUS:
                         Take up a skewer and plant it in the ground
before your feet.

(Peisthetaerus, Euelpides, Xanthias, and Manodorus
stick the skewers in the ground like a palisade.)

EUELPIDES:

But what about my eyeballs?

PEISTHETAERUS:

Use a bowl or saucer

to shield them.

(Peisthetaerus, Euelpides, Xanthias, and Manodorus
put bowls on their heads to serve as helmets.)

EUELPIDES:

Genius! How inventive! How strategic! When it comes
to cleverness, you are a greater general than Nicias!°

CHORUS LEADER:

Charge at them! Raise your beaks and charge! No shrinking from the fray!
Tear them, peck them, beat them, slay them! First, though, take that kettle
    out!

(Tereus steps between the Chorus, on one side, and
Peisthetaerus and Euelpides, on the other.)

TEREUS: *(to the Chorus)*
O cruelest of the creatures, why do you intend to kill,
to mutilate this pair of men? They've never done you any harm.   370
They are, in fact, the relatives and fellow tribesmen of my wife.°

CHORUS LEADER:

Why should we show more mercy to these humans than to wolves? There are
no enemies more execrable that we could take vengeance on.

TEREUS:

Suppose that, though your enemies by nature, they are friends at heart?
They've come to give you valuable advice.

CHORUS LEADER:

How could these men, the foes
to our great-great-grandfathers, ever give us valuable suggestions
or sound advice?

TEREUS:

The wise learn much from foes. Foresight secures all things—
a lesson that you cannot learn from friends but that an enemy
forces you into. For example, it was enemies, not friends,
who taught our cities how to build high walls and fit out ships for war.   380
This is the knowledge that protects our families, households and wealth.

CHORUS LEADER: *(to the Chorus)*
Alright. I guess it's better if we hear them out. One can be taught
something constructive even by a foe.

PEISTHETAERUS:

Their wrath, it seems, is cooling.
Fall back.

TEREUS: *(to the Chorus Leader)*
It's just that you should do this. You will thank me for it later.

CHORUS LEADER:
Trust me, I never meant to act against your counsel till today.

EUELPIDES:
They are behaving in a less aggressive manner now.

PEISTHETAERUS:

They are.

(to Xanthias, Manodorus, and Euelpides, singing)

Put down the bowls, now. Put the kettle down.
Shoulder your spear—that skewer, I mean.

*(Peisthetaerus, Euelpides, Xanthias, and Manodorus put
down the kettles and bowls and shoulder the skewers.)*

Now we should march around within
the bounds of our encampment, looking out   390
along the kettle's rim.
We must not retreat.

EUELPIDES:

Tell me, if we do get killed,
where will our bodies find a home?

PEISTHETAERUS:

We will be planted in the field
for military heroes. Yes,
we'll tell the generals we died
fighting our country's foes
at Finchburg.°

CHORUS LEADER:

Re-form your ranks and ground your spirit beside   400
your anger, as the hoplites° do.
Let's find out who
these men are, where they're from
and why they've come.
Hoopoe, hello? I'm calling you.

TEREUS:

What are you summoning me for?

CHORUS LEADER:

Who are these humans and from where?

TEREUS:

Two strangers out of Greece,
the country of the wise.

CHORUS LEADER:

> What need or circumstance   410
> has brought them to the birds?

TEREUS:

>   A great desire
> to live the way you live,
> to share your home with you
> and do all that you do.

CHORUS LEADER:

> What do you mean? What are their plans?

TEREUS:

> They're marvelous! Beyond belief!

CHORUS LEADER: *(pointing at Peisthetaerus)*

> What, is he hoping to receive
> some benefit by being with me?
> To overpower an enemy?
> To help his friends advance?   420

TEREUS:

> He speaks of great prosperity,
> marvelous, unbelievable
> good fortune. He
> insists that you can have it all,
> what's here, there and beyond.

CHORUS LEADER:

> Is he insane?

TEREUS:

>   His mind
> is most emphatically sane.

CHORUS LEADER:

> Is he a clever man?

TEREUS:

> The slyest fox resides in him.
> He is all cleverness   430
> and cunning, he is ingenuity's
> crème de la crème.

CHORUS LEADER:

> Get him to tell me, tell me, then.
> Hearing what you've been saying
> has set my spirit flying.

TEREUS: *(to the Attendant Birds)*
Alright, then, you and you collect this gear
and hang it in the kitchen, solemnly,
above the tripod near the fire.

> *(The Attendant Birds pick up the kettles, bowls, and
> skewers and carry them out through the stage door.)*

> *(to Peisthetaerus)*

> And you
address the birds, apprise them of the reasons
why I have summoned them to me today.   440

PEISTHETAERUS:
I won't address them, not until they make
the selfsame deal with me the knife-maker
(who was an ape)° made with his wife: to wit,
no using teeth, no yanking on the balls,
no poking in the—

EUELPIDES:

> Hold on, not the—

PEISTHETAERUS:

> No.

I mean the eyes.

CHORUS LEADER:

     I promise.

PEISTHETAERUS:

     Swear.

CHORUS LEADER:

     I swear
and, if I keep my promise, may the judges°
and audience unanimously give me
the victory.

PEISTHETAERUS:

     I'm certain you will win.

TEREUS:

And, if I break my promise, may I win 450
by one vote only.

PEISTHETAERUS: *(to Xanthias, Manodorus, and Euelpides)*
     Everybody, listen.
You foot soldiers may pick these weapons up
and go back home. Be sure to keep an eye out
for future orders posted on the boards.°

    *(Xanthias and Manodorus carry the makeshift weapons
    and armor out through the stage door, then return.)*

CHORUS: *(to Tereus)*

    Strophe
    Man has evolved a character that is
    wholly deceptive. Still, do make your case.
    There may well be some power you have found
    in me, some possibility my simple mind
    has overlooked. Speak up. It's in your own
    best interest as much as it's in mine: 460

whatever benefit you find for me
will benefit us all collectively.

CHORUS LEADER: *(to Peisthetaerus)*
Now, about this scheme of yours you've come to sell us on—
don't be afraid to speak your piece. I promise we won't break
the truce beforehand.

PEISTHETAERUS:
                                I'm just bursting with desire to tell you.
I've mixed my speech's dough, and nothing's going to prevent me
from kneading it into a loaf.

                    (to Xanthias and Manodorus)

                                Bring me a garland, boy,
and one of you get water so that I can wash my hands.

EUELPIDES:
Are we preparing for a feast, or what?

PEISTHETAERUS:
                                No, no, by Zeus;
it's nice and juicy words that I've been after for a while now,   470
words that will melt the hearts of birds.

                    (to the Chorus)

                                I feel so bad for you—
you once were kings . . .

CHORUS LEADER:
                                Us, kings? Of what?

PEISTHETAERUS:
                                Of everything that is,
of me, and this man here and even Zeus himself, and you
were born long, long before the Titans, Cronus, even Earth.°

CHORUS:
Before the Earth?

PEISTHETAERUS:
I swear to you, it's true.

CHORUS:
I'd never heard that.

PEISTHETAERUS:
Well, that's because you are, by nature, ignorant and heedless.
What's more, you've never read your Aesop.° He's the one that tells us
the Lark was born before all other things, before Earth even.
Her father died of sickness and, because the Earth did not
exist yet, lay there uninterred for four whole days. The Lark
was at a loss and out of desperation laid her father
to rest in her own head.

EUELPIDES:
And so the father of the Lark
lies dead in Headley Park.°

PEISTHETAERUS:
Thus, since the two of them existed
before the Earth and gods, the kingship properly is theirs
through primogeniture.

EUELPIDES: *(to the Chorus)*
That's right, but hone your beaks for battle.
Zeus won't be quick to hand the woodpecker his royal scepter.

PEISTHETAERUS:
Long long ago it wasn't gods who ruled mankind as kings,
but birds. I have a thousand ways of proving this. For starters,
I'll point you to the cock who ruled the Persians long before
all those Dariuses and Megabazuses.° And so,
in memory of that time, he's called the Persian Bird today.

480

490

EUELPIDES:
Even now the rooster struts about like the Great King,
the only bird to wear his crown uncocked upon his head.

PEISTHETAERUS:
So great and powerful and formidable was the rooster
that still today, because of the authority he had,
everyone jumps up out of bed as soon as he proclaims
daybreak: blacksmiths and potters, shoemakers and tanners, bathmen,
grain dealers, lyre-makers, armorers—they all put on their shoes
and head out . . .

EUELPIDES:
                    So it was for me. One time I, wretched moron,
lost a cloak made out of Phrygian wool because of him.   500
I'd been invited to a newborn infant's name-day party°
in Athens and had gotten drunk and passed out back at home
when, hungrier than all the rest, I guess, this rooster started
crowing early. I assumed that dawn was near, so I
set out for Halimus. Soon as I slip outside the walls,
this mugger comes up on me from behind and whacks me good,
and down I go. Well, I'm there just about to shout for help,
but he's already made off with my cloak.

PEISTHETAERUS: *(to the Chorus)*
                                        What's more, the bird
they call the "kite"° once ruled as despot over all the Greeks.

CHORUS LEADER:
The Greeks?

PEISTHETAERUS:
       It's true, and when he was the king, he taught the Greeks the custom   510
of rolling on the ground in front of kites.

EUELPIDES:
                                        Of course! One time
I saw a kite and started rolling and, while I was leaning

back with my lips agape, I up and unintentionally
swallowed an obol that was in my mouth.° I had to drag
my shopping bag home empty.

PEISTHETAERUS:

Furthermore, the cuckoo once
was king of Egypt and Phoenicia.° When he called out "cuckoo,"
all the Phoenicians rushed to reap their fields of wheat and barley.

EUELPIDES:

Oh, that explains the proverb, "Cuckoo! Dicks up. Hit the field."°

PEISTHETAERUS:

The birds had such authority, in fact, that if some Agamemnon
or Menelaus° ever was a king in Greece, a bird   520
would perch atop his royal staff and take a share of all
the presents he received.

EUELPIDES:

Of course! I used to wonder when,
at the performance of a tragedy, I saw, say, Priam°
enter with a bird. That bird, of course, was perching there
to reckon up the offerings Lysicrates embezzled.°

PEISTHETAERUS:

But here's the strongest proof of all: Zeus, who is now in charge,
stands with an eagle on his head to symbolize his kingship.
His daughter Athena has an owl, and his attendant god,
Apollo, has a hawk.°

EUELPIDES:

That's right. But why do they have birds?

PEISTHETAERUS:

So that when someone makes the customary sacrifice   530
and offers Zeus the guts, the birds can snatch them up *before*
Zeus gets his portion. In those days nobody would swear
in gods' names. No, they swore by birds instead, and still today

Lampon,° whenever he is keen to rip somebody off,
swears "by the goose."

It's clear, then, that you once were great and sacred,
but now you are looked upon as slaves, as idiots,
as being like Manes.° Nowadays people
pelt you with stones as if you were madmen.
Even in temples the hunters of birds
go after you with nooses and snares,   540
limed twigs and toils, meshes and nets
and baited traps. And when you're caught,
you're sold in bulk, and customers grope you.
Nor are they content to serve you up
roasted—they add on grated cheese,
oil, vinegar and silphium.°
They whip up a second sweet, slick sauce,
which is poured, hot, on your heated backs,
as if you fowl were rotten meat.

CHORUS:

> *Antistrophe*
> Human, the tale that you have shared with us   550
> is horrible. Our fathers' cowardice,
> their failure to bequeath to this my age
> their own forefathers' special privilege,
> has made me weep. But fortune or a god
> has sent you here today to give us aid.
> From here on out I shall entrust you with
> my own life and my chicks'. You've earned my faith.

CHORUS LEADER:

Now tell us quick what we should do. Our life will be insufferable
if we do not try to regain our sovereignty by every means.

PEISTHETAERUS:

Alright, the first thing I prescribe is this: that all you birds construct   560
a single city and surround the space between the earth and sky
with walls of large baked bricks, just like the builders did at Babylon.°

CHORUS LEADER:
O Cebriones! O Porphyrion!° How strong a citadel!

PEISTHETAERUS:
Then, when the wall is done, you should demand that Zeus return his
    kingship.
If he does not agree, if he refuses and does not give in,
you should proclaim a holy war against him and deny the gods
the right to pass through your domains with boners, like, you know,
they used to do to screw their Semeles, Alcmenas and Alopes.°
If they keep on passing through your realm, then fit their wieners all
with too-tight cock rings, so they can't fuck mortal females anymore.   570

Then you should send a second messenger, this time to humankind,
to tell them that they must make sacrifice henceforth to birds because
the birds are kings. (Henceforth the gods get seconds.) Furthermore, mankind
must find appropriate avian counterparts for all the former gods:
If they are making sacrifice to Aphrodite, they should offer
nuts to the penis-bird.° If they are offering Poseidon sheep,
bestow granola on a duck. Instead of giving Heracles
sacrifice, give a cormorant a honey cake. If they are giving
a ram to King Zeus, they should give a gnat that has its nuts intact
to the king bird, the nuthatch, first, before they sacrifice to Zeus.   580

EUELPIDES:
Gutting a gnat! That's beautiful! Now let the great Zan° boom away.

CHORUS LEADER:
How, though, will humans come to see us as divinities, not jays?
We all wear wings and fly around.

PEISTHETAERUS:
                            That makes no sense. Consider Hermes:
he is a winged god and he flies around, and so do many other gods.
Victory flies around on golden wings, and so, of course, does Eros.
The poet Homer even likens Iris to "a trembling dove."

EUELPIDES:

Won't Zeus hurl thunder at us and deploy his "wingéd lightning bolt"?

PEISTHETAERUS: *(ignoring Euelpides)*

Finally, if humans in their blindness still insist that you are nothing
and go on venerating the Olympian gods, then clouds of sparrows,
jackdaws, and starlings should descend upon their fields and eat their
    seeds up.   590
Then, when mankind is starving, we'll see if Demeter doles out grain.

EUELPIDES:

I bet she'd welch on humans then. Oh yeah, she'd come up with excuses.

PEISTHETAERUS:

And then the crows will come and peck the eyes out of the oxen harnessed
to till the field. We'll see if Dr. Phoebus° heals them—and gets paid.

EUELPIDES:

No, don't send crows. At least not till I've sold my little pair of oxen.

PEISTHETAERUS:

If, on the contrary, they do accept you as divinities
such as Poseidon, Cronus and the Principle of Life Itself,°
they will be loaded down with blessings.

CHORUS LEADER:

                                        Blessings? Give me an example.

PEISTHETAERUS:

First off, the locusts won't be eating all the vine blooms any longer—
a company of owls and kestrels will devour the infestation.   600
Secondly, bugs like mites and gallflies won't be ruining the figs—
a single flock of thrushes will exterminate the lot of them.

CHORUS LEADER:

How will we make the humans wealthy? That's the thing they covet most.

PEISTHETAERUS:

When they consult the omens, you will show them where the richest mines are
and tell the prophets which sea voyages will be most profitable,
and never will another sailor perish in a shipwreck.

CHORUS LEADER:

Why?

PEISTHETAERUS:

Because, when someone comes to read the signs before a trip abroad,
some omen from a bird will always say, "Don't go! A storm is brewing,"
or else, "Proceed. This business venture will be very profitable."

EUELPIDES:

I'll buy a ship and go to sea. No way I'm staying here with you.   610

PEISTHETAERUS:

Also, you will reveal to them where all the ancient treasures lie,
because you know. People are always saying, "No one but a bird
knows where my treasure is."

EUELPIDES:

I'll sell my boat and buy a spade
and dig up troves!

CHORUS LEADER:

But who will give them health, the gods' prerogative?

PEISTHETAERUS:

The greater part of health is happiness. The miserable man
is never well.

CHORUS LEADER:

Longevity dwells on Olympus. How will humans
get access to it? Must they die in what must feel like early youth?

PEISTHETAERUS:

No, because birds will give them an additional three hundred years.

CHORUS LEADER:
From whom, though, will these years be taken?

PEISTHETAERUS:

From the birds themselves, of course.
Doesn't the raucous raven live five times the lifetime of a man?   620

EUELPIDES:
My goodness, but these birds would make far better kings for us than Zeus!

PEISTHETAERUS:
Far better. To start with, we won't have to build
temples out of stone for birds
and gild their gateways. No, they'll dwell
in shrubberies and oak-tree groves.
The most revered of all the birds
will have no other temple than
the branches of the olive tree.
There won't be any need to go
to Delphi or Ammon° to sacrifice—   630
No, standing amid the wild olives
and strawberries, we'll hold out handfuls
of barley and implore the birds
please to allow us some small portion
of all the blessings they enjoy,
and we'll be granted them at the price
of just a couple of grains of wheat.

CHORUS LEADER:
You were my biggest foe, old man, but now you are my dearest friend.
It's inconceivable that I could disregard this plan of yours.

CHORUS:
Your words have made me brave: 640
I give notice and swear
that, if you bring just, holy and sincere
proposals to my cause,
if you align

your thoughts with mine
and help me fight the gods above,
not much longer will they abuse
the sacred staff I should possess.

CHORUS LEADER:
We birds will deal with all things that demand the use of strength;
you, on your side, take care of what requires deliberation.   650

PEISTHETAERUS: *(gesturing toward the stage door)*
Listen, now's not the time to stand around
and lollygag like General Nicias.°
We need to act as swiftly as we can!

TEREUS:
First, though, come to this nest, my nest built out
of brush and straw; and tell your names to me.

PEISTHETAERUS:
That's easy: you can call me Peisthetaerus
and him Euelpides of Crioa.°

TEREUS:
My greetings to you.

PEISTHETAERUS:
                    We thank you for your greetings.

TEREUS:
Come in.

PEISTHETAERUS:
        We're coming. You're the one who must
escort us in and introduce us.

TEREUS:
                    Come, then.   660

PEISTHETAERUS:

Hey, wait! Come back down here. Come back and tell us
how we are going to follow you in there,
when you can fly and we cannot.

TEREUS:

                              I see.

PEISTHETAERUS:

Remember Aesop's fables. There's this one
in which things turned out badly for the fox
because she made a treaty with an eagle.°

TEREUS:

Rest easy. All you need to do is eat
a certain root, and then you will be fledged.

PEISTHETAERUS:

Let's go in, then.

                    (to Xanthias and Manodorus)

              Xanthias, Manodorus,
take up our baggage.

              (Xanthias and Manodorus pick up the baggage.)

CHORUS LEADER: *(to Tereus)*
                    Hoopoe, hey, you hear me?   670

TEREUS:

What do you want?

CHORUS LEADER:

                    You go to dine with them,
but please call out the nightingale for us,
the sweet-toned warbler in the Muses' choir.
Let her come out so we can play with her.

PEISTHETAERUS:
I beg you, please agree to their desire.
Lead the chick out of the rushes.

EUELPIDES:
                                        Yes,
by all the gods, bring out the nightingale,
so that we all can take a look at her.

TEREUS:
Your wish is my command.

                    (calling through the stage door)

                    O Procne, Procne,
come meet these strangers who have come to visit.   680

                    (Procne enters through the stage door. She is
                    wearing a bird mask with a beak.)

PEISTHETAERUS:
My goodness, what a gorgeous little bird!
How trim! How bright her plumage!

EUELPIDES:
                                        Do you know
how badly I would like to part her thighs?

PEISTHETAERUS:
She's gold all over, like a wealthy virgin!

EUELPIDES:
Oh, how I want to kiss her!

PEISTHETAERUS:
                                Idiot,
look at the two sharp ridges on her beak.

EUELPIDES:
I'd treat her like an egg. In just the same way
that we remove the shell before we eat
an egg, I'll take her mask off,° then I'll kiss her.

TEREUS:
Let's go.

PEISTHETAERUS:
      Lead on, and may success attend us.   690

      (Peisthetaerus exits behind Tereus through the stage door.
      Xanthias, Manodorus, and Euelpides follow them inside.)

CHORUS: *(to Procne)*
      Ah dear, dear bird, ah gorgeous thing,
      ah musical companion,
      you've come here to be seen;
      you've come to bring me sweet,
      sweet song.

      Weaver of tunes in spring,
      introduce with your fair-toned flute
      anapests on the run.

CHORUS LEADER: *(to the audience)*
Insubstantial confections of clay, frail mortals, ephemeral featherless beings,
ineffectual weaklings who live in a dream and who perish like leaves,
    evanescent   700
generations of shadow, obscurities, listen to us who, ethereal, ageless
and immortal, have minds that consider perennial thoughts. We will teach
    you the business
of the sky, you will thoroughly fathom the nature of birds and the primal
    beginnings
of the gods and the rivers, of Chaos and Erebus. Thanks to us, even the
    famous
intellectual Prodicus° soon will be jealous of all you have learned.
                                 First came Chaos,

Night next, the diffuseness of Erebus, then the voluminous Tartarus. There
    was
no earth, no air, no sky; but obscure-winged Night, at the very beginning,
in the limitless bosom of Erebus, laid a tempestuous egg. From the egg
    hatched,
when his term was attained, irresistible Eros, a god like impetuous
    whirlwinds,
who had glittering wings on his back. He had sex one night with opaque-
    winged Chaos   710
in immeasurable Tartarus. There he begat birdkind. He was first to lead us
to the sunlight. The race of immortals did not come about until later, when
    Eros
intermingled the cosmic ingredients. From his admixture of elements Heaven,
Sea, Earth, and the race of the deathless ones sprang into being. And so we are
    older
than the whole blest race of the gods.
                                    That we birds are the offspring of Eros is proven
by innumerable proofs: We have wings and are often with lovers. Though
    beautiful young men
quite often have vowed to have nothing to do with the pleasures of sex until
    marriage,
they have opened their thighs through the power of us birds:° they have
    yielded to lovers who gave them quails, waterfowls, roosters and geese.
                                And we birds are the ones who bestow all
the significant blessings on mortals. For starters, we mark off, as seasons for
    humans,   720
fall, winter and spring. When the crane flies shrieking to Libya, then it is high
    time
to be sowing the fields, it is time for the helmsman to hang up his tiller and
    sleep in,
it is time for Orestes to weave new clothing,° so that he does not steal others'
on account of the cold. The return of the kite tells mortals that spring is
    returning
and the fleeces of sheep must be clipped. When the swallow is seen, all hasten
    to trade in
thick jackets for lighter attire.
                              We are Ammon to you, and Dodona and Delphi;

we are Phoebus Apollo. Before you attempt new ventures—a business
    transaction,
or the buying of produce, or marriage—you check with the birds, and you call
    all omens
of predestined events "birds." Sneezes and words can be "birds"; providential
    encounters
can be "birds," and mysterious rustlings, "birds." "Birds" also are good-luck
    servants   730
and the brayings of donkeys. To you we are clearly the same as Apollo the
    Prophet.

If you regard us birds as gods,
we shall be seers for you and Muses,
and winds, and winter, and mild summer,
and hot summer. We shall never
run off and sit snobbily in the clouds
like Zeus but, ever present among you,
shall give to you yourselves, to your children
and your children's children, wealth-healthiness,
prosperity, happiness, peace, youth,   740
good humor, choral dances and festivals
and bird's milk. You'll all be so well off
you could knock yourselves out with your blessings!

CHORUS:
    Strophe
    Country Muse of varied note,
    I sing with you on mountain summits and in groves:
    Tio tio tio tio tinx.
    I pour out of my vibrant throat
    music for Pan from the ash-tree leaves.
    Tio tio tio tio tinx.
    With mighty choirs I sing a harmony   750
    in praise of Mountain Mother Cybele.
    To to to to to to to to to tinx.
    Thence bee-like Phrynichus°
    sips ambrosial melodies;

that's why he can emit
song so sweet:
Tio tio tio tio tinx.

CHORUS LEADER:
If any of you audience members want to spend what's left of life
pleasantly with us birds, then step right up. Believe me, all the actions
that lead to shame down here on earth are praiseworthy among the birds.   760
Though, for example, it is shameful here to beat your father, there
they praise whoever rushes at his papa, hits him and proclaims,
"Put up your spur if you are spoiling for a fight." And if you are
a slave who runs away, gets caught again, then has his brow tattooed,°
there you would simply be a dappled francolin. And if you are
as much a Phrygian as Spintharus,° there you would be
a pigeon of Philemon's dovecote. If, like Execestides,°
you are a Carian slave, go generate a pedigree up there,
and noble forebears will appear. Lastly, if Peisias's son
decides to yield the gates to brigands, let him turn into a partridge,   770
an old cock's fledgling, since such partridge tricks are fine among the birds.

> *Antistrophe*
> Thus do the swans, while gathered on
> the Hebrus River's banks,° sing Phoebus serenades:
> *Tio tio tio tio tinx.*
> They beat their wings in unison.
> Their music shoots beyond the clouds.
> *Tio tio tio tio tinx.*
> They rouse the various tribes of animals.
> The waves go tranquil as the clear wind falls.
> *To to to to to to to to to tinx.*   780
> Olympus echoes the tune;
> amazement grips the pantheon.
> The Graces and Muses repeat
> each cheerful note:
> *Tio tio tio tio tinx.*

CHORUS LEADER:

Nothing is nicer or of greater use than sprouting wings. For starters,
let's say a member of the audience is hungry and has gotten
tired of listening to tragic choruses. If he had wings,
he could just fly away, go home for lunch and come back full. Let's say
some Patrocleides° needs to take a dump. Rather than soil his cloak,   790
he could just fly away, let loose a few farts, catch his breath and land
back in his seat. Let's say some one of you were an adulterer
and saw the husband of his mistress sitting in the front-row seats,
he could just fly away and fuck her good and then fly back again.
Being endowed with wings is, of all gifts, the most desirable.
Take Dieitrephes.° Though his wings were wine-jar handles, he was chosen
tribe chieftain, then commander of the cavalry and now, though he
began as nothing, he is thriving like a parti-colored cock-horse.°

*(Peisthetaerus and Euelpides enter through the stage
door. They are wearing wings and feathers.)*

PEISTHETAERUS:

Well, here we are! I've never seen a sight
more comical.

EUELPIDES:

                    What are you laughing at?   800

PEISTHETAERUS:

Those wings you got. Know what you look like most?
A goose some very cheap artiste has painted.

EUELPIDES:

And you're just like a blackbird with a buzz cut.

PEISTHETAERUS:

Yes, we are tricked out like this, in the words
of Aeschylus,° "by no means due to others',
but our own feathers."

CHORUS LEADER:
                    What should we do now?

PEISTHETAERUS:
First, we should name our city something big
and grand, then give the gods a sacrifice.

EUELPIDES:
Yes, I agree with you.

CHORUS LEADER:
                    Well, alright then,
what should we call our city?

EUELPIDES:
                         How about   810
the great Lacedaemonian name of "Sparta"?

PEISTHETAERUS:
No way! You think I'd call my city Sparta?
A hateful name! I'd never use esparto
twine° on my bed, though it were nothing more
than bands of reeds.

EUELPIDES:
                  What should we call it, then?

TEREUS:
A wispy sort of name, something suggestive
of clouds and airy spaces.

PEISTHETAERUS:
                      Do you like
Cloudcuckooland?

CHORUS LEADER:
                  I do, I do indeed!
You've found a great, great name, a handsome one.

EUELPIDES:

Cloudcuckooland—is that the city where   820
Theogenes keeps most of what he owns,
and Aeschines his whole estate?°

PEISTHETAERUS:

                              Not there,
but on the Plain of Phlegra where the gods
outdid the Giants in the Braggart War.°

CHORUS LEADER:

Oh, what a splendid city! But what god
should be our Keeper of the Citadel?
For what god should we weave the Sacred Robe?°

EUELPIDES:

Why not just choose Athena Polias?°

PEISTHETAERUS:

How can a city be controllable
when a woman deity stands armed   830
from head to foot, while Cleisthenes sits spinning
yarn from wool?°

EUELPIDES:

                              Which of the gods will guard
the city's fortress, then?

TEREUS:

                              One of our brood,
the Persian Bird, who is regarded as
the most intimidating fowl of all,
a battle chick.

EUELPIDES:

                              O royal chick! You are
the perfect god to live among the rocks.

PEISTHETAERUS: *(to Euelpides)*
Take off into the air, now. Help the builders
working on the ramparts; bring them gravel,
strip down and mix the mortar; pass a trough   840
above your head; fall off the scaffolding;
post watchmen; keep the fire alive
beneath the embers; march around the boundaries,
bell in hand, and make your bed on-site.
Dispatch one messenger up to the gods,
one down to men, and then come back again.

EUELPIDES:
And you can stay right here and go to hell!

PEISTHETAERUS:
Go now, my friend, where I have sent you. Nothing
of what I've planned will be achieved without you.
As for myself, I need to give the gods,   850
the new bird gods, a sacrifice, so I
will go and find a priest to organize
the ceremony

(Euelpides exits, stage left.)

(to Xanthias)

Hey there, slave! Hey, slave!
Bring out the basket and the lustral water.

CHORUS:
    Strophe
    All that you want, I want. What's more,
    I ask you please to send the gods on high
    a powerful and solemn prayer.
    Also, to thank them, sacrifice a sheep.
    Let's all send up a Pythian cry,°
    and, while we sing, let Chaeris° play his pipe.   860

(The Piper comes out and plays. He is dressed as a raven.)

PEISTHETAERUS:

Enough of that. Egads! What's this? I've seen
a lot of crazy things but never, what?,
a raven decked out like a piper.

> *(The Priest enters from stage right. Xanthias enters through*
> *the stage door holding a basket and leading a small, skinny*
> *goat. Manodorus enters carrying a basin of lustral water.)*

Priest,
the time is now! Start making sacrifice
unto the new bird gods.

PRIEST:

I will begin,
but first, where's the attendant with the basket?

> *(Xanthias holds the basket out for the Priest.)*

Pray to the avian form of Hestia,
the kite who filches from altars,° and to all
the Olympian god- and goddess-birds . . .

PEISTHETAERUS:

O Hawk of Sunium, O Lord of Storks

870

PRIEST:

. . . to the Pythian and the Delian swan,
to Leto, the Mother of the Quails,
and the goldfinch goddess Artemis . . .

PEISTHETAERUS:

The "gold-tressed" Artemis is now a goldfinch.

PRIEST:
. . . and to Sabazius the Finch
and the Ostrich, Mother of Gods and Men . . .

PEISTHETAERUS:
Queen Cybele, Cleocritus's mom!°

PRIEST:
. . . to grant security and health
to all Cloudcuckoolanders and Chians . . .

PEISTHETAERUS:
Charming! The Chians always must be mentioned.   880

PRIEST:
. . . and to hero birds and the sons of heroes,
to porphyrions and pelicans,
to spoonbills and redbreasts, grouse and peacocks,
horned owls, teals, bitterns, herons, petrels,
figpeckers, of course, and tufted titmice . . .

PEISTHETAERUS:
Hey, go to hell, pal. Stop! Just stop! How big,
you moron, do you think the victim is
that you're inviting eagles in, and vultures,
to have a portion of it? Don't you see
that goat's so paltry that a single kite   890
could whisk the whole thing off. Get out of here,
both you and all your garlands. I myself
am going to perform the sacrifice.

(The Priest exits. The goat remains.)

CHORUS:
        Antistrophe
        To help you, we will sing a tune
        fit for the pouring of the lustral water
        and call the gods—well, only one,

because the victim will have to be shared
among us all, and what you've got here
is nothing more than goat horns and a beard.

PEISTHETAERUS:
Now, as we sacrifice, let us address   900
our prayers to the feathered gods above.

> (*The Poet enters, stage left. He has long hair and*
> *is wearing threadbare, ragged clothing.*)

POET:

O Muse,
come use
your songs of praise
to recommend
our blest Cloudcuckooland!

PEISTHETAERUS:
Where did *this* come from? Tell me, who are you?

POET:

"The Muses' willing slave
when I sing a song,
I have   910
a honey-tongue."°
So Homer sang.

PEISTHETAERUS:
Oh really, you're a slave? A longhair slave?°

POET:

"Each of us who excels in song
is the Muses' fervent
servant."
So Homer sang.

PEISTHETAERUS:

It's no surprise, then, that your little cloak
is full of holes. But poet, why the heck
did you come traveling all the way up here?   920

POET:

In celebration of Cloudcuckooland
I've made a hundred gorgeous dithyrambs,
maiden-songs and Simonidean ditties.°

PEISTHETAERUS:

When did you make them, though? How long ago?

POET:

Oh, it's been ages, ages now that I've
been writing songs in honor of this city.

PEISTHETAERUS:

But I've just started giving sacrifice
to celebrate its being ten days old.°
I only just now gave a name to it,
like parents do when they've a newborn baby.   930

POET:

> "Swift are the Muses' voices,
> swift as the hooves of steeds. But you,
> whose name is as revered as sacrifices,
> founder of Aetna, father, please impart
> whatever gift to me your generous heart
> is willing to bestow."°

PEISTHETAERUS: *(to Xanthias and Manodorus)*
This plague will drive us crazy. We had better
give him something to get rid of him.

(to Xanthias)

You there, you've got a jacket *and* a vest.
Take off the vest and hand it over to   940
this genius of a poet.

(giving the vest to the Poet)

Here you go.
It looks like you have got the chills all over.

POET:

Gratefully does my Muse
accept the boon you give.
Now let your mind receive,
in turn, what Pindar° says . . .

PEISTHETAERUS:
He just won't go away and leave us be.

POET:

"Among the Scythian nomads, far from home,
wanders a man attired in nothing woven by a loom.
The man is sad   950
since he has nothing on
except an animal hide."°

Do you get what I mean?

PEISTHETAERUS:
I understand you want the jacket, too.

(to Xanthias)

Take it off. We need to help the poet.

(offering the jacket to the Poet)

Alright, now, you come take it and be gone.

POET:
I'm off but, when I come back, I'll compose
verses like this to celebrate your city:

> "O Muse upon your golden throne,
> come celebrate a cold and shivering town.
> Through many-pathed, snow-blown
> plains I have made my way.
> Hurray!"

960

PEISTHETAERUS: *(to the Poet)*
Well, now that you have put that jacket on,
you sure must not be freezing any longer.

(The Poet exits, stage right.)

(to the audience)

There goes a problem I had not foreseen.
How did he find this town so soon?

(to Manodorus)

Boy, take
the lustral water, walk around the altar.

(Manodorus walks around the altar sprinkling water.)

Let ritual silence be maintained throughout!

*(The Oracle Collector enters from stage left. He
is carrying a book under one arm.)*

ORACLE COLLECTOR:
Don't sacrifice that goat.

PEISTHETAERUS:
                    And who are you?   970

ORACLE COLLECTOR:
Me, I'm an oracle collector.

PEISTHETAERUS:
                    Screw off.

ORACLE COLLECTOR:
It's dangerous to mock religious matters.
Look here, there is an oracle of Bacis°
clearly referring to Cloudcuckooland.

PEISTHETAERUS:
Why didn't you divulge these words *before*
I set about establishing a city?

ORACLE COLLECTOR:
Religiosity prevented me.

PEISTHETAERUS:
I guess I'd better hear the words themselves:

ORACLE COLLECTOR: *(reading from the book)*
"But when the wolves and grizzled ravens share
the same abode twixt Sicyon and Corinth . . ."°   980

PEISTHETAERUS:
But what does "Corinth" have to do with me?

ORACLE COLLECTOR:
By "Corinth" Bacis clearly means the sky:

"First sacrifice a white ram to the Earth,
then to whoever first interprets me
provide a gleaming cloak and fresh-made sandals—

PEISTHETAERUS:
"Sandals" are really in there?

ORACLE COLLECTOR: *(offering Peisthetaerus the book)*
                                    Here's the book.

(continuing to read)

". . . give him the goblet, fill his hands with entrails—

PEISTHETAERUS:
"His hands with entrails," really?

ORACLE COLLECTOR:
                                    Here's the book.

(continuing to read)

". . . If, pious youth, you do as here is written,
you will become an eagle in the clouds.   990
If you refuse, you will become not even
a turtledove, nor rock thrush, nor woodpecker."

PEISTHETAERUS:
All that is really in there?

ORACLE COLLECTOR:
                                    Here's the book.

PEISTHETAERUS:
That oracle is nothing to the one
Apollo gave me.° Look, I wrote it down:

(reading from a book)

"And when a shyster shows up uninvited,
disturbs the sacrifice and asks for entrails,
then you must jab at him betwixt the ribs—

ORACLE COLLECTOR:
You're only joking with me.

PEISTHETAERUS: *(offering the book to the Oracle Collector)*
Here's the book.
". . . and spare no eagle in the clouds, not even   1000
Lampon or the lordly Diopeithes."°

ORACLE COLLECTOR:
Those words are really in there?

PEISTHETAERUS:

Here's the book.

(hitting the Oracle Collector with the book)

Get lost, now! Go to hell!

ORACLE COLLECTOR:

Ouch! Ow! Oh my!

(The Oracle Collector runs off, stage left.)

PEISTHETAERUS:
Go somewhere else and sell your oracles!

*(Meton° enters from stage right, carrying various
rulers and wearing high leather boots.)*

METON:
I've come to you—

PEISTHETAERUS: *(aside)*
                          And here's a new annoyance.

                          (to Meton)

What have you come to us to do? Your plan,
what shape is it? What sort of grand idea
is now en route? What buskin is strutting in?

METON:
I want to measure out the air for you
and separate it into acres.

PEISTHETAERUS:
                                    Goodness,   1010
who in the world *are* you?

METON:
                              Who am I?
Meton, a man whose name resounds through Greece,
and all Colonus too.°

PEISTHETAERUS: *(pointing to the equipment)*
                          What's this equipment?

METON:
Rulers for measuring the air. You see,
the sky in its entirety is like
a rounded shell for baking. So, by laying
this rounded ruler over it and sticking
a compass in it . . . Do you catch my drift?

PEISTHETAERUS:
I don't.

METON:
              . . . and laying out this level ruler
along the side, I'll take a measurement,   1020

so that you'll end up with a circle squared.
There'll be a market in the middle of it,
and all these straight streets running toward that market'll
come together at the very center
and look like beams of starlight emanating
in all directions from a star that's round.

PEISTHETAERUS:
This guy's a Thales.° Meton . . .

METON:
                                        Yes, what is it?

PEISTHETAERUS:
. . . because we're pals, I'll give you this advice:
Get out of here.

METON:
                        What's wrong?

PEISTHETAERUS:
                                        It's like in Sparta:
they're driving out the foreigners, and fists   1030
are flying frequently throughout the city.°

METON:
Is there a civil war here?

PEISTHETAERUS:
                        No, not that.

METON:
What, then?

PEISTHETAERUS:
                        We have resolved, unanimously,
to beat up all the frauds.

METON:

> I'd best be going.

PEISTHETAERUS:

Yes, but I doubt that you'll escape in time.
Those fists I warned you of are near at hand.

> *(Peisthetaerus punches Meton.)*

METON:

Oh miserable me!

PEISTHETAERUS:

> But I've been trying

to get this message through since you arrived:
Get lost! Go use those rulers on yourself!

> *(Meton runs off, stage right. The Inspector enters,*
> *stage left. He is carrying two ballot boxes.)*

INSPECTOR:

Where is the legislative body?

PEISTHETAERUS:

> Who's this

Sardanapallus?°   1010

INSPECTOR:

> I've come from Athens

as the Inspector to Cloudcuckooland.

PEISTHETAERUS:

"Inspector," huh? Who sent you out to us?

INSPECTOR:

Teleas° did. He passed a bill for it.

PEISTHETAERUS:
Hey, wouldn't you prefer to take your fee
and just get out instead of making trouble?

INSPECTOR:
Sounds good to me. I should be back in Athens
speaking to the Assembly, since I'm taking
care of some business for Pharnaces.°

PEISTHETAERUS:
Good, take your pay and vanish. Here it is!   1050

(Peisthetaerus punches the Inspector.)

INSPECTOR:
Hey, what was that?

PEISTHETAERUS:
                    Assembly business for
Pharnaces.

INSPECTOR:
                    Witnesses! I, an inspector,
am being beaten up!

(The Inspector runs off, stage left.)

PEISTHETAERUS: *(to the Inspector)*
                    Get lost and take
your ballot boxes with you!

(to the audience)

                    This is awful.
Inspectors have already been dispatched
to us before we've even had the chance
to give our founding offerings to the gods.

(The Decree Seller enters, stage right. He is carrying a
number of scrolls and is reading from one of them.)

DECREE SELLER:
"If a Cloudcuckoolander harms a man
of Athens—

PEISTHETAERUS:
            What is that vile piece of writing?

DECREE SELLER:
I am a vendor of decrees, and I   1060
have come to sell your settlement new laws.

PEISTHETAERUS:
Like what?

DECREE SELLER:
        "The people of Cloudcuckooland
must use the same law code and weights and measures
the Olophyxians° use."

PEISTHETAERUS:
                    All that I'm fixing
to use is fists on you!

            (Peisthetaerus punches the Decree Seller.)

DECREE SELLER:
                Hey, what's your problem?

PEISTHETAERUS:
Take your decrees away, or else I'll show you
some very stringent laws indeed.

            (The Decree Seller retreats upstage. The
            Inspector reenters from stage left.)

INSPECTOR:
                          I summon
Peisthetaerus to appear in court
for hubris in the month Munychium.°

PEISTHETAERUS:
Really? You're back again?

DECREE SELLER:
                          "And if a man   1070
expels court officers and fails to hear them
according to the terms of the decree—

PEISTHETAERUS:
I'm cursed it seems. Are you still here as well?

INSPECTOR:
I'll ruin you, I'll sue you for ten thousand
drachmas!

PEISTHETAERUS:
            And I'll smash both your ballot boxes!

            (The Inspector runs off, stage left.)

DECREE SELLER:
Do you remember when you used to shit
on law codes in the evening?°

PEISTHETAERUS: *(to Xanthias and Manodorus)*
                          Please, somebody
grab ahold of him.

            (to the Decree Seller, who runs off, stage right)

            Won't you stand still?

            (to Xanthias and Manodorus)

Quick now, let's go inside and sacrifice
this goat and give him to the gods in there.   1080

(Peisthetaerus exits, with Xanthias, Manodorus,
and the goat, through the stage door.)

CHORUS:
Strophe
All humankind henceforth
will honor me with hymns and offerings.
All-powerful, surveyor of all things,
I keep watch over all the earth.
I safeguard crops by snapping up those breeds
of insects that, with greedy jaws,
devour the fruit that plumps in pods
and flourishes on trees.
I slay those who debase
sweet-smelling gardens with impurities.   1090
Under the violence of my wings
destruction falls on all that bites and stings.

CHORUS LEADER: (addressing the audience)
Today's the day we hear the following especially proclaimed:
"Whoever kills Diagoras of Melos° will receive a talent."
Also, "Whoever kills a long-dead tyrant will receive a talent."
Well now, we want to make our own announcement: "He who kills
Philocrates of Sparrowtown° will get a talent. If you catch him
and bring him in alive, you'll get four talents. Why? Philocrates,
you see, runs spits through finches and then sells them seven for an obol.
He tortures thrushes by inflating them with air so they look bigger,   1100
and he plucks blackbirds and sticks the feathers in their nostrils,
and he catches pigeons, cages them and makes them serve in nets
as bait." So runs the proclamation that we want to make to you.
What's more, if you keep birds in cages in your courtyard, we demand
they be released at once. All those who fail to do so will be caught
by birds and bound with rope and forced to play the decoy in their turn.

CHORUS:

Antistrophe
Happy our feathered race
that in the winter needs no woolen clothes,
nor do the summer sun's extended rays
with roasting swelter torment us.   1110
At noontime when the crazed cicada heaves
shrill hymns into the air, I roost
among the flowers and leaves
that fill the meadow's breast.
All winter in a cave
we revel with the nymphs. In spring we have
pure myrtle berries in their white
blossoms, we have the Graces' garden fruit.

CHORUS LEADER: *(to the audience)*
I want to speak now to the judges° there about the prize in question.
If they vote for us, we will bestow more gifts by far upon them   1120
than Paris took in. First, the owls from Laurium,° which every judge
covets above all else, will never fly away and leave you—no,
they'll settle in your house, roost in your money bags and breed small change.
What's more, you'll live in houses that resemble temples, since we'll peak them
with eagle gables. Plus, if you get picked for some official post
and want to pilfer money, we'll endow you with the hawk's sharp talons.
When you go out to dine in town, we'll send you off with boundless stomachs.
However, if you vote against us, well, you'd better have yourselves
fitted for copper coverings, like statues.° Otherwise, whenever
you have a white robe on, you'll pay by getting shat on by the birds!   1130

(Peisthetaerus enters through the stage door,
followed by Xanthias and Manodorus.)

PEISTHETAERUS:
The sacrifice, dear birds, was favorable.
But where's the messenger who should have come
to give us a report on wall construction?
Ah yes, here comes the fellow on the double,
all out of breath like an Olympic sprinter.

(The First Messenger enters, running, from stage left.)

FIRST MESSENGER: *(panting)*
Where—where is—where—where—where is—where—where—where is
our leader Peisthetaerus?

PEISTHETAERUS:
                            I'm right here.

FIRST MESSENGER:
Your wall has been constructed.

PEISTHETAERUS:
                                        Excellent!

FIRST MESSENGER:
A most magnificent and beautiful
accomplishment! The top is so expansive   1140
that Proxenides of Blusterburg
and Theogenes° could each hitch up
a chariot to horses as gigantic
as the Trojan one° and still have room
enough to pass each other when they met.

PEISTHETAERUS:
Truly remarkable!

FIRST MESSENGER:
                    As for its height,
I measured it myself: six hundred feet.

PEISTHETAERUS:
That's quite a height! Who built it up so tall?

FIRST MESSENGER:
Birds did it, birds. No brickmaker from Egypt,
no carpenter, no mason, only birds.   1150
It was astounding: thirty thousand cranes

swallowed foundation stones in Libya
and flew them in, and corncrakes used their beaks
to shape the blocks. Ten thousand storks made bricks
while curlews and the other river birds
kept hauling water through the air to them.

PEISTHETAERUS:
Who brought the mortar?

FIRST MESSENGER:
                              Herons did, in hods.

PEISTHETAERUS:
How did they get the mortar in the hods?

FIRST MESSENGER:
A truly brilliant method was invented!
It was the geese—they used their feet like shovels   1160
to scoop the mortar up and drop it in
the heron's hods.

PEISTHETAERUS:
                              Indeed, what can't feet do?

FIRST MESSENGER:
And there were all the ducks, with aprons on,
laying bricks. And swallows flew to help
with mortar in their mouths and trowels strapped
like children to their backs.

PEISTHETAERUS: *(to the audience)*
                              Why do we pay for
construction workers?

                    (to the First Messenger)

                    Hmm, now. Tell me also.
Who did the woodwork?

FIRST MESSENGER:
                              It was birds again,
this time those rather clever carpenters,
the woodpeckers. They used their beaks like axes
to square the gates. The ruckus of their chopping
evoked a shipyard. All the gateways now
have gates and bolts, and there are guards around them,
and bell ringers are ready with alarms,
and signal fires are waiting in the towers.
Me, I am heading off to take a bath now.
You can attend to all the rest yourself.

(*The First Messenger exits, stage right.*)

CHORUS LEADER:
You there, what's wrong with you? Are you astounded
because the wall was built so speedily?

PEISTHETAERUS:
Yes, by the gods, I am, and so I should be:
that sounded like a fairy tale. But look,
here comes a sentry from the wall with news,
no doubt. He looks just like a battle dancer.°

(*The Second Messenger enters, running, from stage right.*)

SECOND MESSENGER:
Red alert! Red alert! Red alert!

PEISTHETAERUS:
What's going on?

SECOND MESSENGER:
                     A great emergency!
One of the deities attached to Zeus
has flown in through a gate and violated
our airspace. Somehow he escaped the notice
of all the jays, our daytime sentinels.

PEISTHETAERUS:
A terrible misdeed, and quite illegal!   1190
Which of the gods has done it?

SECOND MESSENGER:
                              We don't know.
All that we know for sure is: he has wings.

PEISTHETAERUS:
Shouldn't you have dispatched the border guard
against him right away?

SECOND MESSENGER:
                         Three thousand hawks,
our mounted archers, have been mobilized,
and every bird with claws has gone with them—
vulture and buzzard, eagle, owl and kestrel.
The air is quivering beneath the rush
and rummage of their wings as they pursue
the god that must be somewhere near at hand,   1200
oh yes, quite close to us.

PEISTHETAERUS:
                        To arms! To arms!
Take up your slings and bows! Move in, reservists!
Shoot! Pummel! Someone, arm me with a sling!

CHORUS:
        Strophe
        A war is breaking out between us and the gods,
        a war beyond description. Come, now, everyone,
        guard Erebus's son, the Air,° the region girt with clouds.
        Make sure that no divinity sneaks in.

CHORUS LEADER:
All of you, everywhere, look out—I hear
the god's wings whirring in the air nearby.

(Iris enters, winged, suspended from the stage crane.)

PEISTHETAERUS: *(to Iris)*
Hey, woman, where, where, where you flying to?   1210
Halt there! Stand still! Stop darting to and fro!
Who are you, and from where? You'd better tell me
where you've come from.

IRIS:
                         I have flown down here
from the abode of the Olympian gods.

PEISTHETAERUS:
And what's your name? The *Salaminia*?
The *Paralus*?°

IRIS:
                    I am the Speedy Iris.

PEISTHETAERUS:
Boat or dog?

IRIS:
                    What do you mean by that?

PEISTHETAERUS: *(to the Chorus)*
One of you buzzards, fly up there and grab her!

IRIS:
"Grab me"? What do you mean by all these insults?

PEISTHETAERUS:
You're gonna get it!

IRIS:
                    How unprecedented!   1220

PEISTHETAERUS:
Which gateway did you use to penetrate
our walls, you whore?

IRIS:
                    Which gateway? No idea.

PEISTHETAERUS: *(to the Chorus)*
Do you hear her voice, how insolent
she is?

                              (to Iris)

          Did you present yourself before
the Sergeants of the Jays?

IRIS:
                    I'm sorry—what?

PEISTHETAERUS:
Do you have a passport that the storks
have stamped?

IRIS:
                    What is this nonsense?

PEISTHETAERUS:
                              Do you have one?

IRIS:
Are you insane?

PEISTHETAERUS:
                    And no official bird
was present to approve a visa for you?

IRIS:
No, no one has approved a visa for me,   1230
you idiot.

PEISTHETAERUS:
            So you have stolen passage
through air into a city not your own?

IRIS:
What other roads are gods supposed to fly on?

PEISTHETAERUS:
That's not my problem, but they won't be flying
through here. In fact, you're here illegally
and, if you were to get what you've got coming,
there is no other Iris more deserving
of summary arrest and execution.

IRIS:
But I'm immortal.

PEISTHETAERUS:
            You'd be executed
all the same. The way I see it, we'd   1240
be in a bad position if we birds
were in command here and you gods continued
acting out and failing to accept
you must submit to your superiors
now that your time has passed. So go on, tell me:
Where are you flying with those wings of yours?

IRIS:
I am a messenger of Zeus en route
to order men to offer, at their altars,
oxen and sheep to the Olympian gods
and fill the streets with smoke of sacrifice.   1250

PEISTHETAERUS:
What gods are you referring to?

IRIS:

                              What gods?
Why, us, of course, the gods up in the sky.

PEISTHETAERUS:
You all are gods?

IRIS:

                    What other gods are out there?

PEISTHETAERUS:
Birds now are the humans' gods, so humans
must offer sacrifice to birds and not,
by Zeus, to Zeus.

IRIS:

                       You fool! You fool! Don't rouse
the gods' dread violence against yourself,
lest Justice, armed with Zeus's spade, root out,
entirely, the race of aviankind,
lest lightning smite you with Licymnian force,°   1260
burn up your person, melt your porticoes!

PEISTHETAERUS:
Now you listen. Stop your threatening.
Just stand there without moving. Did you think
I was some Lydian or Phrygian°
you could intimidate with big, loud words?
You need to know that, if Zeus troubles me
again, I will incinerate his palace
and Amphion's, too,° with fire-breathing eagles.
I shall deploy against him in the sky
porphyrions, more than six hundred of them,   1270
all clad in leopard's skins. (And in the past
just one Porphyrion° gave Zeus a lot

of trouble.) As for you, his messenger,
the "goddess" Iris, if you make me angry,
I'll push your thighs apart and screw you good.
You'll marvel that a geezer like myself
can keep it up for three successive rammings!

IRIS:
Die, wretch, along with your obscenities!

PEISTHETAERUS:
Get out of here, and quickly. Scat, girl, scat!

IRIS:
My father Zeus, I swear, will put an end   1280
to your aggression!

PEISTHETAERUS: *(sarcastically)*
        Oh, I'm really scared!

                (sincerely)

Why don't you fly off somewhere else and frighten
some younger person with your talk of lightning?

        (Iris flies off on the stage crane.)

CHORUS:
    Antistrophe
    We have forbidden all the gods derived from Zeus
    any further passage through our town. No more
    shall human beings send the savory smoke of sacrifice
    upward to heaven this way through the air.

PEISTHETAERUS:
I can't stop worrying about the herald
I sent to humankind. What if he never
comes back again?

(The First Herald enters from stage left. He is carrying a golden crown.)

FIRST HERALD:
                    Hail, blessed Peisthetaerus!   1290
O most wise, most distinguished . . . O most wise,
most cunning, triply happy . . . O most . . . break in
anytime.

PEISTHETAERUS:
          What do you have to say?

FIRST HERALD:
In honor of your wisdom all the people
want to bestow this golden crown upon you.

(The First Herald puts the crown on Peisthetaerus's head.)

PEISTHETAERUS:
I welcome it. But why give me this honor?

FIRST HERALD:
O founder of this most illustrious city
set in the air, do you not realize
in what esteem men hold you and how many
now can be called adorers of this land?   1300

Before you built this city, everyone
was mad for all things Spartan.° People grew
their hair out long and fasted, never bathed,
behaved like Socrates and went around
with walking sticks,° but now the fad has changed,
and they are mad for all things avian.
They take delight in copying whatever
we birds do.
                    To start with, right at dawn,
like birds, they all get out of bed and then go scratch
around for legal cases. Then they go   1310
and hone their bills among the civic archives.

So glaring is their avian craziness
that many of them have assumed bird names.
There is a barkeep with a limp who goes by
"the Partridge," and Menippus° calls himself
"the Swallow," and one-eyed Opuntius,°
"the Crow." Their "Lark" is Philocles;° their "Fox-Goose"
Theogenes. Lycurgus° is "the Ibis,"
and Chaerephon° "the Bat." "The Magpie" is
this guy named Syracosius;° "the Quail,"   1320
Midias° (who, one must admit, resembles
a quail hit on the noggin by a finger).°

Ornithophiliacs, they won't stop singing
songs with swallows in them and with teals
in them and geese and pigeons, or with feathers
in them or at least a bit of fluff.
That is the situation down on earth.

There's one more thing that I should tell you: people
are coming here, more than ten thousand of them,
to ask for feathers and a raptor's talons,   1330
and you will have to find a good supply
of wings to outfit all the immigrants.

PEISTHETAERUS: *(to Xanthias and Manodorus)*
Now listen up: we should stop wasting time.
Fill all those bags and baskets to the rim
with wings.

(to Manodorus)

Manes, you carry them to me
outside the nest, and I'll be there to welcome
everyone who comes to live with us.

(Xanthias and Manodorus exit through a stage door.)

CHORUS:

> Soon some human immigrant
> will come to make this settlement
> even more populous.   1340

PEISTHETAERUS:

> With any luck!

CHORUS:

> The urge to settle here is everywhere!

> *(Throughout this scene, Manodorus exits and enters*
> *through stage door carrying baskets full of wings.)*

PEISTHETAERUS: *(to Manodorus)*

> Bring in those wings, now. Quick, be quick.

CHORUS:

> All that an immigrant might want
> we've got in stock:
> Ambrosia, Graces, Smarts, Desire
> and kind Tranquillity's sweet face.

PEISTHETAERUS: *(to Manodorus)*

> Hurry up there! You lazy clod!

CHORUS: *(to Manodorus)*

> Quick, now, we need some wings outside!

> *(to Peisthetaerus)*

> Tell him again to hurry up.   1350

PEISTHETAERUS: *(striking Manodorus)*

> I will, by beating him like this!

CHORUS:

> Oh, he is slow, slow, slow, slow as an ass.

PEISTHETAERUS:

    Manes is a waste of space!

CHORUS:

    First you must group
    these wings according to their type:
    the musical go here; the prophetic, there;
    the naval, here, and then be sure
    you accurately gauge
    the man you fledge.

PEISTHETAERUS: *(to Manodorus)*

    Oh, by the kestrels you   1360
    are going to catch it now!
    How very slow you are!

      (Xanthias and Manodorus have assembled a large pile
      of wings and placed a whip beside it and a stool. The
      Father-Beater enters, singing, from stage right.)

FATHER-BEATER:

    I wish I were an eagle and could fly
    high in the sky
    above the azure motion
    of the barren ocean!

PEISTHETAERUS:

It seems the messenger has given me
no false report. Here comes a person singing
a song of eagles.

FATHER-BEATER:

      Oh my, my. There's nothing
sweeter than flight. Oh yes, I'm mad for birds.   1370
I want to fly up, make my nest among you
and live according to your laws.

PEISTHETAERUS:

                          Which laws?
The birds have many laws.

FATHER-BEATER:

                          Well, all your laws.
Especially the one that says it's noble
both to strangle and to peck one's father.

PEISTHETAERUS:
We do indeed regard a younger bird
who's beaten up his dad as rather manly.

FATHER-BEATER:
That's why I want to nest here—so that I
can break my father's neck and seize his wealth.

PEISTHETAERUS:
But there is also this quite ancient law   1380
inscribed upon the Tablet of the Storks:
"After the father stork has reared his storklings
and taught them how to fly, the storklings must,
in turn, support their father."

FATHER-BEATER:

                          What a waste
it's been for me to travel all this way,
since here I'd even have to feed my father.

PEISTHETAERUS:
No, not a waste. My friend, since you have come here
so proactively, I want to fit you
with wings as if you were an orphan bird.
What's more, young man, I'm going to pass along   1390
some good advice that I myself received
when I was just a lad: Don't beat your father.
Now take these wings in one hand; in the other
take these spurs and then, regarding this

here as a cockscomb on your head, go serve
as sentry or as soldier. Make your way
by working. Let your father live his life out.
Since you are keen to fight, fly off to Thrace
and do your fighting there.

FATHER-BEATER:

What sound advice!
I'll act on it.

PEISTHETAERUS:

You would be wise to do so.   1400

(*The Father-Beater exits, stage left. Cinesias°*
enters, singing, from stage right.)

CINESIAS:
"I flutter to Olympus on ethereal wings.
I fly, now here, now there, on roads of songs . . ."

PEISTHETAERUS:
He's gonna need a whole boatload of wings.

CINESIAS:
". . . seeking a new route
with fearless body, fearless thought . . ."

PEISTHETAERUS:
Greetings, Cinesias, you rail! Why have
you whirled your lame leg round and wound up here?

CINESIAS:
". . . I wish I were a fowl,
a tuneful nightingale . . ."

PEISTHETAERUS:
Stop singing and just tell me what you want.   1410

CINESIAS:

Wing me, and I will fly into the aether
and gather novel preludes from the airborne,
snow-like exhalations of the clouds.

PEISTHETAERUS:

You want to gather preludes from the clouds?

CINESIAS:

A poet's whole craft hangs upon the clouds!
A dithyramb's most striking parts are airy
and misty, darkly bright and flighty.
Just listen, and you'll understand . . .

PEISTHETAERUS:

                              No thanks.

CINESIAS:

By Heracles you simply must! Here now,
I'll sing this one for you from start to finish: 1420

    "O dreams of feathered beings who cleave the aether,
    long-necked, together . . ."

PEISTHETAERUS:

Whoa now.

CINESIAS:

    "Borne on the breath of a gale,
    I soar above the ocean swell . . ."

PEISTHETAERUS:

Believe you me, I'll stop your breath for good!

CINESIAS:

    ". . . Now traveling in the regions where
    the South wind issues forth,

now bringing my body near the North,
cleaving a harborless furrow of air . . ."

(Peisthetaerus lashes Cinesias with pairs of wings.)

You coot, that is a charming trick indeed!

PEISTHETAERUS:
Don't you get off on being wing-propelled?

CINESIAS:
To treat me thus, the dithyrambic poet
for whom the various tribes will not stop fighting!

PEISTHETAERUS: *(sarcastically)*
Oh please, please reside with us and teach
Leotrophides° choral songs for flocks
of flying corncrakes!

CINESIAS:
                    You are mocking me,
that's clear. Regardless, I shall not relent
until I get my wings and climb the air!

*(Cinesias exits, stage right. The Informer enters, singing,
from stage left. He is wearing a tattered cloak.)*

INFORMER:
        "Who are these dappled birds that look like transients?   1440
        O long-winged swallows, subtle ones!"

PEISTHETAERUS:
My goodness, this is no small infestation
that threatens us. Here comes another warbler.

INFORMER:
        Again I sing: "O long-winged subtle ones!"

PEISTHETAERUS:

He's singing to his cloak. That thing needs more
than just a couple swallows.°

INFORMER:

                         Where's the man
that hands out wings to everyone who comes here?

PEISTHETAERUS:

Right here. But you must tell me why you want them.

INFORMER:

It's wings I want and wings that I must have.
Don't make me ask for them a second time.   1450

PEISTHETAERUS:

What, do you want to fly off to Pellene?°

INFORMER:

Not there. I am a server of subpoenas
who trolls the islands, an informer and . . .

PEISTHETAERUS:

What glorious work you do!

INFORMER:

                         . . . a sniffer-out
of lawsuits. And I need a pair of wings
to fly to island states and serve subpoenas.

PEISTHETAERUS:

Would wingpower help you better serve subpoenas?

INFORMER:

No, but that way the pirates couldn't get me.
I could return to Athens with the cranes,
once I had loaded up with tons of lawsuits   1460
as ballast.

PEISTHETAERUS:

That's the way you make your living?
Though you are a hale and hearty youngster,
you inform on foreigners?

INFORMER:

Why not?
I mean, I don't know how to use a shovel.

PEISTHETAERUS:

Surely there must be nobler types of work
from which so big a man could make an honest
living instead of pettifogging lawsuits.

INFORMER:

Buddy, don't nag me. I just want my wings.

PEISTHETAERUS:

And I will give you wings by talking to you.

INFORMER:

How can mere words fit someone out with wings?   1470

PEISTHETAERUS:

It's words, you see, that set us all aflutter.

INFORMER:

All of us?

PEISTHETAERUS:

Have you never heard boys' fathers
in barbershops complaining, for example,
"It's terrible how Dieitrephes's words
have set my son aflutter to be racing
horses!" and then another of them says,
"My son is all aflutter to be writing
tragedies. His wits have up and flown
out of his head!"

INFORMER:

      So they get wings from words?

PEISTHETAERUS:

They do indeed. Words elevate the mind   1480
and move the man. And so I hope to use
these beneficial words to set you all
aflutter for a better line of work.

INFORMER:

But I don't want one.

PEISTHETAERUS:

      What, then, will you do?

INFORMER:

I *won't* disgrace my family name. Informing
has been our business since my great-grandfather's time.
So, quick, now, fit me out with light and speedy
hawk or kestrel wings, so that I can
subpoena foreigners, obtain a judgment
in Athens, then fly back out to the islands.   1490

PEISTHETAERUS:

I see. That way the foreigner will lose
his case before he even reaches Athens.

INFORMER:

That's right.

PEISTHETAERUS:

      And while he's on his way to Athens,
you'll be flying back out to the islands
to grab his property.

INFORMER:
                    You've got it all, now.
I'll have to zip from one place to another
as swiftly as a top.

PEISTHETAERUS:
                    "A top"—I see.

                    (picking up the whip)

Well, by chance I've got some rather handsome
Corcyrean wings° right here beside me.
How do you like them?

INFORMER:
                    Oh no, that's a whip!   1500

PEISTHETAERUS:
Nope, it's a pair of wings. I'm going to use them
to make you zip as swiftly as a top.

INFORMER:
Oh no!

                    (The Informer exits, running, stage left.)

PEISTHETAERUS:
                    Won't you go "flying" out of here?
Git, now, you goddamn good-for-nothing, git!
I'll treat you to some shyster double-dealing!

                    (to Xanthias and Manodorus)

You two, collect the wings and come with me.

                    (Peisthetaerus, Xanthias, and Manodorus exit through
                    the stage door with the baskets full of wings.)

CHORUS:

> *Strophe*
> In my ethereal flights I have seen
> many amazing novelties:
> there is a tree near Cowardtown,
> a strange tree called Cleonymus.°   1510
> It has no heartwood. A useless thing,
> voluminous, with a yellow rind,
> it spouts perjuries every spring
> and in fall sheds shields on the ground.
>
> *Antistrophe*
> Then there's a land at the edge of creation,
> a lampless waste, where people meet
> the great heroes for conversation
> and banqueting, but not at night—
> that's when it's dangerous to be there
> because, if someone ran into   1520
> Orestes,° he'd be stripped down bare
> and beaten from top to toe.

> *(Peisthetaerus enters through the stage door. Prometheus*
> *enters from stage left, masked and carrying a parasol.)*

PROMETHEUS:

Oh no, oh no! I hope that Zeus won't see me!
Where's Peisthetaerus?

PEISTHETAERUS:

                              Whoa, what's this? A masked man?

PROMETHEUS:

Do you see any of the gods behind me?

PEISTHETAERUS:

Nope, none of them are back there. Who are you?

PROMETHEUS:
What time is it?

PEISTHETAERUS:
                What time? Just after midday.
Who are you?

PROMETHEUS:
                Time to loose the oxen? Later?

PEISTHETAERUS:
Ah, this is nauseating!

PROMETHEUS:
                What's Zeus doing?
Breaking the clouds up or collecting them?   1530

PEISTHETAERUS:
Screw off!

PROMETHEUS:
        Alright, then, I'll unmask myself.

                (Prometheus removes his mask.)

PEISTHETAERUS:
Prometheus my friend!

PROMETHEUS:
                Hush, now. Don't shout.

PEISTHETAERUS:
What's wrong?

PROMETHEUS:
                Hush, hush. Don't say my name out loud.
If Zeus finds out I'm here, I'll be a dead man.
Alright, I'm going to tell you everything

that's happening up in the sky, but take
this parasol and shield my head with it
so that the gods don't see me from above.

(Prometheus hands Peisthetaerus the parasol.)

PEISTHETAERUS:
A very clever plan! How Promethean!

(holding up the parasol)

Quick, hide in here, and speak with confidence.   1540

PROMETHEUS:
Now hear this . . .

PEISTHETAERUS:
                    I'm listening, continue.

PROMETHEUS:
Zeus is beaten.

PEISTHETAERUS:
                    Beaten? But since when?

PROMETHEUS:
Ever since you established this encampment
here in the air. Since then no man has offered
sacrifice to the gods; the smoke from victims'
thighbones no longer makes its way to us.
Without burnt offerings we may as well
be fasting at the Thesmophoria!°
All the barbarian gods have grown so hungry
that they are screaming like Illyrians°   1550
and threatening to descend in arms on Zeus,
if he does not reopen all the markets.
so that they can import their fill of tripe.

PEISTHETAERUS:
Wait, there are other savage gods that live
beyond you?

PROMETHEUS:
                Yes, of course there are. Where else
would Execestides's forebears° have found
a deity to worship?

PEISTHETAERUS:
                        What's the name
of these barbaric gods?

PROMETHEUS:
                        Triballians.

PEISTHETAERUS:
I see—"Triballian" must be the word
that "tribbing" comes from.°

PROMETHEUS:
                        Yes, that's very likely.   1560
One thing is clear: ambassadors will soon
come here from Zeus and the Triballians
beyond him to negotiate a treaty.
Don't you agree to anything till Zeus
returns his scepter to the birds and gives you
Princess to be your wife.

PEISTHETAERUS:
                    But who is this "Princess"?

PROMETHEUS:
A gorgeous girl who guards the thunderbolts
of Zeus and keeps such things as prudent counsel,
self-restraint, civility, shipyards,
disparagement, paychecks, three-obol fees.   1570

PEISTHETAERUS:
She watches over all those things?

PROMETHEUS:

She does.
Get her as wife, and you'll have everything.
That's why I came—to give you this advice.
I've always been a friend to humankind.

PEISTHETAERUS:
Yes, it's because of you and you alone
that we get barbecues.°

PROMETHEUS:

I hate the gods,
as you well know.

PEISTHETAERUS:

Yes, you were born to hate them.
You are a perfect Timon.°

PROMETHEUS:

Here, going,
so give me back my parasol so that,
if Zeus does see me from above, I'll seem   1580
to be a butler for a basket-bearer.°

PEISTHETAERUS:
And take as well this stool for her to sit on.

(Peisthetaerus hands Prometheus the stool. Prometheus exits, stage
left, holding the opened parasol over his head with one hand and
the stool in the other. Peisthetaerus exits through the stage door.)

CHORUS:
Strophe
Out in the land of Shadefoots there's a fen
where dirty Socrates calls up the souls of men.

Pisander° came there one day to retrieve
the spirit he'd abandoned when alive.

He brought a baby camel, slit its throat
and took a step back like Odysseus.°

Up from the depths came Chaerephon° the Bat,
conjured by that blood sacrifice.   1590

(Poseidon, Heracles, and the Triballian enter from stage left.)

POSEIDON:
Now you can see Cloudcuckooland before you—
that's where we're headed as ambassadors.

(to the Triballian)

Hey you, look what you've done. You've draped your cloak
from right to left. Why not the other way
from left to right? You moron, do you think
you are Laespodias?° Democracy,
what have you come to, if the gods can choose
this person as ambassador? Keep still, now,
dammit. You are by far the most barbaric
divinity that I have ever seen.   1600

(to Heracles)

Heracles, what should we be doing here?

HERACLES:
You know my mind—we should be strangling
the guy who's walled us gods off from the air.

POSEIDON:
Sorry, my friend. We're here as diplomats;
our job is to negotiate a treaty.

HERACLES:
That just makes me want to strangle him
a second time.

> (Peisthetaerus enters through the stage door. He is attended by
> Xanthias and Manodorus, who carry out a barbecue grill.)

PEISTHETAERUS: *(to Xanthias and Manodorus)*
                    Cheese grater, please. Now pass
the silphium.° Somebody bring the cheese in,
and, you there, stir those coals.

POSEIDON: *(to Peisthetaerus)*
                                We three, as gods,
greet you, a mortal man.

PEISTHETAERUS:
                    Hold on a sec;   1610
I'm grating silphium.

HERACLES:
                    What are these meats?

PEISTHETAERUS:
Fowls that have been condemned to death for raising
a coup against the bird-democracy.

HERACLES:
And you will season them with silphium
before you answer us?

PEISTHETAERUS: *(as if seeing Heracles for the first time)*
                    Oh, Heracles,
hello. What's that you said?

POSEIDON:
                    The gods have sent us
to you as diplomats to sue for peace.

PEISTHETAERUS: *(to Xanthias)*
This flask has no more oil in it.

HERACLES:

The fowls,
of course, must be completely drenched in oil.

POSEIDON:
We gods are gaining nothing from this conflict.   1620
As for you, by being friends with us,
you would obtain rainwater for your pools
and endless halcyon weather to enjoy.
On just these terms we have been granted power
to ratify a treaty.

PEISTHETAERUS:
Hold on there—
We weren't the instigators of this war
and even now we're willing to conclude
a peace, so long as you agree to do
what's right, and here's what's right: that Zeus return
his scepter to the birds. If we can reach   1630
agreement on this matter, I invite
you three ambassadors to lunch.

HERACLES:
Sounds good.
I vote for peace.

POSEIDON: *(to Heracles)*
You vote for what, you wretch?
You're nothing but an idiotic pig.
What, would you oust your father from his throne?

PEISTHETAERUS:
But that's not true. The gods will end up being
even stronger if the birds hold sway
throughout the air. At present men can trust

in clouds and bow their heads and not be noticed
when they swear falsely by your names. However,   1640
if the birds were on your side and someone,
after swearing by the crow and Zeus,
should break his oath, the crow could swoop down on him
unawares and peck his eyeballs out.

POSEIDON:
Well spoken, by Poseidon!

HERACLES:
                         I agree.

PEISTHETAERUS: *(to the Triballian)*
You there, what's your opinion?

TRIBALLIAN:
                         Okey yup.

HERACLES:
See? He agrees with us.

PEISTHETAERUS:
                    Now pay attention.
Here's what else we'll do to benefit you:
If someone promises a god a gift
and then tries getting out of it by saying   1650
"Patient are the gods" and welches on
his promise out of greed, we can compel
the man to pay.

POSEIDON:
                    And how would you do that?

PEISTHETAERUS:
While he is counting up his silver coins
or in the bath, a vulture will (surprise!)

descend, exact a two-sheep penalty
and bring it to the god to whom it's owed.

HERACLES: *(to Poseidon)*
I vote, again, to let them have the scepter.

POSEIDON: *(to Heracles)*
Ask the Triballian.

HERACLES: *(to the Triballian)*
                    Hey, Triballian,
you want a beating?

TRIBALLIAN:
                    No thump head wit' bat.   1660

HERACLES:
He says he sides with me.

POSEIDON: *(to Heracles and the Triballian)*
                        If both of you
agree in this, I'll go along with you.

HERACLES:
Hey you—we're gonna let you have the scepter.

PEISTHETAERUS:
Oh, but I remember stipulating
something further: Zeus can keep his Hera,
but the girl "Princess" must become my wife.

POSEIDON: *(turning away from Peisthetaerus)*
It isn't peace that you are lusting after.

                (to Heracles and the Triballian)

Let's head back home.

PEISTHETAERUS:

It's no big deal to me.

(calling into the house)

Hey, cook, be sure to make the gravy sweet.

HERACLES:
You're nuts, Poseidon! Where you running off to?   1670
We're goin' back to war because of just one
little female?

POSEIDON:

What else can we do?

HERACLES:
What else? Conclude a peace.

POSEIDON:

You total moron.
Don't you know that, for a long time now,
you've been getting suckered? You're completely
ruining yourself. If, after giving
the birds his sovereignty, Zeus were to die,
you would have nothing, since you are the heir
to everything he leaves behind at death.

PEISTHETAERUS: *(to Heracles)*
My, but he's feeding you the double-talk.   1680
Come step aside here so that we can chat.

(aside to Heracles)

Poor guy, your uncle's out to screw you over.
The law says you don't get a single straw°
of your paternal property, because
you are a bastard, illegitimate.

HERACLES:

A bastard? Me? What's that you're sayin' to me?

PEISTHETAERUS:

Why, certainly you are. Your mother wasn't
your father's wife. Why else would people call
Athena, who is Zeus's daughter, "Heiress,"°
if Zeus had any sons who could inherit?   1690

HERACLES:

Couldn't my father on his deathbed leave me
all of his property, though I'm a bastard?

PEISTHETAERUS:

The law does not allow it, and your uncle
Poseidon would be quick to claim that wealth
because he's Zeus's full and legal brother.
I'll even quote this law of Solon's° to you:
"If there are full and legal children, bastards
shall not inherit. If there are no full
and legal children, then the next of kin
shall share the wealth among them."

HERACLES:

                         I'll get nothing   1700
whatsoever of my father's stuff?

PEISTHETAERUS:

Nothing at all. And tell me, has your father
ever inducted you into his phratry?°

HERACLES:

He hasn't, and that's always worried me.

PEISTHETAERUS:

Why do you stand there gaping at the sky?
Why are you glaring upward? If you joined us,
you'd be a king and drink the milk of birds.

HERACLES:
It still seems fair to me that you are asking
to wed the girl. I vote to give her to you.

PEISTHETAERUS: *(to Poseidon)*
And what's your vote?

POSEIDON:

I vote against the treaty.   1710

PEISTHETAERUS:
The whole choice hangs on the Triballian.

(to the Triballian)

What do you say?

(Heracles makes a threatening gesture at the Triballian.)

TRIBALLIAN:
                    Me givie birdie tall tall
pretty queen.

HERACLES:
                    He votes to give her up.

POSEIDON:
He isn't saying we should hand her over.
He's simply twittering nonsense like the swallows.

HERACLES:
Alright, he's saying give her to the swallows.

POSEIDON: *(to Heracles and the Triballian)*
I'm done with this. You two negotiate
the terms of the agreement. I'll keep mum
since you've made up your minds.

HERACLES: *(to Peisthetaerus)*

Here's our decision: 1720
We've resolved to give you everything
that you've requested. Now come up with us
into the sky so that you can receive
Princess and all the rest.

PEISTHETAERUS:

Then these birds here
were cut to pieces for my wedding feast.

HERACLES:

You go and, if you like, I'll stay and roast 'em.

POSEIDON:

You're going to "roast" them? More like eat them all.
Aren't you going to come with us?

HERACLES:

Alright.
I would have liked that job, though.

PEISTHETAERUS: *(to Xanthias and Manodorus)*

Someone go
and get a jacket for me for the wedding.

*(During the following chorus, Peisthetaerus receives
his wedding jacket and exits, stage right, with
Poseidon, Heracles, and the Triballian.)*

CHORUS:

Antistrophe
The wicked people of Get-Rich-by-Tongue 1730
reside off in Illusion near a spring.

They use their tongues as harvesters and sowers,
squeezers of grapes and gatherers of flowers.

People like Gorgias and Philippus°
make up the number of their savage gang.

So, throughout Attica, in sacrifice,
we cut out the Philippic tongue.

(The Second Herald enters from stage right.)

SECOND HERALD: *(to the birds)*
O you who have achieved prosperity,
you beings greater than mere words can say,
you triply happy race endowed with wings,   1740
welcome your ruler to his thriving palace.

As he approaches this resplendent house,
he looks more dazzling than a meteor,
more dazzling than the sun's far-shooting glitz
of beams, and he is leading at his side
a woman of ineffable allure,
and he is brandishing the thunderbolt,
winged dart of Zeus.
                              An indescribably
seductive fragrance spreads throughout the air,
and all those wreaths of incense in the breeze   1750
are beautiful.

*(Peisthetaerus enters from stage right. He is holding a
     thunderbolt. Princess, his bride, is at his side.)*

                    Here he is. Holy Muse,
open your lips and breathe auspicious song!

CHORUS:
          Make room! Fall back!
          Advance! Divide!
          Fly round a bridegroom blest with luck.

Oh! Oh! Her youth! Her beauty!
The marriage you have made
is one great blessing for the city.

CHORUS LEADER:

Because of him
good luck has come   1760
upon the avian race.
Welcome him and his Princess home
with songs for weddings, bridal harmonies.

CHORUS:

Strophe
During just such festivities as these
the Fates united Hera and Olympian Zeus,
who rules the gods while sitting on
the summit of his throne.
O Hymen! O Hymenaeus!°
O Hymen! O Hymenaeus!

Antistrophe
Fresh, golden-feathered Eros guided
the chariot with reins pulled tight. Yes, he presided   1770
as best man on the day Zeus made
Hera a happy bride.
O Hymen! O Hymenaeus!
O Hymen! O Hymenaeus!

PEISTHETAERUS:

I love this music; I adore your song.
The words are ravishing.

CHORUS LEADER:

Come now, exalt
Zeus's thunder rattling the earth
and the fiery glory he sends forth—   1780
that awesome blinding thunderbolt.

CHORUS:

> O golden lightning flare!
> O shafts of holy fire!
> O deeply-echoing booms that bring the rain.
> This man now shakes the earth with you.
> He now is master of
> Zeus's prerogative
> and Princess, who
> once was a slave at Zeus's throne.
> O Hymen! O Hymenaeus!   1790

CHORUS LEADER:

> Come, feathered throngs,
> singers of songs,
> follow this happy pair
> to Zeus's palace and the bridal bower.

PEISTHETAERUS:

> O happy wife, hold out your hand
> and grip my wings and dance with me.
> I'll lift you up and swing you round.

CHORUS:

> Hail, Paeon! Hip, hip, hooray!
> O highest of divinities,
> three cheers to your success!   1800

*(The chorus members escort Peisthetaerus and
Princess out through the stage door.)*

Lysistrata

When Aristophanes wrote *Lysistrata*, Athens had been fighting the Spartans, on and off, for almost twenty years. The high hopes of the Sicilian expedition had given way to near desperation in Athens. At the play's opening, an Athenian woman, Lysistrata, devises a two-part plan to end the war: first, the women of Greece will refuse to sleep with their husbands until peace is concluded, and, second, the older women of Athens will seize the treasury of the Delian League (moved from Delos to the Acropolis in 454 BCE). Although the Spartan representative, Lampito, is marked as "other" by her dialect, by joining Lysistrata's plan, she is absorbed into a larger sisterhood of femininity that transcends national boundaries. In fact, all distinctions in the play (except that between master and slave) work toward unification. The chorus, for example, is initially divided into equal semi-choruses of old men and old women. After staging elemental battles between fire and water, male and female, they eventually reconcile and merge into a single group.

During the confrontation between Lysistrata and the Commissioner, the feminine domestic sphere expands to become the *polis*. As females handle domestic economy, they will handle the state treasury; as females work imperfections out of a fleece, they will deal with problematic groups in the civic population:

> Imagine Athens is a fresh-shorn fleece.
> First, what you do is dunk it in a bath and wash out all
> the sheep poop; then you lay it on a bed and take a stick
> and beat out all the nasties, then you pick the thistles out.
> Next, you take those that have clumped together and become
> as thick as felt (to snag up all the civic offices)
> and comb them out and pluck their heads off. Then you go and card
> the raw cleaned wool into the Basket of Reciprocal
> Agreeableness, mixing everyone in there together—
> resident aliens and other foreigners you like
> and those who owe the state back taxes—mix them in there good. (604–614)

Lysistrata thus describes the *polis* as an *oikos*. During the course of the play, the former, the sphere of male action, is systematically collapsed into the latter, traditionally the purview of females.

We see the effects of the sex strike on both females and males. In scenes set several days after the opening one, Lysistrata has to prevent numerous females from running home to be with their husbands, and Harden (my translation of Cinesias, "the Arouser") arrives with an erection to claim his wife Myrrhine. He is left unsatisfied and, approached by Spartan messengers in a similar aroused state, encourages them to send ambassadors and strike a peace. The nude, voluptuous figure of Reconciliation appears, representing the lands of the Greek-speaking world, and once her parts are equitably divided up, male is reconciled with female, Spartan with Athenian. The play ends with festive songs and dances, in which the Spartan Ambassador's foreignness is appreciated.

I have rendered the spoken and sung dialect of the Spartans in *Lysistrata* as a country twang specific to no region. I use, in addition to lexical choices, the following markers:

- -*g* dropped from gerunds and present active participles: *runnin'* for *running*
- -*n* dropped with an indefinite article before a noun beginning with a vowel: *a' honest* for *an honest*
- *a'* for *of*
- *'roun'* for *around*
- contraction *to't* for *to it*
- occasional dropped linking verbs: *you gropin'* for *you are groping*
- *gonna* for *going to*
- *outta* for *out of*
- *fella* for *fellow*
- *git* for *get*
- *ain't* for *isn't*
- *y'all* for the second-person plural pronoun
- *ma* for the possessive adjective *my*
- *'cause* for *because* and *jus'* for *just*
- *nekked* for *naked*
- *Mount Tayeegety* for *Mount Taygetus*

Lysistrata

(Lysistrate)

First produced in 411 BCE

CHARACTERS IN THE PLAY

Lysistrata
Calonice
Myrrhine
Lampito
Female Representa-
    tives from Boeo-
    tia and Corinth
Scythian Slave Girl
Old Men's Chorus
    Leader (Draces)
Chorus of Old Men
Old Women's
    Chorus Leader
    (Stratyllis)
Chorus of Old
    Women
Commissioner
Four Policemen

Four Scythian
    Archers
Three Old Women
Four Women
Harden
Manes the Slave
Baby
Spartan Messenger
Two Spartan
    Ambassadors
Two Athenian
    Ambassadors
Reconciliation
Athenian
    Doorkeeper
Slaves
Piper

(The setting is Athens, Greece, in 411 BCE. Athens has been at war with Sparta and other Greek states, including Boeotia and Corinth, on and off for almost twenty years. There is a backdrop with two doors in it, for the moment representing the fronts of two typical Athenian houses. Lysistrata emerges through one of the doors. It is very early in the morning.)

LYSISTRATA:

If all the women had been called to worship
Pan, Bacchus or the Goddesses of Sex
at Colias,° believe me, there would be
so many drums around you couldn't move,
and now there's not a single female here—

(Calonice emerges from the other door.)

except my neighbor coming out. Good morning,
Calonice.

CALONICE:

              Morning, Lysistrata.
What's wrong with you? Don't look so grumpy, girl.
Scrunching your face up like a tight-drawn bow
is hardly an attractive look for you.   10

LYSISTRATA:

Oh, but my heart's on fire. I'm grieving over
the way we women have been treated. Men
think we are all so wicked.

CALONICE:

                         Aren't we, though?

LYSISTRATA:

I told the girls to come on time to talk
about important business, but they're late.
They must be sleeping.

CALONICE:

                     Sweetie, they'll be here.
It's tough, you know, for wives to get away—
one will be doting on her man; another
waking the slaves. While one of them is putting
the baby down, another will be nursing   20
or giving baths.

LYSISTRATA:

    But there's another matter
far more important to them than such things.

CALONICE:

What is it, Lysistrata? Why have you
convened this female council here today?
Is it a big deal?

LYSISTRATA:

    Yes, it's big.

CALONICE:

      And meaty?

LYSISTRATA:

Meaty. Yes.

CALONICE:

    Why aren't the women here, then?

LYSISTRATA:

That's not my meaning. They'd have been here quick
enough for *that*. But there's this other thing
I've hit on; I've been tossing it about
for many sleepless nights.

CALONICE:

     "Tossing" the thing—   30
by now it must be flimsy.

LYSISTRATA:

     Yes, so "flimsy"
that all of Greece's future rests upon
us women.

CALONICE:

On us women! Then it rests
on very little.

LYSISTRATA:

Yes, the city's future
rests upon womankind. Or else the people
of southern Greece will wholly cease to be—

CALONICE:

It would be better if they did, by Zeus!

LYSISTRATA:

... and all of the Boeotians be destroyed—

CALONICE:

But not their eels, but not their precious eels!°

LYSISTRATA:

... and Athens, but I don't dare utter such   40
an end for Athens. You must guess my meaning.
If the women would just meet here now,
all of them from the South and from Boeotia
and greater Athens, we could save all Greece!

CALONICE:

But what can women do that's excellent
or noble? We just sit around at home
looking all pretty in our saffron dresses,
makeup, cambric gowns, and cozy shoes.

LYSISTRATA:

Those are the very things I hope will save us—
our little saffron gowns, perfumes, and shoes,   50
our rouge and see-through undergarments.

CALONICE:

How, though?

LYSISTRATA:
They will make it so that no man living
will ever lift a spear against another . . .

CALONICE:
Then, by Demeter and Persephone,°
I'm heading out to have a dress dyed saffron!

LYSISTRATA:
. . . or hold a shield . . .

CALONICE:
I'll wear a cambric gown!

LYSISTRATA:
. . . or even a knife.

CALONICE:
I'm off to go shoe shopping!

LYSISTRATA:
I know! Shouldn't they all have come by now?

CALONICE:
"Come," no—they should have *flown* here hours ago.

LYSISTRATA:
Dear, you will find that they are perfectly
Athenian—always later than they should be.°
There aren't even any who have sailed
over from Salamis or the Paralia.°

CALONICE:
Those girls must still be mounted on their broad-beamed
dinghies.

60

LYSISTRATA:

Not even the Acharnian women°
are here. I thought they'd be the first to come.
I counted on them.

CALONICE:

Theogenes's wife,
at least, had raised her mainsail high to get here.°

(Women enter from stage right.)

But look—some of the girls are coming now.

(More women enter from stage left, including Myrrhine.)

LYSISTRATA:

And there are more arriving on this side.   70

CALONICE:

They reek! Where have they come from?

LYSISTRATA:

Stinkydale.°

CALONICE:

Of course: they kicked the stink up when they came.

MYRRHINE:

What's up, Lysistrata? Are we tardy?
What do you have to tell us? Why so quiet?

LYSISTRATA:

Myrrhine, I disapprove of your arriving
so late when there is such important business.

MYRRHINE:

It was so dark at home. I couldn't find
my bra. We're here now. Give us what you've got.

LYSISTRATA:
No, we should wait a bit until the women
come in from Boeotia and the South.   80

MYRRHINE:
That's better, yes.

> (Lampito enters from stage right, with the Female
> Representatives from Boeotia and Corinth and several
> other females. She speaks with a southern twang.)

But look, here comes Lampito!

LYSISTRATA:
Lampito darling, here you are from Sparta.
Sweetie, why, how gorgeous you are looking!
Your skin is glowing, and your body's ripped.
I bet that you could snap a bull's neck.

LAMPITO:
                                    Shee-ute,
I bet I could. I work out regular—
you know, those heel-to-butt kicks people do.

CALONICE: *(groping Lampito's breasts)*
Wow, what a banging rack you have!

LAMPITO:
                                    Whoa, now!
You gropin' me like I'm some animal
you gonna sacrifice.

LYSISTRATA:
                    And this girl here,   90
where is she from?

LAMPITO:

                    She come here representin'
Boeotia.

MYRRHINE:

          With her undulating lowlands,
she looks just like Boeotia!

CALONICE:

                    Yes indeed.

          (looking down the Boeotian Representative's dress at her pubic hair)

Look at that well-cropped herbage.

LYSISTRATA:

                    Who's this woman?

LAMPITO:

She's a great, great lady, outta Corinth.

CALONICE:

She's great alright! Great front and great behind!

LAMPITO:

Now, which a' y'all called for this here meetin'?

LYSISTRATA:

I am the one.

LAMPITO:

                    Then go on, girl. You tell us
what you got to say.

CALONICE:

                    Yes, darling, please
do tell us what this serious business is.   100

LYSISTRATA:
I want to tell you but, before I do,
let me put a little question to you.

CALONICE:
Ask away.

LYSISTRATA:
                Don't all you ladies miss
your children's fathers when they're on campaign?
Each of you has a husband who's away—
I know you do.

CALONICE:
                Five months my man's been gone
up north in Thrace fighting to save Eucrates
the general.°

MYRRHINE:
                Seven months my man's been off
at Pylos.°

LAMPITO:
                Heck, my man no quicker comes
back home to Sparta than he up and straps
his shield on and is gone again.

CALONICE:
                                What's worse,
there aren't even any lover-boys
to have affairs with. And, ever since Miletus
broke away from us, I haven't seen
one of those five-inch dildos,° no, not one,
though they'd have been small consolation to us.

LYSISTRATA:
Ladies, if I could come up with a way
to end the war, would you agree to join me?

CALONICE:
By Demeter and Persephone,
I would agree, though I be forced to sell   120
this gown and on the same day blow the money
getting . . . drunk!

MYRRHINE:
                          Count me in, also. I'd
be cut right down the middle like a flounder
and donate half myself to help you out.

LAMPITO:
I'd climb Mount Tayeegety° if I thought
I'd catch a glimmer a' a peace from there.

LYSISTRATA:
I'll tell you, then. No need to keep the secret.
Alright: If we are going to force our men
to make a treaty, then we must abstain from . . .

CALONICE:
What is it? Tell us.

LYSISTRATA:
                          You will do it, then?   130

CALONICE:
Yes, though we have to sacrifice our lives!

LYSISTRATA:
Alright, then. What we must abstain from is . . .
dick.

            (All the women turn away from Lysistrata, some
                  shaking their heads, some weeping.)

            Hold on, don't turn away from me.
Where are you going? Don't pout and shake your heads.

Why are you turning pale? Why shedding tears?
Will you or won't you do this thing? Decide.

CALONICE:
I just can't do it. Let the war go on.

MYRRHINE:
God no, me either. Let the war go on.

LYSISTRATA: *(to Myrrhine)*
You, too, Ms. Flounderfish? Weren't you just saying
that you would cut yourself in half for peace?   140

MYRRHINE:
Anything else I'd do! If it'd help,
I'd walk through fire. Just, no, no, not the dick.
There's nothing like it, dear.

LYSISTRATA:
                              Are you out, too?

WOMAN:
Me? I would also rather walk through fire.

LYSISTRATA:
What a bunch of nymphos women are!
The tragedies they make about our sex
are true, since all we do is hump and dump.°

But you, my Spartan friend—if you alone
are with me, then we still might save this business.
Vote with me!

LAMPITO:
              It ain't no fun for women   150
to sleep without a woody for companion;
still, I'm with you, 'cause we need the peace.

LYSISTRATA:
You are a perfect dear! The one true woman!

CALONICE:
Hey, now, even if we did abstain from . . .
from what you said (and may we never have to),
would peace be then more likely to occur?

LYSISTRATA:
Sure it would. If we lounged about the house
with makeup on and sauntered past our husbands
wearing no clothes except a see-through gown
and trimmed our pubes into a perfect triangle,   160
and if the men, then, got all hard and burned
to screw us, but we backed off and refused
to touch them, they would cut a peace damn quick.
You can be sure of that.

LAMPITO:
                    Like Menelaus.
When he caught sight a' nekked Helen's peaches,
lickety-split he threw his sword aside.°

CALONICE:
What happens if our husbands just ignore us?

LYSISTRATA:
Well, like a poet says somewhere: In dog days,
dildo away.°

CALONICE:
                    Faux boners are a joke!
And, anyway, what if our men just drag us   170
into the bedroom?

LYSISTRATA:
                    Hold on to the door frame.

CALONICE:
What if they beat us up?

LYSISTRATA:
                          Then grudgingly
submit. Men get no pleasure out of screwing
when they have to make a woman do it,
and there are other ways to make men ache.
They will surrender to us soon, I promise.
No man can live a happy life unless
his wife allows it.

CALONICE: *(to Lampito and Lysistrata)*
                          Well, if this seems best
to you two girls, the rest of us agree.

LAMPITO:
We Spartan girls can surely git *our* men   180
to make a' honest sort a' peace that's good
for everyone. But how can anybody
keep your Athenian mob from acting like
the crazy folk they are?

LYSISTRATA:
                          I promise you
that we will bring our husbands round to peace.

LAMPITO:
Y'all can't—with all them warships under sail
and tons a' money in Athena's temple.°

LYSISTRATA:
That issue has been taken care of. We
are going to occupy the hilltop fortress
of the Acropolis this very morning.°   190
That task has fallen to the older women.
Even as we are working out the terms

of our agreement here, they, on the pretext
of making sacrifice, are up there taking
the citadel.

LAMPITO:
            Well, now, that sounds jus' right,
like all the things you've said to me so far.

LYSISTRATA:
Why don't we swear an oath right now, Lampito,
so that the details will be fixed forever?

LAMPITO:
Lay down the oath, so y'all and I can swear it.

LYSISTRATA:
Very well. Where is my Scythian slave girl?   200

            (The Scythian Slave Girl enters, carrying a shield.)

What are you gaping at? Now put the shield
facedown there on the ground in front of us,
and someone bring the cuttings from the victim.

            (The Slave Girl lays the shield facedown on the stage.)

CALONICE:
What sort of oath will we be swearing for you?

LYSISTRATA:
What sort of oath? The oath that I have heard
Aeschylus had his heroes swear to, after
they slit a victim's throat above a shield.°

CALONICE:
Come on, Lysistrata, please don't make us
swear an oath for peace upon a shield!

LYSISTRATA:
What should the oath be, then?

CALONICE:
                                        What if we got   210
a pure-white steed somewhere and cut it up?°

LYSISTRATA:
A pure-white steed?

CALONICE:
                        Well, then, how will we swear?

LYSISTRATA:
I'll tell you what I think: Let's put a big
black wine cup on the ground right here, top upward,
and sacrifice a jar of Thasian wine into it
and swear never to add a drop of water.°

LAMPITO:
Yee-haw! I can't praise that oath enough!

LYSISTRATA:
Someone go in and bring the cup and jar.

(The Slave Girl fetches a wine cup and wine jar from offstage.)

MYRRHINE:
O my dear ladies, that's a whole wine vat!

CALONICE:
We could get wasted just by touching it.   220

LYSISTRATA: (pretending the wine cup is a sacrificial boar)
Put down the wine cup now, and everyone
come lay her hands upon this sacral—boar.

(She prays while pouring wine from the jar into the cup.)

O Queen Persuasion and O Cup of Mirth,
kindly accept this offering from women.

CALONICE:
The blood looks good and bubbles like it should.

LAMPITO:
It smells a' sweetness, by the gods.

MYRRHINE:
                                        Please, ladies,
let me be first!

CALONICE:
                    By Aphrodite, only
if your number's up.

LYSISTRATA:
                        Hey there, Lampito,
everyone, lay your hands upon the wine cup.
One of you will repeat, for all, the terms   230
of our agreement after me, and then
the rest will swear to keep them once we're done.

No man, be he a lover or a husband . . .

CALONICE: *(stepping up as the representative for all the women)*
No man, be he a lover or a husband . . .

LYSISTRATA:
. . . shall come up to me with a boner. Say it!

CALONICE:
. . . shall come up to me with a boner.
                                        Ah!
My knees are going to buckle, Lysistrata!

LYSISTRATA:
And I shall pass the time in celibacy . . .

CALONICE:
And I shall pass the time in celibacy . . .

LYSISTRATA:
. . . dressed in a saffron gown and all made up . . .   240

CALONICE:
. . . dressed in a saffron gown and all made up . . .

LYSISTRATA:
. . . so that my man gets very hot for me.

CALONICE:
. . . so that my man gets very hot for me.

LYSISTRATA:
Never shall I consent to sex with him.

CALONICE:
Never shall I consent to sex with him.

LYSISTRATA:
And if he forces me against my will . . .

CALONICE:
And if he forces me against my will . . .

LYSISTRATA:
. . . I shall be frigid and shall not grind back.

CALONICE:
. . . I shall be frigid and shall not grind back . . .

LYSISTRATA:
. . . nor raise my fancy slippers toward the ceiling . . .   250

CALONICE:

. . . nor raise my fancy slippers toward the ceiling . . .

LYSISTRATA:

. . . *nor pose my haunches like a lioness's.*

CALONICE:

. . . nor pose my haunches like a lioness's.

LYSISTRATA:

If I fulfill these vows, may I drink wine . . .

CALONICE:

If I fulfill these vows, may I drink wine . . .

LYSISTRATA:

. . . *but, if I fail, this cup be full of water.*

CALONICE:

. . . but, if I fail, this cup be full of water.

LYSISTRATA:

So do you women swear?

ALL THE WOMEN:

                            So do we swear.

LYSISTRATA:

By drinking from this cup, I consecrate it.

                    (Lysistrata takes a deep drink.)

CALONICE: *(eager to take her drink)*

Only your portion, dear. Prove from the start   260
that we are allies.

                *(Shouts are heard from offstage. They are the sound
                of older woman seizing the Acropolis.)*

LAMPITO:

What's that hullabaloo?

LYSISTRATA:

That's what I was explaining to you: women
have just now taken the Acropolis,
Athena's hilltop fortress. Now, Lampito,
head home and see to your side of this business—
just leave these women here as hostages.

(Lampito exits, stage right, with the Representatives from
Boeotia and Corinth, leaving several females behind.)

We, for our part, will march into the fortress
and help the other women bar the gates.

CALONICE:

But don't you think the men will very quickly
march in arms against us?

LYSISTRATA:

Have no fear.   270
Never will they muster threat or fire
enough to penetrate our gates unless
they give in to our terms.

CALONICE:

By Aphrodite,
they won't get in, or else we women never
should wear the names of "nasty" and "impossible."

(The setting refocuses from the houses of Lysistrata and Calonice
to the Acropolis. The two doors now represent the Propylaea,
or gates to the Acropolis. Lysistrata and the remaining women
exit through a stage door. A Chorus of Old Men enter from stage
right, carrying small branches and a smoking pot full of coals.)

CHORUS OF OLD MEN:
Lead on, Draces,° lead on, though your shoulder's aching bad
under that very heavy load of fresh-green olivewood.

> *Strophe 1*
> There will be lots of shocks in lives as long as ours.
> Who would have thought we'd hear that womankind,
> a race we nursed at home, a blatant curse,   280
> would now control Athena's statue and
> my beautiful Acropolis and, even worse,
> have sealed the fortress gates with bolts and bars?

Let's hurry to the citadel as quick as we can go
and make a ring of timber round the women, all those who
have spawned or nurtured this revolt. Let's make a giant pile
of wood, a bonfire, and proceed, with a united will
and torches in our hands, to immolate them, all of them—
and Lycon's drunken wife° should be the first to feel the flame!

> *Antistrophe 1*
> Their sex won't get to mock me while I'm drawing breath.   290
> Cleomenes,° the first to occupy
> that citadel, barely escaped alive.
> Though Spartan-proud, he gave his spear to me
> and slunk off, small-cloaked, starved, in sore need of a shave.
> It had been six years since he had a bath.

Such was the dogged way that we besieged the man—no sleep
by day or night, we stood in ranks seventeen-shieldmen deep.
And now am I just going to do nothing, stand around
instead of chastening the insolence of womankind,
the foes of every godhead, and Euripides as well?°   300
May Marathon no longer feature my memorial.°

> *Strophe 2*
> We're almost there. All that remains, now, is that steep
> stretch to the citadel—my goal, my hope.
> But, oh, without a donkey, how the heck

will we move all this lumber to that height?
For all this pair of tree trunks weighs my shoulders down,
I must bear up, I must go on,
and keep my fire alight.
It must keep burning till I reach the top.

Huff, puff, and alack,   310
the smoke!

Antistrophe 2
Great Lord Heracles!° The smoke has viciously
leapt from the bucket and come after me.
My eyes sting from its crazy-bitch attack.
No doubt ours is the Lemnian sort of fire°—
that's why it's murdering my bloodshot eyes like this.
On, on to the Acropolis!
Rush to Athena, rescue her!
It's urgent: we must save the deity!

Huff, puff, and alack,   320
the smoke!

Thanks to the gods, the fire is very much alive and kicking.
Come on, let's set our loads of wood down here. Then, after sticking
the torches in the pail and seeing that they catch a flame,
let's rush the gates like battering rams. If, when we order them
to yield, the women still refuse, we'll set the gates on fire
and smoke the rebels out. Alright, then, put the logs down there.
That smoke is something. Damn. Hey, generals at the naval base
in Samos, do you want to help us stack this lumber?°

(*The Chorus of Old Men set the branches down.*)

Those
at last are off my back! Now, fire pail, it is up to you   330
to rouse your embers and provide me with a bright flambeau.
Victory Goddess Nike,° be our ally, fight with us,
and we will win a trophy over female brazenness.

(A Chorus of Old Women enter through a stage
door. They are carrying jugs full of water.)

CHORUS OF OLD WOMEN:
I think that I see smoke and ash, like something is aflame.
Faster now, my female soldiers. Hurry. Double-time.

Strophe 1
Soar, women, soar up there before
our fighting sisters have been set on fire.
Look how the fierce winds fan the blaze!
Those old men would commit atrocities
against us. I am terribly afraid   340
we are too late to do the others any good.

I've just come from the well,
where I had trouble filling up this water jug.
Yes, in the predawn ruckus and the glug-glug-glug
and clay-pot clash and shatter of it all,
I fought a tattooed slave and serving maid
and boldly set this vessel on my head
and now, to save my sister rebels from
the threatened fiery demise, have come,
bringing lots of liquid aid.   350

Antistrophe 1
I've heard that homicidal old
fogeys have been let loose into the wild.
Dragging a superhuman weight
of firewood up the slope, they shout and shout,
like stokers in a bathhouse steam room, rash
threats like "We're gonna turn those nasty hags to ash."

Goddess Athena, please,
let me not see my sisters roasting in the fire.
I want to see them save from craziness and war
our fellow citizens and all of Greece.   360
Yes, Golden-Crested Fortress Guardian,°

that is why we have occupied your shrine.
Tritogeneia,° aid us in this fight
and, if a man's hand sets your house alight,
help us pour the water on.

OLD WOMEN'S CHORUS LEADER: (seeing the Chorus of Old Men for the first time)
Halt, women! What is this? They must be execrable villains
because no good and pious men would do what they are doing.

OLD MEN'S CHORUS LEADER:
Here is a difficulty we did not expect to see:
a swarm of them has come out of the gates to help the others.

OLD WOMEN'S CHORUS LEADER:
What, are you frightened? Does it seem that there are lots of us? 370
Well, you are only seeing one small fraction of our horde.

OLD MEN'S CHORUS LEADER:
Men, are we going to let these women yammer on like this?
Someone should take his log and just start walloping them good.

OLD WOMEN'S CHORUS LEADER:
We'd better put our pitchers down so that our hands are free
in case one of those good-for-nothings lays his hands on us.

(The Chorus of Old Women set down the pitchers.)

OLD MEN'S CHORUS LEADER:
By Zeus, if someone socked them in their kissers two or three times—
you know, like Bupe-Bupe-Bupalus,° they would be much more quiet.

OLD WOMEN'S CHORUS LEADER:
Well, here's my kisser. Hit me. I can take it. If you do, though,
no other bitch will ever grab you by the balls again!

OLD MEN'S CHORUS LEADER:
Shut up, or I will knock you right out of your withered hide. 380

OLD WOMEN'S CHORUS LEADER:
Come on and touch me, touch Stratyllis with your fingertip.

OLD MEN'S CHORUS LEADER:
If I used combo punches, what you got to get me back?

OLD WOMEN'S CHORUS LEADER:
I'd use my teeth to rip your lungs and bowels out of your body.

OLD MEN'S CHORUS LEADER:
I swear, no poet's wiser than Euripides. He said:
"No race of beasts exists as pitiless as womankind."

OLD WOMEN'S CHORUS LEADER:
Come on, let's pick our water pitchers up and get them ready.

(The Chorus of Old Women pick up the pitchers.)

OLD MEN'S CHORUS LEADER:
Harridan hateful to the gods, why did you come with water?

OLD WOMEN'S CHORUS LEADER:
Why did you come with fire, you burial mound? To burn your carcass?

OLD MEN'S CHORUS LEADER:
No, to build a big bonfire and burn up all your friends.

OLD WOMEN'S CHORUS LEADER:
And I, well, I have come to put that fire out with my water.   390

OLD MEN'S CHORUS LEADER:
You think you're going to douse my fire?

OLD WOMEN'S CHORUS LEADER:
                                        You'll find out soon enough.

OLD MEN'S CHORUS LEADER:
I think I might just use this torch to roast you where you stand.

OLD WOMEN'S CHORUS LEADER:
Happen to bring some soap along? I'm giving you a bath.

OLD MEN'S CHORUS LEADER:
A bath from you, a shriveled hag?

OLD WOMEN'S CHORUS LEADER:
                              And you, you're quite a bridegroom.

OLD MEN'S CHORUS LEADER: *(to the Chorus of Old Men)*
You hear that disrespect?

OLD WOMEN'S CHORUS LEADER:
                         I'm free, and I will speak my mind!

OLD MEN'S CHORUS LEADER:
I'll make you quit your screeching!

OLD WOMEN'S CHORUS LEADER:
                              You aren't on a jury now!°

OLD MEN'S CHORUS LEADER: *(to the Chorus of Old Men)*
Set her hair on fire!

OLD WOMEN'S CHORUS LEADER: *(pouring water onto the Old Men's Chorus Leader)*
                    Do your work, now, River God.

(The Chorus of Old Women pour water on the Chorus of Old Men.)

OLD MEN'S CHORUS LEADER:
Oh no!

OLD WOMEN'S CHORUS LEADER: *(ironically)*
       I hope it didn't scald you.

OLD MEN'S CHORUS LEADER:
Scald me? Desist! What are you doing?

OLD WOMEN'S CHORUS LEADER:
I'm watering you so you bloom.   400

OLD MEN'S CHORUS LEADER:
I'm dry again from shivering.

OLD WOMEN'S CHORUS LEADER:
Well, since you have a fire, why not sit down and warm yourself?

> (*The Commissioner of Athens enters from stage left. He has four
> Policemen with him and four Scythian Archers. They are all
> wearing disproportionately large, flaccid strap-on penises.*)

COMMISSIONER:
Has feminine licentiousness flared up
again? The kettledrums? The endless cries
to that exotic god Sabezius?°
And all that rooftop worship of Adonis°
I heard while sitting once in the Assembly?
Demostratus (the villain) was proposing
that we dispatch a fleet to Sicily,
and all the while his wife would not stop dancing   410
and shouting, "Oh Adonis! Oh!" Demostratus,
next, was proposing we conscript foot soldiers
out of Zacynthus,° and his wife just kept on
drinking on the rooftop and exclaiming,
"Beat your bosoms for Adonis!" Well,
that god-detested wretched Captain Blather
just went on legislating, while his wife
exhibited the sort of wild behavior
you get from womankind.

OLD MEN'S CHORUS LEADER: (*gesturing to the Chorus of Old Women*)
                         What will you say
when you find out about *these* ladies' cheek?   420
They've gone too far in every way. They've even
soaked us with those jugs of theirs. We stand here
shaking our clothes out like we've pissed ourselves!

COMMISSIONER:

By Poseidon,° we've been asking for it!
We ourselves incite our wives' transgressions;
we positively *teach* them to be wanton,
and so it's no surprise these sorts of plots
are growing up among them. We ourselves
go to the shops and say such things as:

                              "Goldsmith,
you know that necklace that I had you make?   430
Last evening, while my wife was dancing in it,
the post that's on the fastener slipped out of
the hole. Now I am off to Salamis—
gone till tomorrow. If you have the time,
stop by my house this evening, please, and fit
a post into her hole."

                    Another husband goes
to see a shoemaker, a teenage boy
who's got a grown man's cock, and says such things as:

"Shoemaker, there's this strap that's rubbing raw
my darling's pinkie toe. Please come around   440
some early afternoon and stretch her gap out
wider."

          That's the licentiousness that's led us
to this impasse where I, the great Commish,
when I need money from the treasury
to outfit ships with oars, can't get inside
because I'm locked out by our women!

        (to the Policemen and Scythian Archers)

                              You,
what good is standing there? Go get some crowbars.
I'm going to put an end to female brashness
once and for all!

                (to a Policeman)

What are you gaping at,
you dope? The only thing you're looking for's   450
a tavern, I suspect.

(to the Policemen and Scythian Archers)

All of you, come, now,
drive the crowbars underneath the gates
and yank from there, and I'll start yanking mine
from over here.

(The males onstage start prying at one of the stage doors with
the crowbars. Lysistrata enters from the other stage door. She
is wearing a head scarf. Three Old Women attend, carrying a
wreath, ribbons, and a basket containing wool and a spindle.)

LYSISTRATA:
Stop yanking on those things.
I'm coming out all on my own. Besides,
what need is there for crowbars? What you need
are wits and brains.

COMMISSIONER:
Oh really? What a bitch!
Where's a policeman?

(to the First Policeman)

Go and get her. Bind
her hands behind her back.

LYSISTRATA:
Yeah, if that man
dares touch me even with a fingertip,   460
I'll send him home, a state employee, weeping.

(The First Policeman refuses to grab Lysistrata.)

COMMISSIONER: *(to the First Policeman)*
What, are you scared of her?

(to the Second Policeman)

Go help him. Quick, now,
grab her around the waist and bind her hands.

FIRST OLD WOMAN: *(to the Second Policeman)*
If you so much as lay a hand on her,
I'll hit you so hard that you shit yourself!

(The Second Policeman refuses to grab Lysistrata.)

COMMISSIONER:
"Shit himself"? Where's my other officer?

(to the Third Policeman)

You, come and tie this foul-mouthed hag up first.

SECOND OLD WOMAN: *(to the Third Policeman)*
Touch her, and you'll be begging for a cup°
to be warmed up to soothe your big black eye.

(The Third Policeman refuses to grab the First Old Woman.)

COMMISSIONER:
What *is* this?

(to the Fourth Policeman)

Hey there, you, policeman, seize her.   470
I'll stop those hags from charging from the gates.

THIRD OLD WOMAN: *(to the Fourth Policeman)*
Go on and touch her, do it, and I'll rip
your hair out by the roots and leave you screaming.

*(The Fourth Policeman refuses to grab the First Old
Woman. All four Policemen run off, stage left.)*

COMMISSIONER:
Dammit! Now I've got no policemen left.
All the same, men must never be defeated
by women. Form up, Scythians, and charge them!

(The four Scythian Archers form in a line.)

LYSISTRATA:
You will soon learn well that we have four
brigades of fighting women on reserve
inside the gates.

COMMISSIONER:
                Scythians, wrench their hands
behind their backs!

LYSISTRATA:
                March out, O my reservists!   480

(Women march out of the stage door in military formation.)

Onward, my greens-'n'-egg-seed-market-mongers,
my tavern-keeping-bread-'n'-garlic-hawkers!
Take them down! Wallop them! Devastate
and mock them! Be as foul as you can be!

(After a mock battle, the Scythian Archers retreat.)

Stop now! Withdraw. Don't wait to strip the corpses.°

COMMISSIONER:
Goodness! My Scythians have not fared well.

LYSISTRATA:
What did you think would happen? Did you think
you'd be attacking slave girls? Did you think
that women have no fight in them?

COMMISSIONER:

                                        Yes, lots,
so long as someone nearby serves them drinks.   490

OLD MEN'S CHORUS LEADER: *(to the Commissioner)*
Commissioner, you just keep gabbing on and on and wasting words.
Why would you try to come to terms with savage beasts like these?
Do you not understand the sort of bath we got just now?
They left our cloaks all sopping, and they never gave us soap!

OLD WOMEN'S CHORUS LEADER: *(to the Commissioner)*
Buddy, you can't just hit a person anytime you want.
Plus, if you do attack me, you will wind up with a black eye.
I'd rather be at home, seated demurely like a maiden,
troubling no one, crushing not one blade of grass—except,
if someone riles me like a wasp's nest, I will be a wasp.

CHORUS OF OLD MEN:
> *Strophe*
> Great Lord Zeus, what are we going to do about this pack   500
> of monsters? They are unendurable. Come, now, and look
> into this plot along with me until
> we know why they have seized the citadel
> and the whole sacred and restricted space
> that is our great limestone Acropolis.

OLD MEN'S CHORUS LEADER:
Now start the inquisition! Cast suspicion upon all
she says. It's shameful that we let these actions go unchecked.

COMMISSIONER:

Here is the thing I want to find out first of all, by Zeus:
What did you hope to gain by locking up the citadel?

LYSISTRATA:

To keep the money safe and stop the war for lack of it.   510

COMMISSIONER:

We are at war because of money—is that what you think?

LYSISTRATA:

Yes, and that's why so many other things got screwed up, too.
Pisander and the other would-be officeholders kept on
stirring up trouble as a pretext to get at the silver.
Now they can keep on stirring up whatever they might scheme—
they will be taking no more money from the citadel.

COMMISSIONER:

What are you going to do with it?

LYSISTRATA:

We'll manage it, of course.

COMMISSIONER:

Women will manage it?

LYSISTRATA:

Why do you think that this is strange?
Don't we already manage your domestic finances?

COMMISSIONER:

That's not the same.

LYSISTRATA:

Why not?

COMMISSIONER:

This money is for waging war.   520

LYSISTRATA:
There doesn't need to be a war.

COMMISSIONER:
How will we be protected?

LYSISTRATA:
We women will protect you.

COMMISSIONER:
What, you women?

LYSISTRATA:
Yes, us women.

COMMISSIONER:
How ballsy.

LYSISTRATA:
We will save you whether you consent or not.

COMMISSIONER:
That's crazy talk!

LYSISTRATA:
Oh, are you angry? Still it must be done.

COMMISSIONER:
It's just not proper.

LYSISTRATA:
Still, you must be saved, my dear, dear man.

COMMISSIONER:
Even if I never asked?

LYSISTRATA:
Yes, all the more for that.

COMMISSIONER:
But why are peace and war of such importance to you now?

LYSISTRATA:
I'll tell you.

COMMISSIONER: *(threatening her with his fist)*
            Do it quick or else you're going to get beaten.

LYSISTRATA:
Listen up, then, and control your hands.

COMMISSIONER:
                                    I can't control them.
I'm so worked up that I can't keep from flailing.

FIRST OLD WOMAN: *(to the Commissioner)*
                                    You're the one   530
who's gonna get a beating!

COMMISSIONER: *(to the First Old Woman)*
                        Croak away, you old hag, croak!

                    (to Lysistrata)

And you there, start explaining what you plan to do.

LYSISTRATA:
                                            With pleasure:
Blessed with self-control, we women have endured in silence,
for quite a long time now, whatever you men did, because
you never let us speak. Believe me: you weren't all we dreamed of—
yes, we took good stock of you. Quite frequently at home
we heard you speaking of some fool political decision
you'd lately made. Then, full of agony but still all smiles,
we'd ask: "What was resolved about the rider to the peace
today in the Assembly?" Well, my husband always answered,   540
"What's it to you?" and "Woman, shut your mouth." And I shut up—

FIRST OLD WOMAN:

Not me: I never would have shut my mouth.

COMMISSIONER: *(to the First Old Woman)*

Well, if you hadn't,

you'd have gotten smacked.

LYSISTRATA.

. . . I shut up, and I stayed at home.
And soon enough we heard about some even more atrocious
legislation you had passed. And I would say, "O husband,
why have you gone and voted in so very bad a law?"
Frowningly he would snap back: "Mind your spinning, now, or else
I'll knock your head around, some. *War is an affair for men.*"°

COMMISSIONER:

Yeah, by the gods, your husband schooled you good!

LYSISTRATA:

What's "good," moron,
about not giving good advice to people who are making   550
awful decisions? When we heard you men all over town
lamenting, "Isn't there a *man* left anywhere in Athens?"
and others crying, "No *men* left," we women met in council,
and we resolved to raise a coup and rescue Greece ourselves.
Why should we waste more time? If you are ready now to shut up
just like you said "shut up" to us and heed our good advice,
we'll tell you how to set the city straight.

COMMISSIONER:

You? You tell *us?*

An outrage! It's impossible!

LYSISTRATA:

Shut up.

COMMISSIONER:
                              "Shut up" for *you*,
a nasty creature with a veil on? Never, on my life!

LYSISTRATA: *(taking her head scarf off and putting it on the Commissioner)*
Well, if my veil's the trouble here,   560
you take it from me, wear it over
your head. Now you're the "shut up" one.

FIRST OLD WOMAN: *(handing the Commissioner a sewing basket)*
Oh, and here's a sewing basket.

LYSISTRATA:
Tuck in your clothes and get some beans
to chew on° while you do your spinning.
War is an affair for women.

OLD WOMEN'S CHORUS LEADER:
Leave your water jugs, now, girls, because the time has come
for us to play our part by helping in a different way.

            (The Chorus of Old Women set down the pitchers.)

CHORUS OF OLD WOMEN:
            Strophe
            I'll never tire of dancing. I'll keep dancing on and on,
            and no exhausting hours of work will make my knees break down.   570
            I'm not afraid of anything because
            I've women with me who are bold as these.
            They've got good breeding, grace and spunk in them.
            They've got street smarts and patriotic vim.

Now most manly grannies, ye maternal stinging jellies,
advance with rage and don't grow soft. Run with a gale astern.

LYSISTRATA:
If sweet-souled Eros and his mother Aphrodite of Cyprus
breathe desire onto our breasts and thighs, if they afflict

the men with big love-clubs of amorous rigidity,
all Greece will come to praise us as the "Looseners of War."   580

COMMISSIONER:
And why's that?

LYSISTRATA:
                    First we will have put a stop to armed men going
around the market and behaving like they're crazy people.

FIRST OLD WOMAN:
Three cheers for Aphrodite!

LYSISTRATA:
                    At this moment, in the market,
among the pottery stalls and grocers, there are men with weapons
walking around like nutjobs.

COMMISSIONER:
                    Men are best when they look manly.

LYSISTRATA:
It's madness when a soldier with a Gorgon on his shield
goes fresh-fish shopping.

FIRST OLD WOMAN:
                    Yes, I saw a mounted man with long hair,
a cavalry commander, buying oatmeal from a woman—
he had her scoop the stuff into his metal helmet! Plus,
this Thracian guy would not stop brandishing his shield and lance   590
as if he were a hoopoe!° Why, he scared the old fig lady
so much she ran away and then he gobbled up the ripe ones.

COMMISSIONER:
What will you women do to fix the mess we have in Greece?
How will you sort it out?

LYSISTRATA:

That's easy.

COMMISSIONER:

How, though? Teach me.

LYSISTRATA: *(taking the wool and spindle from the basket)*

Well,

when everything gets tangled up it's like a mess of wool.
We women hold our wool like *this* and wind strands of it deftly
around the spindle, some in this direction, some in that—
so, if allowed, we'll break this war down by untangling it
with envoys sent out, some in this direction, some in that.

COMMISSIONER:

What, you think your spindles, wool and yarn can put an end   600
to so intractable a crisis? That's just stupid.

LYSISTRATA:

Yes,

That's what I think, and if you had a brain, you would conduct
all the affairs of Athens just as women handle wool.

COMMISSIONER:

How? Make me understand.

LYSISTRATA:

Imagine Athens is a fresh-shorn fleece.
First, what you do is dunk it in a bath and wash away
the sheep poop; then you lay it on a bed and take a stick
and beat out all the nasties, then you pick the thistles out.
Next, you take those that have stuck together and become
as thick as felt (to snag up all the civic offices)
and comb them out and pluck their heads off. Then you go and card   610
the raw cleaned wool into the Basket of Reciprocal
Agreeableness, mixing everyone in there together—
resident aliens and other foreigners you like

and those who owe the state back taxes—mix them in there good.
Next, you should think of all the cities that are colonies
of Athens as if they are scattered bits of wool. You take
these bits and bring them all together and combine them into
one big ball, from which you weave apparel for the people.

COMMISSIONER: *(to the Chorus of Old Men)*
Isn't it crazy how these women prate about their sticks
and balls, while in the war they've never had a thing at stake?   620

LYSISTRATA:
Nothing at stake? Prick, we have more than twice as much at stake
as you have! First off, we give birth to sons and send them out
to battle in your war—

COMMISSIONER:
                    Shut up about that—don't remind me.

LYSISTRATA:
Secondly, when we should be having good times and enjoying
being young, we have to sleep alone because our men
are on campaign. But let's forget about us wives—what hurts
is all the maidens growing old at home.

COMMISSIONER:
                    Don't men age, too?

LYSISTRATA:
It's not the same. A man that comes back home can quickly find
some girl to marry, even if he is a graybeard geezer.
A woman has a briefer season. If she misses it,   630
no one will want to wed her. She will sit at home awaiting
marriage omens.

COMMISSIONER:
                    But whatever guy can still get hard—

LYSISTRATA:
Drop dead. What's stopping you?
Here is your burial plot. Yes, you
may go and buy a coffin, sir,
and I will bake the honey cake
for Cerberus.°

(giving the Commissioner a wreath)

Here, take my wreath.

FIRST OLD WOMAN: *(giving the Commissioner ribbons)*
And I will give these ribbons to you.

SECOND OLD WOMAN: *(giving the Commissioner another wreath)*
And here's another wreath from me.

LYSISTRATA:
What else do you need? Embark.   640
Charon is calling out your name,°
and you are keeping him from sailing.

COMMISSIONER:
Isn't the way they have been treating me
appalling? Yes, by Zeus, I'm going straight off
to show my fellow government officials
what has been done to me.

*(The Commissioner exits stage left with
the four Scythian Archers.)*

LYSISTRATA:
                        You won't be lodging
complaints about the way we laid you out
for burial, will you? Well, I promise that,
two days from now, just after sunrise, we
will make the third-day offerings at your grave!°   650

(Lysistrata exits into the Acropolis. The Three Old Women
follow her, one of them carrying the basket of wool.)

OLD MEN'S CHORUS LEADER:
This is no time for sleeping. Every freeborn man should look alive!
Let's strip, men, strip our jackets off to face this great emergency.

(The Chorus of Old Men remove their jackets.)

CHORUS OF OLD MEN:
> *Strophe*
> My nose has just now caught
> a whiff of something more significant.
> Oh yes, there is the scent
> of Hippias's tyranny° in this.
> I greatly fear that certain Spartan men have met
> at Cleisthenes's house°
> and there agreed upon a plot
> to stir up all the nasty women of   660
> our town so that they seize the treasury
> and by this action take away my life,
> my means—my precious jury pay.

OLD MEN'S CHORUS LEADER:
It's terrible that they, mere women, now are criticizing fellow
citizens and discussing bronze-wrought shields and, what is even worse,
working to reconcile us with the Spartans, men less to be trusted
than famished wolves! In actual fact the plot the women have been weaving
is aimed at tyranny. But they will never tyrannize yours truly—
I'll be prepared and henceforth "hide a sword inside a myrtle bough."
I'll march in arms down to Aristogeiton's statue in the market°   670

(striking a heroic pose)

and stand like *this* right next to him.

(looking at the Old Women's Chorus Leader)

Oh, how I've a got an overwhelming
desire in me to sock this god-despised old woman on the jaw.

OLD WOMEN'S CHORUS LEADER:
Try it, and your own mom won't recognize you when you get back home.
Rouse yourselves, fellow geriatrics! Lay your jackets on the ground.

(The Chorus of Old Women remove their jackets.)

CHORUS OF OLD WOMEN:
> *Antistrophe*
> People, I shall begin
> by giving useful counsel to the state,
> and this is only right,
> seeing as it brought me up in noble splendor:
> at seven, I was Weaver of Athena's Gown;°
> at ten, I served as Grinder   680
> for Artemis the Foundress;° then,
> shedding my saffron robe, I danced as Bear
> at Brauron.° Next, a pretty maiden, back
> in Athens, I was Basket-Carrier
> and wore dried figs around my neck.°

OLD WOMEN'S CHORUS LEADER:
That's why I owe good counsel to the state. Although I am a woman,
don't hold a grudge against me if I give far better counsel than
the nonsense we have now. I've got a stake in Athens: what I've paid
is men. You worthless fogeys haven't got a stake because you wasted
what you inherited, all that your fathers captured from the Persians,   690
and now you pay no taxes to replace it. We are almost ruined
because of you! Do you have anything to grumble in response?

(The Chorus of Old Men make threatening gestures.)

Upset me, and I'll use this rawhide boot to kick you in the jaw!

CHORUS OF OLD MEN:

> *Strophe*
> Don't you think that womankind
> has finally gone too far?
> This mess is only getting worse from here.
> It's time for everyone with balls to make a stand!

OLD MEN'S CHORUS LEADER:

Strip your shirts off, since it's better when a man smells like a man.
We shouldn't be concealed inside our clothes like meat in ravioli.

(The Chorus of Old Men remove their shirts.)

CHORUS OF OLD MEN:

> Come on, White Feet!° When we were in our prime,   700
> we fought a tyrant at Leipsydrium.°
> We must rejuvenate ourselves. It's time
> to cast off this old skin
> so that our carcasses can fledge again.

OLD MEN'S CHORUS LEADER:

If anybody on our side allows those hags the slightest handhold,
they will get their greedy mitts all over everything.
Sure, soon enough they will be building warships and, before we know it,
launching a fleet against us men like Artemisia.° If they turn
to horseback riding, you can cross out all our cavalry, because
women are made for mounting up and riding hard—you see, they never   710
slip out of the saddle! Take a look at Micon's paintings of
the Amazons°—see how they charge on horseback to attack the heroes.
We'd better grab these women by the necks and lock them in the stocks.

CHORUS OF OLD WOMEN:

> *Antistrophe*
> Oh, but when I am on fire,
> I will attack you like
> a feral sow and send you bleating back
> home to your buddies with your hide clipped bare.

OLD WOMEN'S CHORUS LEADER: *(to the Chorus of Old Women)*
Quick, now, strip your outer layers off, so that we emanate
the reek of women mad enough to use their teeth to bite their foes.

(The Chorus of Old Women remove their clothing.)

CHORUS OF OLD WOMEN:
> If someone dares attack me, he will chew   720
> on no more garlic, no more beans. If you
> so much as toss curse words my way, I'll go
> crazy with rage and, like
> the beetle, make your eagle's eggs go "crack."°

OLD WOMEN'S CHORUS LEADER:
I won't be giving all you men another thought, not while Lampito
and Ismenia, that distinguished Theban girl, are still alive.
You have no power, not though you should pass the same law seven times.

(to the Old Men's Chorus Leader)

You, jackass, are despised by everyone—all the Athenians
and all your neighbors. Yesterday in fact, when I was celebrating
Hecate with my friends,° I asked a fine and lovable girl over   730
from just across the way—an eel out of Boeotia—but those neighbors
said that she couldn't come due to a law of yours. You'll go on passing
laws until someone grabs your leg and drags you off and breaks your neck!

> *(The setting refocuses in time to several days later. The sex strike
> has had its effect. Subsequently, all the male characters' strap-
> ons are represented as erect. Lysistrata enters from a stage door.
> She has a parchment in her pocket. For the opening eight lines
> of this scene the characters speak in a mock-lofty pastiche.)*

Queen of our deed and plot, why dost thou enter
from out the palace with so dour a visage?

LYSISTRATA:
Base women's actions and the female heart
cause me to pace about in deep despair.

OLD WOMEN'S CHORUS LEADER:
What sayest thou? What sayest thou?

LYSISTRATA:
'Tis true! 'Tis true!

OLD WOMEN'S CHORUS LEADER:
Pray, what's the matter? Tell your confidantes.   740

LYSISTRATA:
'Tis shame to speak, but cumbrous to conceal.

OLD WOMEN'S CHORUS LEADER:
Do not conceal our miseries from me.

LYSISTRATA:
Well, in a nutshell, then: we need a fuck.

OLD WOMEN'S CHORUS LEADER:
O great Zeus!

LYSISTRATA:
Why call on Zeus? That's just the way things are.
I've tried, but I can't keep them from their husbands
any longer. They keep running off.
The first one that I caught was over by
Pan's Grotto,° digging out the hole; the second
was trying to desert by sliding down   750
a pulley rope. I caught another one
just yesterday—she was astride a sparrow
and hoped to fly to see Orsilochus.°
I had to grab her by the hair. The women
just keep on coming up with lame excuses
to go back home.

(The First Woman enters from the Acropolis.)

Where are you running to?

FIRST WOMAN:
Home. I have fine Milesian wool there, wool
that's being cut to bits by moths.

LYSISTRATA:

What moths?
Get back in there.

FIRST WOMAN:
I'll go and come back quick.
Just let me spread my wool out on the bed.   760

LYSISTRATA:
No spreading on the bed. No going home.

FIRST WOMAN:
So I just have to let my wool be wasted?

LYSISTRATA:
Yes, if necessary.

(The Second Woman enters from the Acropolis.)

SECOND WOMAN:
Oh no, no,
my flax, I left my flax unscutched° at home.

LYSISTRATA:
This other woman here is running off
to scutch her flax. You get right back inside.

SECOND WOMAN:
I'll just go do some shucking and be back.

LYSISTRATA:
No shucking! If I let you do your "shucking,"
the other girls will beg to do the same.

*(The Third Woman enters from the Acropolis. She has a
helmet tucked under her shirt to simulate pregnancy.)*

THIRD WOMAN:
Queen Eileithyia,° please delay my childbirth   770
until I get outside of sacred space.

LYSISTRATA:
What are you saying?

THIRD WOMAN:
                      I am giving birth!

LYSISTRATA:
But you weren't even pregnant yesterday.

THIRD WOMAN:
I am today. Oh, Lysistrata, let me go
home to my nurse as quick as I can run.

LYSISTRATA:
What story are you making up?

(knocking on the helmet)

                            What hard
object are you concealing?

THIRD WOMAN:
                  It's a boy!

LYSISTRATA:
No, not a boy, but something hollow
and made of metal. Well, let's take a look.

(Lysistrata removes the helmet from under the Third Woman's shirt.)

What you are really saying is that you   780
are pregnant with Athena's Sacred Helmet.°

THIRD WOMAN:
I'm pregnant, though. I swear to Zeus I am.

LYSISTRATA:
Why did you have the helmet?

THIRD WOMAN:
                               Well, I thought
that, if I started giving birth while still
up in Athena's temple, I could make
a sort of pigeon's nest out of the thing
and give birth there.

LYSISTRATA:
                         What sort of lie is that?
A lame excuse. Your real intent is clear,
and you will have to stay up here until
your—helmet—has its name-day festival.   790

THIRD WOMAN:
But I can't sleep on the Acropolis,
not since I saw the sacred guardian snake.

(The Fourth Woman enters through a stage door.)

FOURTH WOMAN:
Oh, oh me! I am ruined utterly
because the owls keep going "who-who-who"
all night and I can't get to sleep!

LYSISTRATA:
                                  Enough
lies and excuses, girls. You're acting crazy!

No doubt you miss your men. But don't you think
that *they* miss *you*? You can be sure that they
are spending miserable nights. Good ladies,
be patient and endure a short while longer.   800
There is, in fact, an oracle foretelling
victory for us, if only we
do not become divided. Here it is.

(Lysistrata takes out a parchment.)

THIRD WOMAN:
Go on and tell us what it says.

LYSISTRATA:
                              Hush, now:
When all the swallows settle in a roost
separate from the hoopoes and desist
from congress with the feathered phalluses,
their problems will be solved. Loud-thundering Zeus
will turn all upside down—

THIRD WOMAN:
                              And we will get
to ride on top?

LYSISTRATA:
              . . . but if the swallows fight   810
and fly out of the venerable shrine,
they will be seen as sluts by everyone.

THIRD WOMAN:
Well, that was blunt. Praise be to all the gods!

LYSISTRATA:
Though we are suffering, let's not surrender
but go inside, dears. It would be a shame
for us to act against the oracle.

(Everyone exits into the Acropolis except the members of choruses.)

CHORUS OF OLD MEN:
> *Strophe*
> When I was a child
> I heard the story of a nice young man—
> Milanion.
> Running from marriage, he escaped into the wild   820
> and lived upon the mountain slopes,
> kept a dog, plaited rabbit traps,
> and never thought to go back home
> because he so detested *them*—
> the loathsome members of the female race.
> We hate them like he did, and we are wise.

OLD MEN'S CHORUS LEADER: *(jokingly to the Women's Chorus Leader)*
> I want to kiss you, harridan—

OLD WOMEN'S CHORUS LEADER:
> Stop eating onions, then.

> *(The Old Men's Chorus Leader lifts his leg.)*

OLD MEN'S CHORUS LEADER:
> . . . and raise my leg to kick you good.

OLD WOMEN'S CHORUS LEADER: *(looking at the Old Men's Chorus Leader's crotch)*
> You've got a hairy sack indeed.   830

CHORUS OF OLD MEN:
> General Myronides—
> he had a very shaggy crotch as well
> and flashed his black-haired butt-cheeks at his foes,
> and so did Phormion our admiral.

CHORUS OF OLD WOMEN:

> *Antistrophe*
> I want to tell
> a tale to counter your "Milanion":
> There was a man,
> Timon, a wandering hermit hidden in a veil
> of stubborn thorns, the Furies' child.
> He also went into the wild   840
> and there tongue-lashed the whole male race.
> Yes, he despised you. Yes, like us,
> he thought you worthy of endless odium.
> But women—we were always dear to him.

OLD WOMEN'S CHORUS LEADER:

> Want me to punch you in the jaw?

OLD MEN'S CHORUS LEADER: *(sarcastically)*

> Oh no! You're scaring me!

OLD WOMEN'S CHORUS LEADER:

> You want a kick? Would you like that?

OLD MEN'S CHORUS LEADER:

> Do it, and you'll expose your twat.

OLD WOMEN'S CHORUS LEADER:

> Well, if I do, you men
> won't see my pubes, old lady though I am,   850
> rough as a wilderness and overgrown.
> No, they are tidied by a candle's flame.

> *(Lysistrata appears atop the wooden backdrop and
> spots a man approaching from stage left.)*

LYSISTRATA:

Hip, hip, hooray! Come quick, now, ladies.

> *(Myrrhine and the First Woman appear beside her, above.)*

FIRST WOMAN: ₃
                                        What's up?

Tell us. What's all the hollering about?

LYSISTRATA:

A man, I see a crazed man coming, seized
by orgiastic Aphrodite's powers.
Goddess of Cyprus, Cythera and Paphos,
the road you're coming down is very straight.

FIRST WOMAN:

Where is this mystery man?

LYSISTRATA:

                                Beside the shrine

of Chloe.

FIRST WOMAN:

                        Ah yes, now I make him out.   860
Who is he, though?

LYSISTRATA:

                                Look closely, all of you.
Does anybody recognize the man?

MYRRHINE:

Oh, that's my "better half"—my husband Harden.

LYSISTRATA:

Your mission is to spit him, roast him, turn him,
to trick him, to adore and not adore him,
to give him everything except those items
the bowl that we have sworn by has forbidden.

MYRRHINE:

No need to worry. I'll do what you ask.

LYSISTRATA:
Still, I will stay close by to help you roast
and trick him. All you other women, go.

870

(*The First Woman and Myrrhine disappear from the
top of the backdrop. Harden enters from stage left,
wearing a disproportionately large, erect strap-on penis.
With him is Manes the Slave carrying the Baby.*)

HARDEN:
Oh, how I am afflicted! Cramps and spasms
torturing me like I'm on the rack!

LYSISTRATA:
Who there has penetrated our defenses?

HARDEN:
Me.

LYSISTRATA:
        A man?

HARDEN: (*gesturing to his erection*)
                Yes, very much a man.

LYSISTRATA:
Then very much get out of here.

HARDEN:
                        And who
are you to drive me off?

LYSISTRATA:
                Me, I'm the day watch.

HARDEN:
Oh god! Just tell Myrrhine to come out here.

LYSISTRATA:

What's with that "tell Myrrhine"? And who are you?

HARDEN:

Her husband Harden, up from Dickersdale.°

LYSISTRATA:

Hello, you darling. Yes, the name of "Harden"   880
is hardly seldom-heard and unrenowned
among us. You are always in your wife's mouth.
Always, when she eats an egg or apple,
she sighs, "If only this could be for Harden."

HARDEN: *(suffering a spasm of pain)*
Damn, the pain!

LYSISTRATA:

                    So help me, Aphrodite,
she says that. When we talk about our husbands,
she blurts out right away, "Compared with Harden,
all other husbands are just so much garbage."

HARDEN:

Go on, then, call her out.

LYSISTRATA:

                    What will you give me?

HARDEN: *(gripping his erection)*
Well, if you want it, I've got this for you.   890
It's all the bribe I've got, but you can have it.

LYSISTRATA:

Alright, I'll go and call Myrrhine.

                    (Lysistrata disappears, above.)

HARDEN:

Just hurry!

(to the audience)

My life has had no pleasure in it, none,
since she has gone away. When I come home,
I only ache, and everything feels empty.
Not even food has any pleasure for me.
Damn, it's hard!

(Myrrhine appears above.)

MYRRHINE: *(as if speaking to Lysistrata)*
           I do adore him, yes,
adore him, but the man does not know how
to be adored. Don't make me go and meet him.

HARDEN:
Myrrhie my sweet, why are you doing this?   900
Get down here, please!

MYRRHINE:
               I absolutely won't.

HARDEN:
You won't come down here when I ask you to?

MYRRHINE:
You ask, but you don't really, really need me.

HARDEN:
Not need you? Life is agony without you.

MYRRHINE:
I'm leaving.

HARDEN:
>   Wait, wait—listen to the baby.

>   *(to the Baby)*

Hey, baby, call for Mama.

BABY:
>   Mama! Mama!

HARDEN:
What kind of mother are you? Six days now
your child has gone without a bath, unnursed,
and you feel nothing?

MYRRHINE:
>   Oh, I feel for *him*.
His dad, though, doesn't give a damn about him.   910

HARDEN:
You crazy girl, come down and see your baby!

MYRRHINE:
What a thing it is to bear a child.
I must go down to him.

>   *(Myrrhine disappears from above.)*

HARDEN: *(to the audience)*
>   What can I do?
Myrrhine seems so much younger than before.
Her glances have a sultry look, and all
her getting mad and flouncing back and forth
just makes me burn with passion even more.

>   *(Myrrhine enters from the Acropolis. She*
>   *goes immediately to the Baby.)*

MYRRHINE:

O sweetie little baby! What a naughty
daddy you have. Let Mommy give you kisses.

HARDEN:

Why are you acting like this, troublemaker?   920
Why are you listening to all those women?
You're killing me and injuring yourself.

(Harden tries to drag Myrrhine off.)

MYRRHINE: (resisting)
Don't do it—don't you lay your hands on me.

HARDEN:

But you are letting everything at home,
all of our possessions, go to ruin.

MYRRHINE:

I really couldn't care at all about that.

HARDEN:

It matters very little to you that
chickens are ripping up the tapestry
you had been working on?

MYRRHINE:

                    Yes, very little.

HARDEN:

For too long now the rites of Aphrodite   930
have gone uncelebrated by us. Please,
won't you come home?

MYRRHINE:

                    I'll come back home as soon
as all you men make peace and end the war.

HARDEN:

That's what we'll do . . . if we decide to do it.

MYRRHINE:

I'll come home when you men decide to do it.
I've sworn an oath to stay right here till then.

HARDEN:

Will you just lie down with me for a bit?
It's been so long.

MYRRHINE:

          I won't. But I won't say
that I don't love you.

HARDEN:

          Do you love me? Then
won't you lie down with me for just a little?   940

MYRRHINE:

You joker. With the baby watching us?

HARDEN: *(to Manes the Slave)*
Manes, take the baby home.

(Manes takes the Baby off stage left.)

(to Myrrhine)

          Alright,
the kid's no longer an impediment.
Won't you lie down?

MYRRHINE:

          Where will we do it, though?

HARDEN:

Pan's Grotto will be fine.

MYRRHINE:

How could I go
back up to the Acropolis, unbathed, impure,
after the act?

HARDEN:

No problem. Take a bath
in the Clepsydra.°

MYRRHINE:

Are you saying, love,
that I should break the oath I took?

HARDEN:

May all
the consequences light upon my head.   950
Don't think about the oath.

MYRRHINE:

Alright, but first
I need to go and get a bed.

HARDEN:

No way.
The ground will be just perfect for us.

MYRRIIINE:

Never.
I'd never let you do it on the ground,
whatever sort of man you are.

(Myrrhine goes offstage and returns with a cot.)

HARDEN: *(to the audience)*

My wife
really does love me. Nothing could be clearer.

MYRRHINE:
Here it is! You just take a load off there
and I will get undressed. But, darn, a mattress—
I should get a mattress.

HARDEN:
                    What, a mattress?
No need.

MYRRHINE:
            It would be awkward on the bed frame.   960

HARDEN:
Just kiss me.

MYRRHINE:
            Muh.

HARDEN:
                Damn, get that mattress quick!

            (Myrrhine goes offstage and returns with a mattress.)

MYRRHINE:
Here it is! You just lie back down right there
and I will get undressed. But, darn, a pillow—
I should get a pillow.

HARDEN:
                I don't want one.

MYRRHINE:
                        I do.

                (Myrrhine goes offstage.)

HARDEN: *(to the audience)*
What, is my dick voracious Heracles
forever waiting for his dinner now?°

(Myrrhine returns with a pillow.)

MYRRHINE:
Up, up. Sit up, now. Is that everything?

HARDEN:
Yes, everything. Come here, my precious one.

MYRRHINE:
Yes, I'm just getting off my bra. Remember:
Don't let me down about the peace agreement.   970

HARDEN:
Great Zeus, destroy me if I do.

MYRRHINE:
                              Oh, but
you need a blanket.

HARDEN:
                    I don't need a blanket—
I need a fuck!

MYRRHINE:
                  And, never fear, you'll get it—
right after I get back.

(Myrrhine goes offstage.)

HARDEN: *(to the audience)*
                        The girl will drive me
crazy with all this bedclothes talk.

(Myrrhine returns with a blanket.)

MYRRHINE:

Get up.

HARDEN:

Oh, I am "up" already.

MYRRHINE:

Want some scent?

HARDEN:

God no.

MYRRHINE:

By Aphrodite, I want scent,
whether or not you want some.

HARDEN:

Great Lord Zeus,

then pour it on.

(Myrrhine goes offstage and returns with a flask of scent.)

MYRRHINE:

Hold out your hand and take some.
Rub yourself with it.

HARDEN:

This is no sweet scent—   980
it feels like much delay and doesn't smell
like conjugal relations.

MYRRHINE:

Oh, how silly,
I brought the scent from Rhodes.

HARDEN:

It's good. Just leave it,

goofball.

MYRRHINE:

> What are you going on about?

> *(Myrrhine goes offstage.)*

HARDEN: *(to the audience)*
My curses on the man who first made scent!

> *(Myrrhine returns with another flask of scent.)*

MYRRHINE:
Here, use this flask.

HARDEN: *(grabbing his erection)*
> I've got a big one here.
Lie down now, minx, and don't you go and get me
anything more.

MYRRHINE:
> Just as you say, and now
I'm taking off my shoes. Be sure, though, dearest,
to vote to make the peace.

> *(Myrrhine silently exits through a stage door.)*

HARDEN:

> I'll think about it.   990

> *(realizing that Myrrhine has left)*

She has destroyed me! Killed me! Even worse:
she got me all worked up and then just left.

HARDEN:

> Oh, what I'm going through! Where will I find a lover
> now that the fairest of them all has screwed me over?

> *(gesturing to his erection)*

How will I feed this offspring here? Where is the pimp
Foxhound?° Let him come rent me out a nurse to pump.

OLD MEN'S CHORUS LEADER:
    Terrible horrible pain
    must now be torturing your soul.
    I pity you, poor man—
    you have been played the fool.   1000

    What kidney could endure this much?
    What soul? What balls? What loins? What crotch
    strained like a victim on the rack?
    And, in the morning hours, no fuck!

HARDEN:
    O Zeus, the ache is back!

OLD MEN'S CHORUS LEADER:
    Your utterly revolting and appalling
    wife has done these things to you.

HARDEN:
    No, she is gorgeous and enthralling.

OLD MEN'S CHORUS LEADER:
    No, by Zeus, she's wicked through and through.

HARDEN:
    Yes, by Zeus, she's wicked through and through.   1010

    Zeus, send a firestorm or a great typhoon
    to strike her like a little pile of grain
    and set her spinning. Sweep her up, up, up,
    then make her drop
    back down toward earth again
    and land precisely on my boner's tip.

*(A Spartan Messenger runs on from stage left. He is wearing a
disproportionately large, erect strap-on penis hidden crudely
beneath his robe. He speaks with a southern twang.)*

SPARTAN MESSENGER:
Where do y'all keep the Senate House in Athens?
Y'all's Assembly? I got news to tell.

HARDEN:
What are you, then, a man or boner-monster?

SPARTAN MESSENGER:
Me, I'm a messenger, ma boy, and I   1020
come here from Sparta to discuss a peace.

HARDEN:
Is that a spear tucked up beneath your arm?

SPARTAN MESSENGER:
I swear it ain't.

HARDEN:
                    Why have you turned away?
Why tugged your cloak out there in front of you?
What, are your balls all swollen from the ride?

SPARTAN MESSENGER:
You're crazy.

HARDEN:
                    Dirty dawg, you've got a woody.

SPARTAN MESSENGER:
Naw, naw, no woody. Cut out all your guff.

HARDEN:
What do you call that thing?

SPARTAN MESSENGER:

A Spartan staff.

HARDEN: (gesturing to his erection)
Well, if it is, then here's my "Spartan staff."
Listen, I understand the situation.   1030
Now tell me truly: How are things in Sparta?

SPARTAN MESSENGER:
Sparta is up in arms, and all her allies
are scared stiff. What we need's that whore Pellene!°

HARDEN:
Who sent this plague upon you? Was it Pan?

SPARTAN MESSENGER:
Naw, but Lampito was the one, I think.
Then all together, jus' like they were runners
leavin' a startin' gate, our other ladies
locked us menfolk outta their vaginas.

HARDEN:
How are you holding up?

SPARTAN MESSENGER:

We got it, bad.
We hobble 'roun' the town a' Sparta doubled   1040
over like we luggin' lamps about.
Our ladies—they won't let us even touch
their nether cherries till we men agree
as one to make peace with the rest a' Greece.

HARDEN:
So all the women everywhere in Greece
conspired to work this plot. I get it now.
Go back to Sparta quick as you can ride
and tell them there to send ambassadors

up here with absolute authority
to make a peace.

(gesturing to his erection)

After presenting this—   1050
my cock—as evidence, I'll ask our council
to choose our own ambassadors as well.

SPARTAN MESSENGER:
I'm flyin' off, now. What ya said's jus' right.

(The Spartan Messenger exits stage left. Harden exits stage right.)

OLD MEN'S CHORUS LEADER:
Nothing, no, no animal, not even fire, is more unruly
than woman. Womankind is even more ferocious than a leopard.

OLD WOMEN'S CHORUS LEADER:
You admit all that but still insist on waging war on us.
It's possible, you naughty boy, for us to have a lasting friendship.

OLD MEN'S CHORUS LEADER:
No, I never shall desist from loathing women. Never. NEVER!

OLD WOMEN'S CHORUS LEADER:
Whenever you are ready. Now, though, well—I just can't let you go
around half-naked like that. Take a good look at yourself: you are   1060
ridiculous. I'm coming over there to help you put your shirt on.

*(The Old Women's Chorus Leader helps the Old
Men's Chorus Leader put his shirt back on.)*

OLD MEN'S CHORUS LEADER:
Why, what you did for me just now was right, not wrong. I must admit
that it was wrong of me to strip it off in rage a while ago.

OLD WOMEN'S CHORUS LEADER:

The first thing is that you look like a man again; the second thing,
that you no longer look ridiculous. If you weren't such a grump,
I'd have removed that insect from your eye for you. It's still there now.

OLD MEN'S CHORUS LEADER:

So that's what has been irritating me! You take this little ring
and plow the thing out of my eye. Then, when you're done, please show it
    to me.
By Zeus, that insect has been gnawing on my eye for ages now!

OLD WOMEN'S CHORUS LEADER:

Alright, I'll do it for you. Just you don't be such a grumpy-face.   1070

      (*The Old Women's Chorus Leader takes the ring and uses it to*
      remove the mosquito from the Old Men's Chorus Leader's eye.)

By Zeus, what a gargantuan mosquito you had in your eye!
Just look at this! A monster spawned within the swamps of Tricorysia!°

OLD MEN'S CHORUS LEADER:

Thanks very much. That monster had been digging pits in me for days.
Now that you've gotten rid of my mosquito, I can't keep from weeping.

OLD WOMEN'S CHORUS LEADER:

Though you are quite a naughty boy, I'll wipe your tears away . . . and kiss you.

OLD MEN'S CHORUS LEADER:

No kissing!

OLD WOMEN'S CHORUS LEADER:

      I am going to kiss you whether you consent or not.

OLD MEN'S CHORUS LEADER:

I wish you all bad luck.

      (*The Old Women's Chorus Leader kisses*
      the Old Men's Chorus Leader.)

You women were just born to be persuasive.
There is a proverb that has got the thing just right: we men can live
neither *with* nor *without* all you wretches. All the same, I now
declare a peace: henceforth we'll never do you wrong, and, you all, never   1080
do us wrong as well. Let's join together and begin our song:

(*The Old Men's Chorus Leader and the Old
Women's Chorus Leader unite.*)

CHORUS:

Strophe
Gentlemen, we're not here to make a scandal of
some citizen's behavior. No, instead,
we only want to say and do what's good.
Your present troubles are already quite enough.

Let every man and wife
who need a little money—say,
a whole year's salary—
come ask us for a loan.
We've got that sum at home and bags to put it in.   1090
And, if we ever get to live at peace again,
our debtors need not pay us back—
because they won't have gotten jack!

Antistrophe
This evening we will entertain distinguished, gracious
gentlemen from Carystus.° We have soup.
We have a suckling pig, which I cut up
for sacrifice. (I kept the choice and juiciest pieces.)

Come over to my house this
evening. Be sure to take a bath,
but come on over with   1100
your wife and kids in tow.
Trust me, you won't need anyone's permission—no,
just walk on up as if the place belonged to you.

What will be waiting for you there?
A stiffly locked and bolted door!

(Two Spartan Ambassadors enter from stage left. They are
wearing disproportionately large, erect strap-on penises
beneath their cloaks. They speak with a southern twang.)

CHORUS LEADER:
Here come the Spartan Ambassadors—bearded
gentlemen wearing something like wicker
pig-cages strapped between their thighs.

First off: my greetings to you, men of Sparta.
Second: please tell me how you have been doing.   1110

SPARTAN AMBASSADOR:
Heck, what's the use a' gabbin' on and on:
Y'all can see quite clear jus' how we're doin'.

(The Spartan Ambassadors remove their
cloaks, exposing their erections.)

CHORUS LEADER:
Goodness, what awful diplomatic tension.
This mess was hot but now looks even hotter.

SPARTAN AMBASSADOR:
Words jus' can't say it. Let some fella come
and make a treaty any way he fancies.

(Two Athenian Ambassadors enter from stage right. They, too,
are wearing disproportionately large, erect strap-on penises.)

CHORUS LEADER:
And now I see these native sons of Athens
letting the robes hang forward from their stomachs
like wrestlers crouching for a hold. It looks
like they have got some bad groin injuries.   1120

ATHENIAN AMBASSADOR:
We'd like to know where Lysistrata is.
We men are here, as you can clearly see.

CHORUS LEADER:
These men's afflictions match up with the others'.
The spasms—do they strike worst late at night?

ATHENIAN AMBASSADOR:
Yes, and we can't stop getting chafed down there.
If someone doesn't reconcile us soon,
we'll all be forced to go fuck Cleisthenes.

CHORUS LEADER:
Be careful, now, and cover up or else
someone will come and mutilate your . . . Herms.°

ATHENIAN AMBASSADOR:
Thank you. That is excellent advice.   1130

SPARTAN AMBASSADOR:
Sure is. Come on, let's put our cloaks back on.

     (The Ambassadors all cover up their erections with their cloaks.)

ATHENIAN AMBASSADOR: *(to the Spartan Ambassadors)*
Spartans, hello. We've suffered quite a bit.

SPARTAN AMBASSADOR:
Buddy, we're sufferin' something fierce as well.

              (gesturing to the audience)

I hope them choppers a' the Herms don't see us!

ATHENIAN AMBASSADOR:
Spartans, let's get down to the nitty-gritty.
Why have you come here?

SPARTAN AMBASSADOR:
                        As ambassadors
to make a peace.

ATHENIAN AMBASSADOR:
                    Great news. That's why we're here
as well. Why don't we call in Lysistrata?
She's the one to bring us all together.

SPARTAN AMBASSADOR:
Heck, if you like, go call her brother, too.   1140

                (*Lysistrata enters from the Acropolis.*)

ATHENIAN AMBASSADOR:
Why, there's no need to call her—here she is.
She must have heard us when we said her name.

CHORUS LEADER: *(to Lysistrata)*
Greetings to you, most manly of women.
It's time for you to be clever and gentle,
classy and trashy, severe and sweet—
in sum, a universal lady.
Seduced by the power of your amorous magic,
important men have gathered together
from all over Greece to lay their many
disputes before your arbitration.   1150

LYSISTRATA: *(to the Chorus Leader)*
They're not so hard to manage if you catch them
when they are aroused and not attacking
one another. Well, we'll find out soon.
Where is Reconciliation?

                (*Reconciliation, a voluptuous female,
                enters, nude, from a stage door.*)

(to Reconciliation)

Go
and bring those Spartans over here by me.
Do not be rough or overbearing with them
or paw them boorishly the way our husbands
have handled us, but touch them like a woman—
domestically. If he won't offer up
his hand, you'll have to grab him by the dick.   1160
Now go get those Athenians as well.
Take hold of what they offer up and drag them
over here.

(to the Spartans and Athenians)

You Spartans, stand right here
beside me; you Athenians, right here.
Now listen to my words: I am a woman,
yes, but I have a brain. Although I've got
plenty of intellect in my own right,
I've also listened frequently to what
my father and his friends were talking over,
so I've become quite educated, too.   1170
Now that I have you here, I want to scold you,
both sides, in common, as is only just.

Both Spartans and Athenians, like kinsmen,
sprinkle the altars from a single bowl
of sacred water at Olympia,
at Pytho, at Thermopylae°—how many
other places could I add to make
the list still longer? But, though there are foreign
enemies out there with their armies, you
wage war against Greek men and towns in Greece.   1180
One point, my first, has now been driven home.

ATHENIAN AMBASSADOR:
My dick's about to burst out of its skin!

LYSISTRATA: *(to the Spartans)*
Next, Spartans, I will turn my words on you.
Have you forgot how Pericleidas° came
and, though a Spartan, took a seat upon
a shrine in Athens as a suppliant,
a pale man in a vivid red cloak, begging
for military aid? Your subject state
Messenia had attacked you, and Poseidon
had shocked you with a quake. Our Cimon took   1190
four thousand infantry and saved all Sparta.
Since you have received such benefits
from the Athenians, why do you Spartans
ravage the land that gave you so much aid?

ATHENIAN AMBASSADOR:
They've done us an injustice, Lysistrata!

SPARTAN AMBASSADOR:
We sure did.

           (looking at Reconciliation's behind)

      Dang, she's got a luscious ass.

LYSISTRATA: *(to the Athenians)*
Now, don't assume that I'll be letting you
Athenians off scot-free. Don't you remember,
when you were dressed in sheepskin clothes like slaves,
how Spartans showed up with their spears and killed   1200
many Thessalian men and many allies
and friends of Hippias as well?° That day
they were the only ones who helped you kick
the tyrant out. Don't you remember how
they came and liberated you and how
they wrapped your people in a cloak again?

SPARTAN AMBASSADOR: *(gawking at Reconciliation)*
Me, I never seen a nicer woman.

ATHENIAN AMBASSADOR: *(looking at Reconciliation's crotch)*
And me, I've never seen a finer pussy.

LYSISTRATA:
You've done so many favors for each other.
Why are you fighting? Why not put an end   1210
to all this turmoil? Why not make a peace?
Come on, what's stopping you?

SPARTAN AMBASSADOR: *(looking at Reconciliation's buttocks)*
                              We come 'roun' to't, if one
a' y'all come 'roun' to giving us this here
round mountain on her backside.

ATHENIAN AMBASSADOR:
                              What round mountain?

SPARTAN AMBASSADOR:
Why, Pylos, that's the thing that we been gropin'
and hankerin' after for a long time now.

ATHENIAN AMBASSADOR:
No, by Poseidon, you will not get Pylos!°

LYSISTRATA: *(to the Athenian Ambassador)*
Be a good man, now, and give it to them.

ATHENIAN AMBASSADOR:
Where will we go to get some loving, then?

LYSISTRATA:
Just ask for somewhere else as compensation.   1220

ATHENIAN AMBASSADOR: *(looking at Reconciliation's front)*
Alright, then. Give us this, er, mound right here,
Echinous, and the Malian Gulf behind it,
and both these long legs stretching out of Megara.°

SPARTAN AMBASSADOR:

Dang, we ain't gonna give y'all everythin'!

LYSISTRATA: *(to the Athenian Ambassador)*

Just let it drop. Why wrangle over legs?

ATHENIAN AMBASSADOR: *(looking at Reconciliation's crotch)*

I want to strip right now and start my plowing!

SPARTAN AMBASSADOR: *(looking at Reconciliation's buttocks)*

I'll git up with the sun and spread manure!

LYSISTRATA:

After you both have sworn to the agreement,
you each can get down to your business. Now,
if it seems best to you to make this peace,   1230
go and present your allies with the terms.

ATHENIAN AMBASSADOR:

Allies, my dear? Just look how hard I am.
Won't all our allies reach the same decision—
to fuck?

SPARTAN AMBASSADOR:

      Our allies sure will do the like.

ATHENIAN AMBASSADOR:

Our Carystian men—they'll go along.

LYSISTRATA:

Alright, then. You must purify yourselves
so that my girls and I can entertain you
on the Acropolis and share with you
the food we have inside our wicker baskets.
There you will conclude the peace with oaths   1240
on both sides. Then you all may claim your wives
and go back home.

ATHENIAN AMBASSADOR:
> Well, let's get going, then.

SPARTAN AMBASSADOR:
Y'all fetch me where I need to go.

ATHENIAN AMBASSADOR:
> And quickly!

(Everyone exits into the Acropolis except the members of the Chorus.)

CHORUS:
> *Strophe*
> Embroidered tapestries, nice clothing, fancy gowns,
> even my gold, all this—I willingly provide
> to everybody to supply their sons
> or dress their daughters for the Big Parade.
> I welcome you to come and take
> everything that I have in stock.
> Nothing is sealed up so well   1250
> that you can't break the seal
> and take whatever you might find inside.
> Ah, but unless you're blessed with better eyes than me,
> there won't be anything to see.
>
> *Antistrophe*
> If anyone is out of bread and has a lot
> of slaves to feed and lots of little children, too,
> come borrow flour from me—small grains of it,
> but, taken all together, they would grow
> into a healthy-looking loaf.
> And all you who are paupers, if   1260
> you bring your own bags to my house,
> my servant boy Manes
> will pour in little grains of flour for you.
> Be careful, though: if ever you come to my door,
> you'll find a killer watchdog there.

*(The Athenian Ambassador emerges with another Athenian
from a stage door. They are very drunk. The first Athenian
Ambassador is carrying a torch. A Doorkeeper and several
Slaves are sitting on the ground near the door.)*

ATHENIAN AMBASSADOR: *(to the Doorkeeper)*
Open the door there, you. You should have moved.

(to the Slaves)

You slaves, what are you doing sitting there?
Yeah, maybe I should burn you with this torch.
That's shtick, though. I would never do it.

(addressing the audience)

                           Well,
if you *insist* I do it, then I'll go   1270
all-out and do the audience a favor.

(He chases the Slaves off with the torch.)

ATHENIAN: *(helping to chase the Slaves off)*
Me, too. I'll go all-out along with you.

(to the Slaves)

Git, now! I'll burn your hair until you scream.

ATHENIAN AMBASSADOR:
Yeah, git, so that the Spartans, when they come out
after the feast, enjoy some peace and quiet.

ATHENIAN: *(to the Athenian Ambassador)*
I've never seen a party so fantastic!
The Spartans, for their part, were charming guests,
and we were pretty clever in our cups.

ATHENIAN AMBASSADOR:
That's what I would expect, since, when we're sober,
we go astray. If the Athenians   1280
would only listen to me, we would always
go on ambassadorial missions drunk.
As things are now, when we arrive in Sparta
sober, we look for ways to cause a ruckus;
and we don't hear whatever they are saying
and, when they don't say boo, we turn suspicious.
So we wind up with rival versions of
the same events. But everything was perfect
this time around. When someone started singing
the *Telamon*, when he should have been singing   1290
Cleitagora,° we all just whooped and swore
that there was no mistake.

        (The Slaves return and sit down again.)

            Those slaves have all
come back again. Get out of here, you vagrants!

      (He chases the Slaves off with the torch again.)

ATHENIAN:
Here are the Spartans right now, coming out.

        *(The Spartan Ambassador emerges with
          other Spartans and a Piper.)*

SPARTAN AMBASSADOR:
Hey, piper, grab your flute, now, 'cause I'm gonna
dance a two-step while I sing a pretty
Spartan ditty for the men a' Athens.

ATHENIAN AMBASSADOR:
Piper, by all the gods, take up your flute.
I just love watching Spartans do their dances.

SPARTAN AMBASSADOR: *(singing while he dances)*

> O Goddess a' Rememberin', rouse   1300
> for me a Muse who knows
> all a' the Spartans' and Athenians' deeds—
> how, off the Cape a' Artemisium,
> the men a' Athens spread their sails like gods
> and beat the navy a' the Medes,
> while Spartans under Leonidas fought on land°
> like boars. Like boars, we gnashed our tusks, and foam
> ran from our jaws, and sweat ran down our thighs.
> The Persian troops outnumbered grains a' sand
> upon the shore.
>   O Goddess a' the Wilderness,   1310
> Beast-Slayer Virgin Power, come
> join in this treaty, help us live
> in harmony a good long time.
> Let lots a' amity attend
> always this sacred peace.
> Let us forever put a' end
> to foxy guile and stratagem.
> O Virgin Huntress, come here, please.

ATHENIAN AMBASSADOR:

Well, now that everything has come together,
you Spartans may reclaim your spouses here.   1320
Let every husband stand beside his woman,
and every woman by her man. Let's hold a dance
in honor of the gods to celebrate
today's successes, and let's promise never,
ever again, to make the same old blunders.

CHORUS:

> Begin the dancing, bring the Graces in
> and Artemis and her dance-leading twin,
> Apollo, the kindhearted healing power,
> and Dionysus with his eyes aflame,

guiding the madwomen who follow him,   1330
and King Zeus brandishing his bolts of fire
and Hera, prosperous wife of Zeus,
and many other deities
to serve as witnesses
of the magnanimous Peace
that Aphrodite made for us.

Hip, hip, hooray!
Hooray, it's like a victory!
Lift your legs up high.
Hip, hip, hooray!   1340

ATHENIAN AMBASSADOR:
My Spartan friend, since we have sung a new song,
share a new song of your own with us.

SPARTAN AMBASSADOR: *(singing while he dances)*
        Come, Spartan Muse, from handsome Tayeegety
        and celebrate this friendship with a ditty
        in honor a' the gods
        Apollo and Athena a' the Brazen House°
        and both the sons a' King Tyndareus
        riding their steeds
        beside the Eurotas.°

        Come on and leap,   1350
        now! Up, now, up!
        Let's sing in praise a' Sparta where
        everyone in the sacred choir
        sings, and the sound of dancing gives
        off echoes, where the girls like fillies raise
        dust clouds while running with the Eurotas,
        where they have great fun, waving sacred staves
        under the tutelage a' Leda's daughter,°
        their fine and pious chorus leader.

(to the Chorus)

Come, now, and tie your hair up with a ribbon. Like a deer now, leap,   1360
and make a brouhaha to keep the people dancin', while you sing
in honor a' invincible Athena a' the Brazen House.

(The ensemble dances together and then exits stage left and right.)

women of
the assembly

At the beginning of *Women of the Assembly*, the women of Athens have plotted, at an exclusively female festival called the Scira, to disguise themselves as men and vote in the Assembly to hand the government over to women. Under the leadership of Praxagora, they succeed. The major male character Blepyrus, Praxagora's husband, left only with his wife's slip and slippers to wear, is systematically effeminized. Praxagora eventually explains to him that what had been a capitalistic democracy will henceforth be a communistic one, and in a great monologue their neighbor addresses all of the chattel in front of his house that is to be turned over to the common fund. A skeptical Athenian male approaches this neighbor and mocks him for complying but, in the end, suffers for his refusal by being excluded from the communal feast.

Sexual relations also will be communalized, and there will be no more marriage. The citizens will be free to have sex with whomever they wish, so long as they have sex with an undesirable person first. Aristophanes provides a scene that shows the implications of this policy. The setting shifts from Blepyrus's and the Neighbor's house to another pair of houses, one occupied by a young girl and the other by an old woman. A young man named Epigenes enters to visit the girl, but he is informed, to his horror, that he must service the old woman first—it's the law. When she eventually withdraws, two other older women appear and drag him offstage against his will.

That salacious interlude gives way to a scene of mirth in which, as part of the new civic order, all are invited to enjoy a feast:

Now there will be served, en masse,
limpet, saltfish, dogfish, shark,
mullets, sardines in pickle sauce,
rooster, crusted wagtail, lark,
thrush, blackbird, dove and slices
of mulled-wine-marinated hare,
all drenched in oil and vinegar,
silphium, honey, all the spices. (1316–1323)

The elimination of private property and marriage and the inversion of traditional gender roles result in a state of festive blessedness.

women of the assembly

(Ecclesiazusae)

First produced in 392 BCE

CHARACTERS IN THE PLAY

Praxagora
First Woman
Chorus Leader
Second Woman
Chorus of Athenian
    Women
Blepyrus
Neighbor
Chremes
Sicon the Slave

Parmenon the Slave
Man
Female Herald
First Old Woman
Girl
Epigenes
Second Old Woman
Third Old Woman
Slave Girl

(The setting is Athens, Greece, in 392 BCE. The time is just before dawn. There are two stage doors in a backdrop, with windows above them. Praxagora enters through one of the doors carrying a lit lamp. Already onstage are boots, a cloak, a fake beard, a walking stick, and a garland.)

PRAXAGORA: *(in a mock-lofty tone)*
Bright eye inside of this ceramic lamp,
beautiful innovation of our craftsmen,
I shall disclose your origin and duty:
wrought on the wheel the potter's zeal spins round,
you, through your nostrils,° serve a solar office.

(waving the lamp)

Send out the fire signal we agreed on.
It's fitting that you should be privy now,
since even in our bedrooms late at night
you stand nearby while we complete our acts
of Aphrodite. No one thinks to move   10
your supervisory gaze out of the room
while lying legs-up on a mattress. You
and you alone, agleam between our thighs,
shine on the depths that dare not speak their name
when we are singeing off the hair down there.
You stand beside us when we raid the pantry
for bread and Bacchic beverages. A loyal
confidant, you never run to tell
the neighbors. That is why you will be privy
to what we women plotted at the Scira°   20
to do today.

                        (to the audience)

          They were supposed to be here,
but none of them have come. It's almost dawn,
and the Assembly will be starting soon.
We "congress-whores" (at least that is the way
that Pyromachus° put it once—remember?)—
we need to take our seats and not attract
any attention.
          Why are they so late?
Haven't the women got the phony beards
they were supposed to get? Or has it proved
too hard for them to steal their husbands' clothing   30
without anybody noticing?

Oh, I can see another lamp approaching.
I'll duck down here in case it is a man.

          (The First Woman opens the stage door next to Praxagora's.)

FIRST WOMAN:

Time to be up and at 'em since the herald
has crowed out twice already, while we got
ready to go.

(The First Woman closes her door again.)

PRAXAGORA:

    I sat up all night long
waiting for you.
     Hmn, I will have to call
my neighbor out by scratching on the door
gently, so that her husband doesn't hear.

(Praxagora scratches on her neighbor's door. The First
Woman enters through that door. She is carrying
a fake beard, boots, and a walking stick.)

FIRST WOMAN:

I heard you. I was getting dressed. I heard   40
that scratching of your fingers at my door,
since I was wide awake. The man I live with
hails from Salamis, the land of sailors,
and he was up the whole night driving me
though waves of bedding, so that I was able
only just now to steal this cloak of his
from him and come.

(Three females enter, stage right, the Chorus Leader with them.)

PRAXAGORA:

    I see Sostrata coming,
and here's Cleinarete, and here as well's
Philainete.

CHORUS LEADER:

    You hurry up, now, girls.
Glyce has vowed the last girl here will have   50

to pay a fine of twenty pints of wine
and one whole bag of chickpeas.

(Another female enters, stage left.)

PRAXAGORA:

Look, here comes
Smicythion's wife Melistiche wearing
a man's big boots. She is the only one,
it seems, who had no trouble sneaking from
her husband's side.

(Another female enters, stage right.)

FIRST WOMAN:

And, look, there's Geusistrata,
the tavern-keeper's wife. She's got a torch.

(More females, including the Second Woman, enter, stage left.
They are all carrying fake beards, boots, and walking sticks.
They will constitute the Chorus of Athenian Women.)

PRAXAGORA:
Here comes the wife of Chaeretades, here's
Philodoretus's, and here come lots
more women—all the best of them in town.   60

SECOND WOMAN: (to Praxagora)
I had a hard time getting out the door
and sneaking over here, my dear. My husband
sucked down a bunch of anchovies at dinner
and coughed all night.

PRAXAGORA:

All of you, please, be seated.
Now, since I see that everybody's here,
I want to ask you whether you have done
those things we all agreed on at the Scira.

FIRST WOMAN:

I have. To start, I've grown my armpit hair out
bushier than a thicket, as stipulated.
Plus, when my husband went out to the market,   70
I would anoint myself with oil and stand
all day out in the sun to get a tan.°

SECOND WOMAN:

I have as well. I threw my razor out
after the Scira so that I would get
hairy and be no longer lady-like.

PRAXAGORA:

And do you have the phony beards that you
were told to have whenever we met next?

FIRST WOMAN: (holding up a fake beard)
By Hecate, I've got a fine one here!

SECOND WOMAN: (holding up a fake beard)
The one I've got's a fair bit more attractive
than Epicrates's beard.

PRAXAGORA:

                    The rest of you,   80
what do you say?

FIRST WOMAN:

                    They all are nodding "Yes."

PRAXAGORA:

I see they've taken care of all the other
matters, too—they have their Spartan boots,°
their walking sticks and men's cloaks, as requested.

FIRST WOMAN: (holding up a cane)
And I've brought Lamius's cane°—I stole it
while he was sleeping.

SECOND WOMAN:
This must be the cane
he leans on when he farts!

PRAXAGORA:
By Zeus the Savior,
if he were dressed in All-Eyes' goatskin jacket,°
he would be just the man to tend and feed
the cattle of the executioner!   90
Come, now, let's move on and address the next
order of business while there still are stars out,
since the Assembly that we will attend
begins at dawn.

FIRST WOMAN:
That's right. We need to claim
the seats right underneath the speaker's platform,
right at the chairmen's feet.

SECOND WOMAN: *(taking out a basket)*
Yes, that's the reason
why I have brought this spinning basket with me,
so I can do some work while the Assembly
is filling up.

PRAXAGORA:
"Is filling up"? You're nuts!

SECOND WOMAN:
Why would I listen any worse while spinning?   100
My kids need clothes to wear.

PRAXAGORA:
You and your spinning!
You should be wholly in disguise, revealing
nothing the men can notice. It would be
just glorious if some woman clambered over
the men and hitched her clothes up and exposed her—

Phormisius!° If we all sit down first,
no one will notice that we have our cloaks
pulled tight around our bodies. When we break
our fake beards out and tie them to our faces,
who will not take us, at a glance, for men?   110
Now that he has on Pronomus's beard,°
Agyrrhius° is passing for a man and yet
this "man" was once a woman. Now, just look,
he is by far the most important person
in town. I tell you by this dawning day
he is the reason we must dare to try
to seize control and do some good for Athens,
which is now becalmed and rudderless.°

FIRST WOMAN:
How can a women's group, with woman-thoughts,
hope to address the people?

PRAXAGORA:
                              We will be   120
the best at it by far. They say the young men
whose holes get fucked the most are also best
at public speaking. Well, as luck would have it,
we are by nature made for getting reamed.

FIRST WOMAN:
But I don't know. We lack experience,
and that is risky.

PRAXAGORA:
                    Isn't that why we
assembled here, to run through all the things
we need to say up there?

                    (to the First Woman)

                    Be quick, now, tie
your beard on.

(to the rest)

You, too, ladies, since I know
you have been practicing your chattering.   130

FIRST WOMAN:
Who here, my friend, does not know how to chatter?

PRAXAGORA:
Go on, then, tie your beards on and, like that,
you'll be a man.

(They put on the fake beards.)

I'll put these garlands down
and tie my own on, just in case I feel
like speaking, too.

(Praxagora puts down the garland and ties on her fake beard.)

SECOND WOMAN: *(holding up a mirror)*
                    Praxagora, come see
just how ridiculous this getup is.

PRAXAGORA:
Ridiculous?

SECOND WOMAN:
                    It's like a beard was stuck on
a squid, a grilled white squid.

PRAXAGORA:
                              Hey, purifier,
walk round, now, with the sacrificial cat.°
And, you all, move inside the sacred space.   140
Stop gabbing, Ariphrades!° Come, sit down.

(They sit facing Praxagora.)

Who here would like to speak to the Assembly?

FIRST WOMAN: *(raising her hand)*
I would.

PRAXAGORA: *(offering the garland)*
          Then put this garland on and utter
words that are of some use.

FIRST WOMAN: *(putting on the garland)*
                              Alright; I'm set.

PRAXAGORA:
You may begin.

FIRST WOMAN:
                    But don't I get a drink first?

PRAXAGORA:
A drink?

FIRST WOMAN:
              Why else, man, did I don a garland?

PRAXAGORA:
Get down from there. You would have done the same thing
up on the podium.

FIRST WOMAN:
                    What, don't they drink
in the Assembly?

PRAXAGORA:
                    What's this "don't they drink"?

FIRST WOMAN:

They drink, I swear, and straight stuff, too. Consider   150
how much the laws they pass sound like a drunk man
raving. They pour libations, too, I know it.
Why else would they recite those endless prayers,
if there were no wine handy? Plus, they shout
at one another like a bunch of drunks,
and the police drag off the violent ones.

PRAXAGORA:

You go and take your seat. You're bad at this.

FIRST WOMAN:

I'd have been better off without this beard—
I'm nearly dead of thirst.

PRAXAGORA:

                              Does any other
among you wish to speak?

SECOND WOMAN: *(raising her hand)*
                              I want to speak!   160

PRAXAGORA:

Put on the garland. Now at last our scheme
is underway. Step up and speak out loudly,
manfully. Lean your weight upon your staff.

             (The Second Woman puts on the garland.)

SECOND WOMAN:

I'd have preferred it if some other person,
one of the usual speakers, had proposed
the wisest counsel. Then I could have sat
in silence. Now, as far as I'm concerned,
we will forbid, in bars, the installation
of water kegs.° They're just a bad idea,
by Demeter and Persephone.°   170

PRAXAGORA:
"By Demeter and Persephone,"
you idiot? What were you thinking?

SECOND WOMAN:
                                    What's wrong?
I didn't ask for wine.

PRAXAGORA:
                        True; but you swore
by goddesses. A man would not have done that.
The rest of what you said was so smart, too.

SECOND WOMAN:
How about "by Apollo"?

PRAXAGORA: *(taking the garland from the Second Woman)*
                        Just stop speaking.
I won't take a step toward making you
orators in the Assembly till we get
it all just right.

SECOND WOMAN:
                    Hey, give me back the garland.
I want to try again. I think I've got   180
enough rehearsal in.

                (beginning her speech again)

            In my opinion,
ladies of the Assembly—

PRAXAGORA:
                        Idiot,
this time you have referred to men as "ladies."

SECOND WOMAN: *(pointing to a member of the audience)*
That man Epigonus°—he made me do it,
that creature over there. One glimpse of him,
and I assumed I was addressing "ladies."

PRAXAGORA: *(to the Second Woman)*
Get down from there! Go sit down, too.

(ascending to the platform and putting on the garland)

To judge
from your performances, I'd better put on
this garland here and give the speech myself.

I ask the gods on high to help me prove   190
successful in this day's deliberations.
I have just as much at stake in Athens
as you all do, and what's been going on here
has greatly irritated and depressed me.
I know that Athens always seems to choose
criminals as her heads of state. If one
turns good for one day, he will prove a scoundrel
for ten days after. If you try another,
he will do even worse things than the guy
before him. It is hard to have discussions   200
with men as obstinate as you are, men
who fear all those inclined to benefit them,
men who tend to dote on those who aren't.
There was a time when we had no Assemblies.°
Back then at least we knew Agyrrhius
was nasty. Now we do convene Assemblies
and, while the men who draw pay worship him,
all those who don't attend for pay insist
that those who do ought to be executed.

FIRST WOMAN:
By Aphrodite, you expressed that well!   210

PRAXAGORA:
That's bad—you swore your oath by Aphrodite.
It would have been a charming thing indeed
if you had said her name in the Assembly.

FIRST WOMAN:
I wouldn't have.

PRAXAGORA:
        It's time to break the habit.

               (continuing her speech)

About our late alliance:° When we were
considering the matter, people said
Athens would be destroyed if we did not
approve it. When it finally was approved,
people were very angry, and the speaker
who did the most to get the measure passed   220
was forced to skip town quick.
                We need to launch
a new armada.° All the poor vote "yes,"
and all the rich folks and the farmers, "no."
You rage at the Corinthians,° and they
rage back at you. Now, though, they're being pleasant,
so you "play nice" as well. Argives are dunces,
and Hieronymus a mastermind.°
Salvation starts to peep in at us, but
Thrasybulus° gets mad because you didn't
ask him to be in charge.

FIRST WOMAN:
             This man is wise!   230

PRAXAGORA:
Now you are cheering properly!

               (continuing her speech)

                                        And you,
the people, are to blame for this. Although
the money you receive comes from the state,
you each look after only your own interest.
The common interest flails, like Aesimus.°
If you abide by my suggestions, you
may yet be saved. What I propose is that
we hand the city over to the women
to rule. They have already proved themselves
as managers and treasurers in our homes.   240

FIRST WOMAN:
Well said, by Zeus! Well said!

SECOND WOMAN:
                                        Please, sir, continue.

PRAXAGORA:
I shall prove the female character
is better than the male. First off, they all
adhere to ancient precedent in that
they use warm water when they dye their wool.
No, you would never see them making any
innovations, while the city of Athens
won't stick to any customs even though
they work quite well. Oh no, the men would have
to mess with them and try out something novel.   250
Meanwhile the women cook the meals like always
and carry burdens on their heads like always.
They celebrate the Thesmophoria°
like always, and like always, bake sweet rolls.
Like always they annoy their husbands and
like always stash their lovers in the house.
They purchase extra goodies for themselves
like always and like always love their wine
unmixed. Like always they are fond of fucking.
So, in conclusion, gentlemen, let's hand   260
the rule of Athens over to the women.

No blabbering about it, no inquiring
what they are planning to accomplish. No,
let's simply let them rule, considering
that, first, as mothers they will want to keep
our soldiers safe, and, second, who would sooner
send the soldiers rations than the ones
who gave them birth? Women are very clever
when it comes to getting funds, and they
will not be cheated when they are in power   270
because they all, themselves, are expert cheaters.
I will omit my other points. If you
accede to my proposal, you will all
lead happy lives.

FIRST WOMAN:
                       O sweet Praxagora,
well said, and rightly said. Where did you learn,
darling, to make so fabulous a speech?

PRAXAGORA:
We were displaced awhile, my man and I,
and living on the Pnyx.° That's where I learned
the art of speaking from the orators.

FIRST WOMAN:
It's no surprise, then, that you were so clever   280
and penetrating. Furthermore, we women
hereby do choose you as our general,
if you can carry what you have in mind
in the Assembly. But if Cephalus°
flings insults at you, how will you respond?

PRAXAGORA:
I'll say that he's a madman.

FIRST WOMAN:
                      Everybody
knows that he's nuts already.

PRAXAGORA:
                              Then I'll say
he's got a nasty sickness.

FIRST WOMAN:
                              Everybody
knows that he's sick already.

PRAXAGORA:
                              Then I'll say
a man like him who makes bad pottery   290
will do a great job shattering the city.

FIRST WOMAN:
What if that squinter Neocleides° starts
insulting you?

PRAXAGORA:
                    I'd tell him to go squint up
a dog's behind.

FIRST WOMAN:
                    What if they try to screw you?

PRAXAGORA:
I'll screw them back. I'm quite familiar with
the art of screwing.

FIRST WOMAN:
                    But there's one more thing
we should discuss: What if policemen grab you?

PRAXAGORA: *(making a violent gesture with her elbow)*
I'll elbow them like *this*. They'll never get
the chokehold on me.

CHORUS LEADER:

        If they lay hands on you,
we'll—we'll—entreat them please to let you go.   300

FIRST WOMAN:

It's good we've gotten all that figured out,
but there's another thing we should consider: How
will we remind ourselves to raise our hands
to vote? Our legs are what we're used to lifting.

PRAXAGORA:

That is a hard one.

    (undraping her right arm and then raising her right hand)

        All the same, try this—
undrape your right arm, then hold up that hand.

Lift up your hems, now. Quick, put on these boots
just as your husband does when he goes out
to the Assembly or on other business.

        (The women start putting on their boots.)

Then, when you have your boots put on just right,   310
tie on your beards.

        (The women start putting on their beards.)

        Then, when you've got the beards
positioned just exactly as they should be,
dress yourselves in the cloaks you swiped.

        (The women start putting on the cloaks.)

        Be sure
to drape them properly. Now, as you walk,

lean on your staffs and sing an old man's song—
something that farmers from the sticks might sing.

CHORUS LEADER:
What good advice!

PRAXAGORA: *(to the First and Second Woman)*
              Let's go ahead before
these other ladies here, because I think
the women coming from the country will proceed
straight to the Pnyx. Let's get a move on, too,   320
because the rule up on the Pnyx is that
you must be in by dawn or go back home
with nothing for your troubles, not one clothespin.

              (Praxagora and the First and Second Woman
                exit to the Assembly, stage right.)

CHORUS LEADER: *(speaking to the chorus members)*
Men, it is time for us to march. We always must remember
that we are men. That we are men must never slip our minds.
There's no small risk to us if we get caught in these disguises
while we are perpetrating such a dark and risky deed.

CHORUS:
              Strophe
              Let's march to the Assembly, gentlemen.
              The magistrate has sounded out his warning:
              anyone not there early in the morning,
              dust-covered, stuffed with an entire tureen
              of garlic pickles for his morning meal,°
              will not receive his pay: three obols.° Hey,
              Smicythus, Draces, Charitimides,°
              buddies, make certain that you strike the right
              notes in the manly role you've got play.
              After we've checked in, let's be sure to sit
              with one another so that we can raise
              our hands in favor of whatever bill

              330

this coterie of women may propose.   340
Oops, "men" is what I meant to say.

Antistrophe
Let's jostle the Assemblymen from town
who never showed up when the pay was less
but sat in garland shops and flapped their jaws.
Now they fight like crazy to get in.
Never in the glorious days of yore,
when brave Myronides was all the rage,
would anyone have dared to cast a vote
in expectation of a daily fee.
No, we would show up for the privilege   350
with our own lunches: several onions, three
olives, wine to drink and bread to eat.
Now everybody wants three obols for
doing his sacred duty to the state
as if he were a common drudge.

(*The Chorus exit toward the Assembly, stage right. Blepyrus enters
from a stage door, wearing a yellow slip and women's slippers.*)

BLEPYRUS:
What's the deal here? Where's my wife gone off to?
It's getting on toward dawn, and I can't find her.
I was lying there in bed a long time
needing to shit and groping everywhere
around in darkness looking for my shoes   360
and cloak. Well, I kept reaching all around
but couldn't find them, and the poop-man kept on
trying to break my door down. So I up
and grabbed this slip here of my wife's and put
her Persian slippers on.
                          Where can a fellow
shit in private? Where indeed? It's night,
so anywhere will serve the turn, I guess.
No one is going to see me shitting here.
How dumb I was—a geezer like myself

taking a young wife. I should get my hide   370
lashed good for it. She hasn't left the house
on any proper errand at this hour.
Oh well, it's time: I've really gotta go.

>   (Blepyrus hunches down as if to defecate. A
>   Neighbor enters through a stage door.)

NEIGHBOR:
Who's that out there? It's not my next-door neighbor
Blepyrus, is it? Yes, by Zeus, that's him.

Hey, what's that yellow stuff all over you?
What happened? Has Cinesias the poet°
hit you with his spray?

BLEPYRUS:
                    I'm out here wearing
a yellow slip, a favorite of my wife's.

NEIGHBOR:
But where's your cloak?

BLEPYRUS:
                    I wish that I could tell you.   380
I searched all over for it in the bedding
but couldn't find it.

NEIGHBOR:
                    And you didn't ask
your wife to tell you where it got off to?

BLEPYRUS:
I tried to, but she isn't in the house.
She slipped away without my noticing,
and I fear she is somewhere misbehaving.

NEIGHBOR:
Hey, the same thing just happened at my house.
The woman I live with has gone somewhere
and must have brought the cloak I like to wear
along with her. It's no big deal, except   390
she also took my boots. I wasn't able
to find them anywhere.

BLEPYRUS:
                                I couldn't find
my boots as well and, since, as it so happens,
I had to shit, I put these slippers on
and rushed outside. I didn't want to soil
the blanket   I just had it washed, you know.

NEIGHBOR:
Why did she leave? Maybe a friend of hers
asked her to breakfast?

BLEPYRUS:
                                That's what I assume.
Far as I know, she isn't cheating on me.

                    (Blepyrus squats again.)

NEIGHBOR:
You must be pooping out a thick ship's hawser.   400
Well, I'd best be off to the Assembly—
if I can find my cloak. I've just got one.

BLEPYRUS:
I'll go there, too, when I have finished here.
I swear a pear has got me all blocked up.

NEIGHBOR:
Is it the same pear that Thrasybulus
introduced to the Spartans?°

BLEPYRUS:
                          Yep, the same.
The thing has got me terribly impacted.

(The Neighbor exits into his house, through a stage door.)

                    (to himself)

What am I going to do? This present pressure
isn't my only problem. When I eat again,
will there be room for still more poop? Already   410
Mr. Nowhere-Else-to-Go has got
my door sealed tight.

                    (to the audience)

                    Who will go and find
a doctor for me, and what kind of doctor?
Can any of you butt-hole virtuosos
suggest a clever cure for my condition?
Can Amynon tell me what to do?
He likely would deny his expertise.
Someone must absolutely go and find
Antisthenes. A connoisseur of grunting,
that man knows when a butt-hole needs to shit.   420
Goddess of Childbirth,° don't you leave me helpless
when I am crammed and bolted. Please don't make me
play the role of comical commode.

(Chremes enters, stage right, carrying an empty shopping basket.)

CHREMES:
What are you doing there? Not shitting, are you?

BLEPYRUS:
Me? I'm done with that. I'm standing upright.

CHREMES:

Wait, do you have your wife's slip on?

BLEPYRUS:

                                    I do.

The house was dark. I took it by mistake.

Where are you coming from?

CHREMES:

                        From the Assembly.

BLEPYRUS:

The session has already been dissolved?

CHREMES:

That's right, before the sun had even risen.   430

Oh dear Zeus, the way they threw around

the red dye that they use to mark the tardy

got lots of laughs.

BLEPYRUS:

                    Did you receive three obols

as payment?

CHREMES:

                    Yeah, if only. I arrived

too late and, I'm ashamed to say, left there

with empty hands.

BLEPYRUS:

                    So you have gotten nothing?

CHREMES:

Yep, I have nothing but my shopping basket.

BLEPYRUS:

Because of what?

CHREMES:

        A whole huge crowd of people,
bigger than ever, gathered at the Pnyx.
They looked as if they were, you know, shoemakers.   440
The whole Assembly seemed so very pale.
So lots of folks (myself included) didn't
receive the payment.

BLEPYRUS:

           What you're saying's that,
if I went now, I wouldn't get the payment?

CHREMES:

How would you? No, not now, not even if
you reached the Pnyx before the rooster crowed
a second time.

BLEPYRUS:

        I am, alas, destroyed.

"Antilochus, sing out the dirge for me,
not those three obols. All I had is lost."°

But what was on the schedule that assembled   450
so very large a crowd at such an hour?

CHREMES:

The chairmen had proposed deliberation
on nothing less than "how to save the city."
The squinter Neocleides was the first up.
While he was stumbling to the platform, people
started to shout as loud as you might guess:
"Isn't it awful that this man presumes
to teach us how to save the city of Athens
when he can't even rescue his own eyelids?"
Squinting here and there, he yelled at them: 460
"What can I do about it?"

BLEPYRUS:

     "Grind up garlic
with figs, throw in a bit of cayenne pepper
and rub the ointment nightly on your eyelids"—
that's what I'd have said, if I'd been there.

CHREMES:

Next came that paragon Euaeon,° wearing
only a shirt, at least that's what it looked like,
but he insisted that he had a cloak on.
The speech he made was very democratic:

"You see that I myself require salvation—
a good four staters' worth.° Well, all the same,   470
I'll tell you how we ought to save the city
and people of Athens. If the clothesmakers
donated cloaks each year at winter solstice
to needy persons, none of us would ever
catch pneumonia again. What's more,
we should permit all those who lack a bed
and quilt to go and, after washing up,
sleep in the tanneries. And, if a tanner
locks anybody out in wintertime,
he should be fined three quilts."

BLEPYRUS:

       A brilliant plan!   480
Everyone would have voted in his favor
if, in addition, he had moved grain dealers
should give three quarts of grain for every meal
to those in need or pay a fine. They could
have gotten something good from Nausicydes!°

CHREMES:

Next, a pale young man as pretty as
the little Nicias° got up and started
addressing the Assembly. He proposed
that we should give the women governance

of Athens. All those pale-faced shoemakers   490
immediately erupted into cheers
and roared, "Well said! Well said!," while all the people
in from the country grumbled in the background.

BLEPYRUS:
They were the smart ones.

CHREMES:
                              But they were outnumbered.
The speaker hushed them with his shouts, insisting
women did only right, and you, much wrong.

BLEPYRUS:
What did he say?

CHREMES:
                First off, he said you are
a crook.

BLEPYRUS:
          Okay. And what did you get called?

CHREMES:
I'll tell you later. Then he said you are
a thief.

BLEPYRUS:
          Just me?

CHREMES:
                That's right. And then he called you   500
a snitch.

BLEPYRUS:
          Just me?

CHREMES: *(gesturing to the audience)*
           Yes, you and all these people.

BLEPYRUS:
Well, there's no denying they are snitches.

CHREMES:
He said that women are idea-people
and money-makers. Furthermore, he said,
they never compromise the Thesmophoria
by broadcasting its secrets, whereas men
blab all that they decide in private council.

BLEPYRUS:
Ain't that the truth?

CHREMES:
                And then he said that women
lend each other clothes, accessories,
money and drinking cups just one on one   510
and not in front of witnesses and still
always return the things and never cheat
like most men, he insisted, do.

BLEPYRUS:
                      That's true.
We even cheat when there are witnesses.

CHREMES:
And he went on extolling womankind
in many other ways: they don't inform
on people; they don't sue; they don't usurp
the government—all winning qualities.

BLEPYRUS:
What was decided?

CHREMES:

That the women ought
to run the government. That seemed to be   520
the only thing we haven't tried.

BLEPYRUS:

It passed?

CHREMES:

That's what I'm saying.

BLEPYRUS:

Women are in charge
of all us citizens had been in charge of?

CHREMES:

That's what has happened.

BLEPYRUS:

So from here on out
my wife, not me, will have to deal with lawsuits?

CHREMES:

And she, not you, will care for your dependents.

BLEPYRUS:

And I won't need to wake up with a groan
each morning?

CHREMES:

Nope, that now belongs to women.
You can quit your groaning, just stay home
and fart the day away.

BLEPYRUS:

But there's a risk   530
for men our age. Once women have assumed
the reins of Athens, they will force us to . . .

CHREMES:
To what?

BLEPYRUS:
      . . . have sex with them. And if we can't,
they will refuse to make us any breakfast.

CHREMES:
Well, you will simply have to find a way
to keep on fucking *while* you eat your breakfast.

BLEPYRUS:
Sex is miserable when you're forced!

CHREMES:
A man must do all that the state decrees.

BLEPYRUS:
There is a certain saying our ancestors
have handed down to us: However thoughtless   540
and idiotic are the laws we pass,
everything will turn out for the best.

CHREMES:
Yes, by Athena and the other gods,
may all be for the best. I've gotta go.
Stay healthy, neighbor.

        (Chremes exits into his house through a stage door.)

BLEPYRUS:
                And you also, Chremes.

    *(Blepyrus exits into his house through a stage door. The Chorus
       of Athenian Women enter from the Assembly, stage right.)*

CHORUS LEADER:

March, now, march!

Are any men behind us? Turn around and look about.

Mind your deportment. There are lots of nasty males around,

and one of them might watch our rears and know us from our movements.

CHORUS:

> *Strophe*
>
> Let's stomp our feet loud as we can.   550
>
> It would be shameful if the men
>
> saw us like this. Stay wrapped up close
>
> and keep tight watch to left and right,
>
> far forward, far behind, so that
>
> there will be no surprise for us.

CHORUS LEADER:

Quick, now, and make the dust fly with your marching. We are near

the place from which we first set out to go to the Assembly.

Now we can see the house in which our Great Protectress lives.

She is the one who came up with the plan that now is law.

CHORUS:

> *Antistrophe*
>
> No need to spend more time with these   560
>
> absurd beards dangling from us.
>
> It's dawn. Some man might catch us here.
>
> Watch for them, as we change ourselves,
>
> under the shadow of the eaves,
>
> back to the sex we were before.

CHORUS LEADER:

Don't drag your feet, now, ladies. Here already we can see

our general coming out of the Assembly. All of you,

quick, now, get rid of those disgusting nets of hair your cheeks

have worn, with indignation, for what seems a long, long time.

(Praxagora enters from the Assembly, stage right.)

PRAXAGORA:

Ladies, we have been fortunate: this business   570
has gone as we had planned. Quick as you can, now,
lose those cloaks before a man can see you.
Undo those Spartan straps and let those boots
cease to impede you. Throw away your staffs.

(The women remove their cloaks and boots and set aside their staffs.)

(to the Chorus Leader)

You, there, arrange these women rank on rank
in military order. I, meanwhile,
will slip back in the house and put this cloak
back where I found it and replace the rest
before my husband catches sight of me.

*(Praxagora exits into her house through a stage door.
The Chorus Leader arranges the chorus members
in a military formation. Praxagora reenters.)*

CHORUS LEADER: *(to Praxagora)*

All has been done according to your orders. It behooves you   580
to keep on training us. What useful deed can we perform
so that you want to keep us on as aids. All I can say is:
I've never met a more outstanding woman than yourself.

PRAXAGORA:

Then stand your ground right there. I will employ you as advisors
to help me with this new authority I have been granted.
Back there in the Assembly, when we faced great shouts and peril,
you proved yourselves to me by acting in a manly way.

(Blepyrus enters from his house through a stage door.)

BLEPYRUS:

Where have you been, Praxagora?

PRAXAGORA:

Is that your business, sir?

BLEPYRUS:

"Is that my business?" That is not the answer
the innocent would use.

PRAXAGORA:

Now don't you start   590
accusing me of being with some lover.

BLEPYRUS:

It's likely you have been with more than one.

PRAXAGORA:
Alright, then, test me.

BLEPYRUS:

How?

PRAXAGORA:

Just smell my hair.
Do I have perfume on?

BLEPYRUS:

What? Can't a woman
do the nasty without perfume on?

PRAXAGORA:
At least I can't.

BLEPYRUS:

Why did you leave so early
without informing me? Why take my cloak?

PRAXAGORA:
A friend went into labor in the night
and asked that I attend her.

BLEPYRUS:

                    Couldn't you
have told me you were going?

PRAXAGORA:

                         And delay,   600
dear husband, giving help to someone
suffering as she was?

BLEPYRUS:

                    You should have told me.
Something isn't right about all this.

PRAXAGORA:

I left just as I was. I swear to you.
Her maid demanded that I come at once.

BLEPYRUS:

Then shouldn't you have worn your own slip there?
You stole the cloak I like to wear and left me
wrapped in your slip as if I were a body
awaiting burial. All I needed was
a wreath and urn.

PRAXAGORA:

                    Well, it was cold outside,   610
and I am delicate and sensitive,
so I put on your cloak to keep me warm.
I left you wrapped, husband, in quilts and comfort.

BLEPYRUS:

Hold on: Why did my boots and staff walk off
with you?

PRAXAGORA:

            I took them too to sound like you,
so that no one would try to steal your cloak.

I stomped along inside the boots and used
the staff to hit at stones.

BLEPYRUS:

Aren't you aware
you've made us lose eight quarts of grain? That's what
I'd planned to use the Assembly money for.   620

PRAXAGORA:

No worries. It's a boy!

BLEPYRUS:

Who had a boy?
The Assembly?

PRAXAGORA:

No, the woman that I helped.
So the Assembly met today?

BLEPYRUS:

Didn't I tell you
about it yesterday?

PRAXAGORA:

Now I remember.

BLEPYRUS:

Don't you know what was decided there?

PRAXAGORA:

I don't.

BLEPYRUS:

Well, you can sit and dine on squid
from here on out. I've heard the city of Athens
has now been handed over to you women!

PRAXAGORA:
For what? For weaving?

BLEPYRUS:
                    No, for governing.

PRAXAGORA:
What will we govern?

BLEPYRUS:
                    All affairs of state.   630

(The Neighbor enters from this house through a stage
door and stands in the background, listening.)

PRAXAGORA:
From here on out, by Aphrodite, Athens
will be a happy place.

BLEPYRUS:
                    And why is that?

PRAXAGORA:
A lot of reasons. Henceforth nobody
will dare commit atrocities; nobody
will bear false witness; nobody will profit
off informing on a neighbor—

BLEPYRUS:
                    Wait!
By everything that's holy, do you mean
to strip me of my daily bread?

NEIGHBOR: *(cutting in on the conversation and moving out of the background)*
                    Excuse me—
let the lady speak.

PRAXAGORA:
> . . . and nobody
will break-and-enter; nobody will envy   640
other people; no more wearing rags;
no more poverty, and no more violence;
and no more dragging people into court.

NEIGHBOR:
That sounds just great—if only it were true.

PRAXAGORA:
I will convince you. You will be my witness,
and this man

> *(pointing to Blepyrus)*

> will be left without objections.

CHORUS: *(to Praxagora)*
> Now is the time to use
> your practical intelligence,
> to waken the savvy mind that knows
> how best to fight for friends.   650

> It's for the good of everyone
> if an inspiring plan
> to improve the lives of citizens
> leaps from your tongue.
> > Now is the time
> to show what brains can do.
> We need a beneficial scheme.
> Fully describe it, making sure
> none of it has been done before:
> the audience hates to watch the same
> old stuff passed off as new.   660

CHORUS LEADER:
Let there be no delaying. Put your plan in action right away.
Swift execution—that is what the audience enjoys the most.

PRAXAGORA:
I feel the changes I will make will be improvements. All I fear
is that the audience members will refuse to "mine new veins of silver"°
and stick too much to worn-out, backward-looking ways of doing things.

BLEPYRUS:
Don't worry—they will "mine new veins." The guiding principles in Athens
are loving change and disregarding all that is traditional.°

PRAXAGORA:
Let no one cut me off and start repudiating me before
he hears and fully understands just what I am proposing to him.
Here's what I say: that every person have a share in everything   670
and there be no more public property. Henceforth there will be no more
rich and poor, no more of one man owning lots and lots of acres
while another lacks sufficient land for his own grave; no more
of one man having slaves in great abundance, while another lacks
even a lone attendant. No, what I propose is that henceforth
there be identical conditions of existence for us all.

BLEPYRUS:
How do you mean "for all"?

PRAXAGORA:
                              You'd want to eat manure before I do.

BLEPYRUS:
Oh, won't manure be shared as well?

PRAXAGORA:
                              No, no, you cut me off too soon.
This is what I have tried to tell you: First off, I will make all land,

all money, all that any person owns, collective property.   680
By proper management, frugality and due consideration,
we all will live off this collective wealth.

BLEPYRUS:

But what about the man
who has no land, but only gold and silver coins, the inconspicuous
kind of wealth?

PRAXAGORA:

He must present them to the common fund or else
be sentenced as a perjurer.

BLEPYRUS:

That's how he got them in the first place.

PRAXAGORA:

Money will not be useful to him, anyway.

BLEPYRUS:

And why is that?

PRAXAGORA:

Nobody will be doing anything out of a desperate lack.
Everyone will have everything he needs: bread, salted fish, wheat cakes,
wine, clothing, garlands, chickpeas. What would be the benefit to him
of *not* surrendering his coins? If you can find one, let me know.   690

BLEPYRUS:

Even right now, though, isn't it the biggest thieves who have the money?

PRAXAGORA:

My friend, that was before, when we were living under backward customs.
Now that we will be taking all we need out of a common fund,
where is his stake in *not* contributing his coins?

BLEPYRUS:

Alright, then, say
he sees a prostitute he wants to screw. He'll get to take her price
out of the common fund and have the commonly desired pleasure
of screwing her?

PRAXAGORA:

No, he'll be able to have sex with her for free.
My plan is all the women will belong to all the men in common
both for screwing and for making babies, as each man might wish.

BLEPYRUS:

How will this work, since every male will hurry to the prettiest female   700
and want to fuck her?

PRAXAGORA:

All the most flat-nosed and unattractive females
will stand beside the cute ones. If a male wants to enjoy the latter,
he first must screw an ugly one.

BLEPYRUS:

But what about us older men?
If we must screw the foul ones first, our cocks will fail before they reach
what you described.

PRAXAGORA:

That's not a problem, since the women won't be fighting
about you. Don't you worry, they won't fight.

BLEPYRUS:

About what, though?

PRAXAGORA:

About
not getting to have sex with you. They don't want sex with you already.

BLEPYRUS:

That works out well for women, since, according to your scheme, no woman's
hole will be left unbunged. But what about us menfolk? All the women
will shun the ugly and pursue the handsome.

PRAXAGORA:

That's why the ugly men   710
will tail the handsome after dinner and observe them out in public,
since it will be illegal for the tall attractive ones to sleep
with women who have not first shared their favors with a shrimp or toad.

BLEPYRUS:

So now Lysicrates's nose° will be as good as shapely ones!

PRAXAGORA:

That's right! This is a democratic policy, and everyone
will laugh at reputable fellows with their fancy signet rings
when someone wearing big clodhoppers tells them, "Step aside
and wait your turn; I'll give you sloppy seconds."

BLEPYRUS:

If we live that way,
how will a man be able to identify which kids are his?

PRAXAGORA:

He won't. The children will consider all the older males their fathers.   720

BLEPYRUS:

They will punctiliously strangle all the old men, one by one,
since even now, when sons know who their fathers are, they strangle them.
Imagine what will happen when the fathers are unknown! The young
will just start shitting on their elders, won't they?

PRAXAGORA:

No, the others present
will stop the violence. In the past, when someone saw an old man beaten,
he wouldn't interfere because it wasn't any of his business.

Now everyone will fear the person being beaten is his father
and battle the assailants.

BLEPYRUS:

                    What you say is not completely crazy,
but it would be just awful if Leucolophas and Epicurus°
came up and called me father.

PRAXAGORA:

                         Still, it would be far, far worse if . . .

BLEPYRUS:

                                                      What?   730

PRAXAGORA:

. . . if Aristyllus° hugged you and addressed you as his dear ol' dad.

BLEPYRUS:

I'd make him howl for it.

PRAXAGORA:

                    You'd reek of mint if he came up and kissed you.°
But he was born before the law was passed, so there's no need to fear
that he will do it.

BLEPYRUS:

                    That would be disgusting. Here's another question:
Who will till the soil?

PRAXAGORA:

                    The slaves will do it. All you'll have to do
is put on scent and go to dinner when the shadow of the sundial
grows to ten feet long.

BLEPYRUS:

                    But tell me this: From where will we get clothing?

PRAXAGORA:

Your current clothes will do at first, and later we will weave you others.

BLEPYRUS:

Another question: If the magistrates impose a fine on someone,
how will he pay it? From the public coffers? That would not be right.   740

PRAXAGORA:

There won't be any lawsuits.

BLEPYRUS:

                              This decision will destroy you.

PRAXAGORA:

                                                            Yes,
it may, of course; but why should there be any lawsuits in the first place?

BLEPYRUS:

For many reasons. First, for when a borrower denies his debt.

PRAXAGORA:

Where would the lender get the funds to lend, if all is held in common?
He'd have to steal it from the state and then would clearly be a thief.

BLEPYRUS:

A clever answer! Tell me this, though: say some men are walking home,
drunk, from a feast and beat somebody up. How would they pay their fine?
I think I've got you this time.

PRAXAGORA:

                              No. Their food allowance would be docked.
Punished with hunger once, they wouldn't misbehave like that again.

BLEPYRUS:

Will no one be a thief?

PRAXAGORA:

                    How can a man steal what he has a share in?   750

BLEPYRUS:
So no more muggings late at night?

NEIGHBOR:
                              Not if you sleep at home.

PRAXAGORA:
                                                  Not even
if you go out like you did in the past. All will be satisfied
with what they have. If someone tries to steal your cloak, you'll let him take it.
Why fight to keep it? You can go and get a cloak at least as good
out of the common fund.

BLEPYRUS:
                    And gambling—men won't gamble anymore?

PRAXAGORA:
What would they gamble for?

BLEPYRUS:
                        And what will be our quality of life?

PRAXAGORA:
The same for everyone. I plan to make this polity one household
by breaking down the walls, so everyone can enter every space.

BLEPYRUS:
Where will you serve up dinner?

PRAXAGORA:
                          In the law courts and the colonnades—
I'll make them into dining rooms.

BLEPYRUS:
                        And what about the podiums?° 760

PRAXAGORA:

They'll serve as cupboards for the bowls and pitchers and provide
places where children can recite poems about bold warriors
and cowards, too, to make the cowards too ashamed to join the meal.

BLEPYRUS:

How charming! And the ballot boxes, what will they be turned into?

PRAXAGORA:

They'll stand beside Harmodius's statue in the market,
and everyone will draw a ticket from them till they all have letters
and head off happy to whatever dining hall they've been assigned.
A herald will direct all those who drew the letter S to go
have dinner in the Stoa Basileus, those who drew an N
to go next door, and those who chanced to get a G to head   770
into the storehouse.

BLEPYRUS:
                            Is that G for "gulp"?

PRAXAGORA:
                                No, as in "get food there."

BLEPYRUS:

But what about those citizens who miss their chance to draw a ticket
for dinner? Will the other ones, the lucky, drive them from the table?

PRAXAGORA:

But that will never happen. Every man will have
all that he needs to live and more. You all will leave
the feast, drunk, torch in hand and with a garland on.
Women will run to meet you in the streets and say,
"Come to my house, you'll find a gorgeous young girl there."
Another from a window on the second floor
will shout at you: "I have a young, fine, fair-skinned one.   780
Except, before you touch her, you must sleep with me."

And all the ugly men, trailing the handsome ones,
will mock them with "Hey, where do you all think you're going?
It doesn't matter. You'll be getting nothing anyway.
The law demands that we, the snub-nosed and the plain,
first fuck the women.
                            You can pass the downtime screwing
yourselves, with both hands on your twin-nut-dangling branch."

Now, tell me, do you like what I've described?

BLEPYRUS:
Yes, very much so.

PRAXAGORA:
                            Good. Then I'll be heading
off to the market to receive the goods   790
as they come in and to select a woman
graced with a powerful voice to be my herald.
I, as the woman voted into power,
have many new responsibilities.
I must arrange for the communal meals
so that you may enjoy the first of them
this very day.

BLEPYRUS:
                            The feasts will start today?

PRAXAGORA:
This very day. And then the prostitutes—
I want to put them out of business.

BLEPYRUS:
                            Why?

NEIGHBOR: (gesturing to the Chorus)
That's obvious. So that these women here   800
can have the produce of the young men's plowing.

PRAXAGORA:
Also, female slaves may now no longer
put makeup on and plunder Aphrodite
from freeborn women. Let those hussies trim
their bushes like a tidy swatch of wool
and sleep with slaves.

BLEPYRUS: *(to Praxagora)*
                        I want to walk beside you
so that the town will see me and exclaim,
"Look at the husband of our Great Protectress!"

NEIGHBOR:
And me, if I am going to bring my goods
down to the marketplace, I'd better get them   810
in order here and take an inventory.

> *(Praxagora exits to the market, stage left, with Blepyrus behind*
> *her. The Neighbor exits into his house through a stage door.)*

> *(The Neighbor enters from his house. The slaves Sicon*
> *and Parmenon enter behind him in a parody of a ritual*
> *procession. They are carrying a sieve, a cooking pot, a table*
> *with a pitcher on it, a grinder, tripods, and a tray.)*

NEIGHBOR:
O gorgeous sieve, finest of my possessions,
you who have strained so many sacks of flour
for me, come gorgeously out here and be
the basket-carrier in the procession
of all my things. Where is the sunshade holder?
Come out here, cooking pot. By Zeus, you're black,
as if you boiled whatever compound dyes
Lysicrates's hair.° You stand right there,
beside the sieve. Come out here, also, table,   820
and, like a pitcher-bearer, bring the pitcher
along with you. You, grinder, who have often
roused me with your aubade for the Assembly

at an ungodly hour, come out and be
musician for us.

(to Sicon)

You there with the tray,
come here and bring the honeycombs. Make sure
you lay the olive branches there beside them.
And bring the tripods and the oil flask, too.
Now, all you little pots, come marching in!

(A Man enters, stage left.)

MAN:
Why would I give up all of my possessions?   830
I'd be a wretched moron if I did.
So, never! Not at least until I duly
scrutinize the situation first.
Never because of words alone will I
give up the produce of my sweat and thrift,
not till I understand how things will go.

(to the Neighbor)

Hey, buddy, why is all this stuff out here?
What, do you plan on moving it somewhere?
Placing the lot of it in pawn?

NEIGHBOR:
                    Nope.

MAN:
Why have you stood it rank on rank? To march it   840
over to Hieron the auctioneer?°

NEIGHBOR:
Uh-uh. I'm going to turn it in to Athens
down in the square, just as the law requires.

MAN:

You're really going to turn it in?

NEIGHBOR:

I am.

MAN:

By Zeus the Savior, you're a wretch indeed.

NEIGHBOR:

How's that?

MAN:

"How's that?" Quite easily.

NEIGHBOR:

Why's that?

Isn't it proper to obey the laws?

MAN:

What laws, you chump?

NEIGHBOR:

The laws that have been passed.

MAN:

"The laws that have been passed"? You are a fool.

NEIGHBOR:

A fool?

MAN:

How not? You are the biggest sucker   850

ever.

NEIGHBOR:

Because I do what I'm supposed to?

MAN:

Oh, so you think a prudent man should do
what he's supposed to do?

NEIGHBOR:

                    That most of all.

MAN:

Only a moron would behave that way.

NEIGHBOR:

You won't be turning over your possessions?

MAN:

I plan to wait until I see what others
decide to do.

NEIGHBOR:

              What will they do besides
get ready to surrender their possessions?

MAN:

Yeah, I will believe it when I see it.

NEIGHBOR:

People are saying that's what they will do.

860

MAN:

Of course they *say* it.

NEIGHBOR:

               They are swearing they'll
surrender all their goods.

MAN:

            Of course they *swear* it.

NEIGHBOR:
Your total skepticism's killing me!

MAN:
Of course they're *skeptical* of it.

NEIGHBOR:

                                God damn you!

MAN:
Of course they say "*God damn* it." Do you truly
believe that anyone who has a brain
will hand their goods in? It's un-Athenian.

NEIGHBOR:
So we should only take things?

MAN:

                                Yes, we should.
That's what the gods do too. Their statues' hands
show clearly what they're after. When we ask them   870
to give us blessings, they just stand there holding
their hands out, palm up, ready to receive,
not give.

NEIGHBOR:
              Hey, let me do my work, you crank.
All this stuff needs packing. Where's my rope?

MAN:
You're really going to give up your possessions?

NEIGHBOR:
Yes, I am. I'm just about to pack
this pair of tripods.

MAN:

You are pretty foolish
not to wait and see what others do
and then at last . . .

NEIGHBOR:

Do what?

MAN:

. . . keep waiting longer
and drag your feet

NEIGHBOR:

But why would I do that? 880

MAN:

Because, you moron, if an earthquake hits,
or lightning strikes, or if a black cat runs
across the street, the women will desist
from taking all our stuff.

NEIGHBOR:

It would be awful
if there were no place I could turn my stuff in.

MAN:

"No place" for your deposit? Don't you worry.
Even if you wait a day, they'll still
be eager to receive your property.

NEIGHBOR:
What do you mean?

MAN:

I know the sort of people
who quickly raise their hands to vote for something 890
can change their minds and scrap what they decided.

NEIGHBOR:
People will bring their stuff in. Trust me, buddy.

MAN:
What if they don't?

NEIGHBOR:
Don't worry. People will.

MAN:
What if they don't?

NEIGHBOR:
We'll make them.

MAN:
What if there
are more of them than you?

NEIGHBOR:
I'll leave them be
and simply walk away.

MAN:
What if they sell
your stuff for profit?

NEIGHBOR:
I wish you would explode!

MAN:
And what if I exploded?

NEIGHBOR:
That would be great.

MAN:

Hey, are you really going to give your stuff up?

NEIGHBOR:

I am, because I see my neighbors turning   900
their stuff in, too.

MAN:

                    Yeah, sure, Antisthenes°
will hand his goods in, though it would be better
if he took a thirty-day-straight shit.

NEIGHBOR:

Aw, go to hell!

MAN:

                    Hey, will Callimachus
the chorus master° hand in anything?

NEIGHBOR:

Far more than Callias.°

MAN: (pointing to the Neighbor and addressing the audience)
                    This sucker's gonna
lose all that he possesses.

NEIGHBOR:

                    You just keep
exaggerating.

MAN:

                    How, exaggerating?
As if I haven't seen such laws before!
Don't you recall the mandate that they passed   910
regarding salt?°

NEIGHBOR:

            I do.

MAN:
                    Don't you remember
when we voted out those copper coins?°

NEIGHBOR:
I do. Those things proved terrible for me,
because, when I had sold my grapes, I stuffed
my whole mouth full of them and went to market
to buy some barley. Then when I held out
my little bag of coins, the herald blared,
"Nobody's taking copper anymore;
We're on to silver now."

MAN:
                    Didn't we all
just lately vow we'd raise five hundred talents   920
for Athens off the tax Heurippides°
had levied? Oh my, yes, Heurippides
was made of gold. But, when we looked more closely,
we saw his tax was just the same old story
and not enough for what we needed. Then,
oh my, Heurippides was tarred and feathered.

NEIGHBOR:
Buddy, it's not the same. Back then we men
were ruling; now the women are in charge.

MAN:
And I will watch them closely, by Poseidon,
or else they'll piss on me.

NEIGHBOR:
                    You're talking nonsense.   930
I just don't understand.

                    (to Parmenon)

            Boy, lift this baggage!

(The Female Herald enters from the market, stage left.)

FEMALE HERALD:
Here is a message to the citizens:
Proceed directly to our Great Protectress
so that you can all draw lots, and chance
can tell you where you will enjoy your dinner.
The tables have been set and plied with goodies.
The couches have been made with coverlets
and pillows. Slaves are mixing wine in bowls
and perfume girls are standing in a line.
Fillets of fish are being grilled, and rabbits   940
are being spitted, rolls are in the oven,
garlands are being woven, and treats are roasting.
Little girls are boiling pots of soup.
Smoeus° is with them in his riding suit,
licking their bowls. And old Geron° is there
wearing a nice new cloak and fancy shoes.
His boots and rags abandoned, he is telling
jokes to a young man. Come on! Come, partake!
A slave is standing by to serve you bread.
You only have to open up your mouths!   950

(The Female Herald exits, stage left.)

MAN:
Alright, then, let's get going! Why am I
still standing here, when Athens has approved
a spread as rich as that?

NEIGHBOR:
                         Where are you going?
You haven't turned in your possessions yet.

MAN:
To dinner.

NEIGHBOR:

    Not you. If they have a brain,
those ladies won't allow you in to dine
until you hand your whole stock in.

MAN:

                    I will.

NEIGHBOR:

When, though?

MAN:

          I won't be the problem, pal.

NEIGHBOR:

What does that mean?

MAN:

            That other men will surely
hand in their possessions after me.   960

NEIGHBOR:

And you will go to dinner all the same?

MAN:

What else can I do? All conscientious
citizens must work to serve the city
as best they can.

NEIGHBOR:

          What if they shut you out?

MAN:

I'll charge on in.

NEIGHBOR:

          What if they whip you back?

MAN:
I'll sue them.

NEIGHBOR:
                And what if they laugh your case off?

MAN:
I'll stand beside the door . . .

NEIGHBOR:
                        And do what? Tell me.

MAN:
. . . and grab the food that they are carting in.

NEIGHBOR:
Then wait and try to sneak in after me.

                (to Sicon and Parmenon)

Hey, Sicon, and you, Parmenon, it's time   970
for us to start to carry out my stuff.

MAN:
Here, let me help you out with that.

NEIGHBOR:
                                No way!
I won't have you pretending that my stuff
belongs to you when I surrender it
to our Protectress.

                (The Neighbor exits, stage left, with Sicon and
                Parmenon, carrying all his possessions.)

MAN:
                What I need's a plan
that will allow me both to keep my things

and have a share of all the delicacies
they are preparing for the people of Athens.
Aha! I think I've got it! I must go in
to dine with them, and I must go there quick!   980

(The Man exits, stage left. The First Old Woman
enters through a stage door, followed by the Piper.
The Girl enters through the other stage door.)

FIRST OLD WOMAN:
Why aren't the men here yet? It's getting late.
Well, here I am, with makeup plastered on me,
posing in a saffron-colored dress,
whistling a little ditty to myself
and acting girl-like so that I can snatch
some fellow as he passes. Muses, come
into my lips,° discover for me some
risqué Ionian tune.°

GIRL:
                      You've beaten me,
you moldy hag. You are the first one out here
looking for boys. You thought that, with me absent,   990
you could pillage an unguarded vineyard
by leading on the young men with your song.
If you start singing, I will sing as well.
And, even if this irritates the audience,
still there is something charming in it, comic.

FIRST OLD WOMAN: (gesturing to her butt)
Complain to this and then get out of here.

(to the Piper)

O piper darling, take your pipes in hand
and play a ditty worthy of us both.
            Whoever wants to learn what pleasure is
            should come inside and sleep with me.   1000

Maturer women understand finesse
better than girls do. No one knows
the art of pleasuring a lover-boy
so well as I. Mademoiselles
fuck once and fly away to someone else.

GIRL:

Don't envy us, the younger girls, because
softness is living in our lissome thighs
and blooming on our breasts. You, horrid crone,
all trimmed and tweezed and plastered over with
foundation, are the darling honeybun   1010
of Death.

FIRST OLD WOMAN:

I pray your twat falls off and, when you ache
for pleasure, you can't find a couch.
I hope that, when you want to smooch
in bed, you find you have embraced a snake.

GIRL:

Alas, poor me, boo-hoo, boo-hoo!
My boyfriend's late. I'm here alone.
I needn't tell you what I'll do,
now that my mother's gone.

(calling inside the house)

O nurse, O nurse, bring in   1020
Sir Dildo. I'll use him instead.
A thousand blessings on your head.

FIRST OLD WOMAN:

So, you wretch,
you have an itch
for the Ionian tool.°

I bet that you
are also inclined
to suck off mankind
the way that all
the Methymnan women do.°   1030

GIRL:

I'll never let you walk off with
my toys, my boys.
I'll never let you spoil my youth
or steal my time.

FIRST OLD WOMAN:
Sing any song you want and just keep looking,
alley cat—no man will visit you
before he stops and visits me.

GIRL:
                              At least
not for my funeral. Hey, that's a fresh one.

FIRST OLD WOMAN:
No it isn't.

GIRL:
              Who could tell a crone
a joke she hasn't heard?

FIRST OLD WOMAN:
                        It's not my age   1040
that's going to make you ache.

GIRL:
                        What will it be, then?
Your rouge? Your war paint?

FIRST OLD WOMAN:
                        Why do you keep talking?

GIRL:
Why do you keep looking out your door?

FIRST OLD WOMAN:
Me, I'm singing for Epigenes,
my lover.

GIRL:
            The only lover you'll be getting
is geriatric Geres.

FIRST OLD WOMAN:
                    Wait and see—
he'll soon be here and come inside my house.

            (Epigenes enters, stage left, carrying a torch.)

Here he is now.

GIRL:
                    Not wanting anything
from you, old bag.

FIRST OLD WOMAN:
                    Not so, not so, you rail.

GIRL:
The man himself will show which one he wants.   1050
I'm heading in.

            (The Girl exits through a stage door.)

FIRST OLD WOMAN:
                    Me, too, so that you know
how much more confident I am than you.

EPIGENES:

>   I wish that I could only do
>   the young and pretty one
>   and weren't required first to screw
>   a flat-nose or a crone.
>   This is intolerable for a freeborn man.

FIRST OLD WOMAN: *(to Epigenes, who does not hear or see her)*
Oh, you'll be sorry if you fuck that girl.
This is no longer Charixena's hour.°
You must obey the law, because we are   1060
now living under a democracy.

> *(to the audience)*

But I'll go in and wait for his decision.

> *(The First Old Woman exits into her house through a stage door.)*

EPIGENES:
I pray, by all the gods, that I may find
the girl alone. It's her I've come to see
now that I'm drunk, her that I've long desired.

> *(The Girl opens a window in the wooden backdrop.)*

GIRL: *(to the audience)*
Ha, I've completely fooled that damn old lady.
She went in thinking I would stay gone, too.
He's here at last, the boy we were discussing.

> *(to Epigenes)*

>   Come here, my dear, come here
>   and vow to be my paramour   1070
>   until the break of day.
>   Desire has set me reeling

over your mass of curly hair.
A strange new feeling
for you will not stop wearing me away.

Only you can release me, Eros, God
of Love. I beg, I plead:
drive this boy into my bed.

EPIGENES:

Come here, my dear, come here.
Run down and open up the door.   1080
If you won't let me in,
I'll pass out on your stoop.
I want to slap your derriere.
I want to languish in your lap.
Why, Cypris, are you driving me insane?

Only you can release me, Eros, God
of Love. I beg, I plead:
Drive this girl into my bed.

Words cannot express
just how excessive is the pain   1090
I'm feeling for you. Lovely one,
I beg of you, oh please, oh please
receive me, open up your door.
It's you I'm aching for.

Well-made golden prize,
Cyprian snippet, O you Muses'
sweet bee, you nursling of the Graces,
O paragon of pleasure, please
receive me, open up your door.
It's you I'm aching for.   1100

(*The Girl closes the window. Epigenes knocks on the door to the
Girl's house. The First Old Woman enters from her house next door.*)

FIRST OLD WOMAN:
Hey, why are you knocking? Are you here for me?

EPIGENES:
No way.

FIRST OLD WOMAN:
        You sure were banging on my door.

EPIGENES:
I'd sooner die.

FIRST OLD WOMAN:
                Who have you come here after,
torch in hand?

EPIGENES:
            I'm here for Master Bates.

FIRST OLD WOMAN:
Who's that?

EPIGENES:
        Not Mr. Fuck, the one you seem
to be expecting.

FIRST OLD WOMAN: (grabbing Epigenes)
            Oh, you're Mr. Fuck,
whether you want to be or not.

EPIGENES:
                    But we
are entering no hearings on the docket
for cases over sixty at this time.
We've pushed them back until some future date.   1110
Right now we're trying cases under twenty.°

FIRST OLD WOMAN:
That is the way things used to be, my sweet.
The law now states you first must "enter" me.

EPIGENES:
It's dealer's choice here in this game of chance.

FIRST OLD WOMAN:
Those weren't the rules back when you ate your dinner.

EPIGENES:
Sorry, but I don't understand what you
are saying. I must knock on this door here.

FIRST OLD WOMAN: *(gesturing to her crotch)*
Not until you knock on this door here.

EPIGENES:
We aren't looking for a knocker now.

FIRST OLD WOMAN:
I know you love me. You were merely startled   1120
by finding me outdoors. Now give me kisses.

EPIGENES:
No ma'am. I'm far too frightened of your boyfriend.

FIRST OLD WOMAN:
Who's that?

EPIGENES:
                The most prolific of the painters.

FIRST OLD WOMAN:
Who?

EPIGENES:

 The one who paints on urns for corpses.
You'd best go in before he sees you lurking.

FIRST OLD WOMAN:

Oh I know, I know what you desire.

EPIGENES:

And I, what *you* desire.

FIRST OLD WOMAN:

      By Aphrodite,
I drew your name by luck out of the jar
and I won't give you up.

EPIGENES:

     You crazy hag.

FIRST OLD WOMAN:

Stop yammering. I'm taking you to bed.   1130

EPIGENES: *(to the audience)*
Why should we purchase tongs to gather buckets
out of a well, when we could send a grasping
crone like this one down and have her snatch them?

FIRST OLD WOMAN:

Quit teasing, dear, and come inside my house.

EPIGENES:

I won't, unless you've paid the city of Athens
the service tax for me.

FIRST OLD WOMAN:

      Oh yes you will.
I love sleeping with nice young men.

EPIGENES:

                              I loathe
the thought of sleeping with a hag like you.
I never will consent.

FIRST OLD WOMAN: *(holding up a scroll)*
                     This will compel you.

EPIGENES:
What's that?

FIRST OLD WOMAN:
            A law that says you have to come   1140
inside my house.

EPIGENES:
               Read it from start from finish.

FIRST OLD WOMAN: *(unrolling the scroll and reading from it)*
I will: "It is the law that, if a young man
wants a girl his age, he may not bang her
until he fucks an old hag first. If he should,
in his desire for the girl, refuse
the prior coitus, then the hag may grab
the young man's pecker with impunity
and pull him off with her."

EPIGENES:
              Oh no, it seems
today I'm going to have to play Procrustes.°

FIRST OLD WOMAN:
The laws must be obeyed.

EPIGENES:
                What if a friend   1150
or neighbor comes and offers bail for me?

FIRST OLD WOMAN:

Men are not permitted to transact
business of greater value than a bushel.°

EPIGENES:

Can't I object?

FIRST OLD WOMAN:

            You won't be wriggling free.

EPIGENES:

What if I get a businessman's exemption?°

FIRST OLD WOMAN:

You'd regret it!

EPIGENES:

            So what can I do?

FIRST OLD WOMAN:

Come into my place.

EPIGENES:

            Must I, really?

FIRST OLD WOMAN:

The mandate has the strength of Diomedes!°

EPIGENES:

Well, strew the funeral bed with marjoram,
break off four boughs and lay them underneath it.   1160
Drape the bed with ribbons, then set urns
on either side and in the doorway place
a water jug.°

FIRST OLD WOMAN:

            When we are done, you'll end up
buying me a wedding garland too!

EPIGENES:
I will, if I can find a garland made
of wax—the kind they use in funerals—
because I bet you will be breaking down
real fast in there.

(The Girl enters from her house through a stage door.)

GIRL:
Where are you taking him?

FIRST OLD WOMAN:
I'm bringing my own man back to my house.

GIRL:
That wouldn't be a prudent thing to do.   1170
Young as he is, he's not the proper age
to go to bed with you. You're much more like
his mother than his wife. If you begin
to live by this new law, you will be making
all the men of Athens Oedipuses.°

FIRST OLD WOMAN: (to the Girl)
You filthy whore, you're jealous. That's why you
came up with that. I'll get you back for it.

(The First Old Woman exits through a stage door.)

EPIGENES: (to the Girl)
By Zeus the Savior, you have earned my thanks,
sweetheart, for driving off that foul old thing.
Tonight, as compensation, I will slip you   1180
a great big, meaty favor in return.

(A Second Old Woman enters, stage right.)

SECOND OLD WOMAN: *(to the Girl, while taking hold of Epigenes)*
Stop that. By dragging off this gentleman,
you are committing an illegal act.
He first must sleep with me—that's what the law says.

EPIGENES:
Oh no! What hole has loosed you on the world,
you damned and horrid thing? This monster looks
even more ugly than the one before.

SECOND OLD WOMAN:
Come here, now.

EPIGENES: *(to the Girl)*
            Please don't let her drag me off!

(The Girl exits into her house through a stage door.)

SECOND OLD WOMAN:
It is the law, not me, that drags you off.

EPIGENES:
Empusa° does, her face a big blood-blister.   1190

SECOND OLD WOMAN:
Come here, you mama's boy, and don't talk back.

EPIGENES:
Please let me go and take a dump first, then
I'll steel myself for sex. If you don't let me,
you'll have to see me be defiled with terror—
that is, I'll have to drop a load right here.

SECOND OLD WOMAN:
Be strong; keep moving. You can poop inside.

EPIGENES:
I fear that I'll do more than poop in there.

(gesturing toward his testicles)

I'll leave two priceless sureties with you
if you just let me go and do my business.

SECOND OLD WOMAN:
Stop making trouble for me.

(A Third Old Woman enters, stage left.)

THIRD OLD WOMAN: *(to Epigenes)*
     Hey you there,   1200
where are you going with that woman?

EPIGENES:
        "Going"?
I'm being dragged. Whoever you might be,
bless you if you, instead of merely watching,
step in and help me in my hour of need.

(seeing the Third Old Woman for the first time)

Great Heracles! Great Pan! O Corybantes!°
O Dioscuri!° Here's another creature
more repulsive than this other one.
Please, someone tell me what this monster is.
An ape in makeup? An abomination
out of the underworld?

THIRD OLD WOMAN:
      Stop cracking jokes   1210
and come along.

SECOND OLD WOMAN:
    Oh no, you come with me.

THIRD OLD WOMAN:
I'll never let you go.

SECOND OLD WOMAN:

No, never, never.

EPIGENES:

You're tearing me in half, you wretched beasts!

SECOND OLD WOMAN:

You're coming back to my house—it's the law!

THIRD OLD WOMAN:

Not if an even fouler hag shows up!

EPIGENES:

Tell me, how will I screw the pretty one
after you two have utterly destroyed me?

THIRD OLD WOMAN:

That's not my problem.

(making an obscene gesture)

You just go *like this*.

EPIGENES:

Which of the two of you must I fuck first
so that I can be free?

THIRD OLD WOMAN:

Me first, of course.   1220

Come on.

EPIGENES:

Then make this other one release me.

SECOND OLD WOMAN:

No way! Come here with me!

EPIGENES:

If she lets go.

THIRD OLD WOMAN:
I never will release you.

SECOND OLD WOMAN:

Me, too: never.

EPIGENES:
You two would make harsh boatmen on a ferry.

SECOND OLD WOMAN:
Why's that?

EPIGENES:

You'd pull your passengers to pieces.

THIRD OLD WOMAN:
Shush, now, and come along.

SECOND OLD WOMAN:

No, come with me!

EPIGENES:
This here is like Cannonus's decree.°
I must appear in court in chains and fuck
the prosecution. How, then, will my oar
drive on two boats at once?

SECOND OLD WOMAN:

You'll do just fine

once you have eaten up a whole potful
of potent bulbs.°

1230

EPIGENES:

Oh no, I'm done for, now!

The creature won't stop dragging me away.

THIRD OLD WOMAN:
You won't escape like that. I will be here
mere steps behind you.

EPIGENES:
                        Help me, gods. I'd rather
fight with a single evil than with two.

THIRD OLD WOMAN:
Whether you will or no, you're coming in.

EPIGENES: *(to the audience)*
I'm three times ruined if I have to fuck
a hag all night and then all day and then,
when I have gotten free of her, start in   1240
again on a decrepit toad who has
a funeral urn just waiting by her jaws.
Am I not cursed? By Zeus the Savior, yes,
I am a heavy-fated, an unlucky man,
because I will be locked up with these beasts!
Well, if the worst befalls me while I'm sailing
into port atop these fallen women,
bury me right there in the channel's mouth.

(gesturing to the Third Old Woman)

And this one—cover her alive in tar
all over, dip her feet in molten lead   1250
up to the ankles, then erect her over
my grave to be my funerary urn.

*(The Second and Third Old Woman drag Epigenes off
through a stage door. A Slave Girl enters, stage left.)*

SLAVE GIRL:
Blest citizens, and happy land, and her,
our most blest leader, and you women standing
before our door, and all you next-door neighbors

and people from the neighborhood, and me
as well, a maid whose hair has been anointed
with the finest perfumes. Praise Lord Zeus!

But all such scents are nothing when compared
with those fine little jugs of Thasian wine.   1260
It stays inside your head a long time after
the perfumes have forsaken their bouquets
and wholly vanished. Yes, this wine's the best
by far, the gods be praised! Serve it unmixed,
and, if you pick the jar that smells the richest,
it will keep you happy all night long.

But women, tell me please where is my master—
um, I mean the husband of my mistress?

CHORUS LEADER:
Just wait right here and he should come along.

(Blepyrus enters stage right.)

Look, here he is now, heading out to dinner.   1270

SLAVE GIRL: *(to Blepyrus)*
How happy you must be, my thrice-blest master!

BLEPYRUS:
Me?

SLAVE GIRL:
    Yes you. The happiest man of all.
Who could be luckier? More than thirty thousand
people in this town, and you alone
have not had dinner.

CHORUS LEADER: *(with irony)*
                Yes, you have described him
as quite a lucky gentleman indeed.

SLAVE GIRL:
Where are you headed now?

BLEPYRUS:
                         I'm off to dine.

SLAVE GIRL:
You'll be the latest to arrive by far.
Nevertheless, your wife instructed me
to come and get you and escort you there,   1280
along with all these girls. There's still some Chian
wine left, and lots of other tasty things,
so come on, hurry up.

                    (to the audience)

                    You audience members,
if you, by chance, have kindly thoughts, you judges,
if you still are watching this production,
come along. We're providing everything!

BLEPYRUS:
Why don't you be a generous hostess, welcome
everyone in and shut out no one? Yes,
freely invite the senior citizen,
the youth, the child. A dinner has been laid   1290
for each and every one of them, and all
they have to do is hurry to their homes.
I'm heading off to dine right now. Thank goodness
I've got this little torch right here to guide me.

CHORUS LEADER: *(to Blepyrus)*
Why are you just standing there? Come, now,
why not collect these girls and get a move on?
While you are heading down to dinner, I
will sing a ditty as an appetizer.

(to the audience)

Oh, but I want to share some humble little
bits of advice with all the judges first: 1300

Let the wiser ones remember what is wise in this and vote for me.
Let the ones who like to laugh remember all the jokes and vote for me.
Yes, it's nearly every one of you I ask to vote for me.°
Don't punish us because we drew the lot that made us go on first
but, keeping this entire production in your mind, don't break your oath:
Always be fair when voting on the choruses. Don't act like bad
prostitutes who remember only their most recent customers.

CHORUS: *(dancing)*
>   Dear ladies, come, make haste.
>   Let's all go to the feast
>   so we can have our share of it.   1310

(to Blepyrus)

>   Let the wild rhythms of Crete
>   put wild movement in your feet.

BLEPYRUS: *(dancing)*
>   I am. I am.

CHORUS:
>   You girls, make sure your light
>   steps, too, keep time.

>   Now there will be served, en masse,
>   limpet, saltfish, dogfish, shark,
>   mullets, sardines in pickle sauce,
>   rooster, crusted wagtail, lark,
>   thrush, blackbird, dove and slices   1320
>   of mulled-wine-marinated hare,
>   all drenched in oil and vinegar,
>   silphium, honey, all the spices.

> Now that you've heard about the feast,
> go grab a plate and raise some dust
> running to get your hands on pudding.

BLEPYRUS:

> Oh yeah, the town's already eating.

CHORUS:

> Lift up your feet, now, hey, hey, hey.
> We're off to eat, hurray!
> Hurray, this feels like victory!   1330
> Hurray! Hurray!

(Blepyrus, the Slave Girl, and the Chorus exit, dancing, stage left.)

NOTES

Clouds

8   *I can't even beat the help*: During the first few years of the Peloponnesian War, the Spartans annually invaded Attica, giving slaves the opportunity to desert to the enemy.

20   *the twentieth of the month*: Interest on a debt accumulated monthly in ancient Athens, and the months were shorter (lunar).

25   *twelve minas*: A large sum of money. The Attic mina was the equivalent of one hundred drachmas.

55-56   *the niece of Megacles / the son of Megacles*: Strepsiades, it seems, has taken a wife from the large and affluent family of the Alcmaeonidae.

57   *Coesyra*: Coesyra, a figure of Athenian folklore, is represented as a spoiled, wealthy woman.

62   *the Goddesses of Sex*: See note on "the Goddesses of Sex / at Colias," *Lysistrata*, lines 2–3.

73-74   *Xanthippus, / Charippus or Kallipides*: The word *hippos* means "horse" in ancient Greek. Strepsiades's aristocratic wife wants the word "horse" to be in their son's name.

110   *Thinkery*: The "Thinkery" is a fictional school in this play, though Socrates's student Plato did go on to found the Academy circa 387 BCE.

123   *Chaerephon*: Chaerephon and Socrates were close friends from youth (Plato, *Apology* 20e). In Aristophanes, Chaerephon is described as looking like a bat and Socrates as "wretched" for being shaggy-haired, barefoot, and poor.

129   *Leogoras's pheasants*: Leogoras was an aristocrat and friend of the leading statesman Pericles until the latter's death in 429 BCE. It seems Leogoras bred pheasants for show.

139   *obol*: In classical Athens, obols were coins made of silver, and six of them equaled a drachma.

142   *Horsemen*: The *Hippeis*, or Horsemen, constituted the second highest of the four Athenian social classes. With an income of at least three hundred medimnoi, they were able to buy and care for a war horse during military duty.

143   *by Demeter*: Demeter was the goddess of grain, and thus it is appropriate that Strepsiades swears "by Demeter" when he threatens to withhold food from Pheidippides and his horses.

158   *the deme Cicynna*: The location of the deme (district) of Athens is unknown, though con-

text suggests it was somewhere on the northern coast of Attica. We are to think of Strepsiades as living "way out in the country."

179   *Persian slippers*: Persian slippers were worn by Athenian women around the house.

208–209   *then went ... somebody's cloak*: The humor in the apparent punch line here has eluded scholars. Socrates, it seems, starts out by sprinkling ash instead of grain because he intends to give the students a lesson by writing geometric figures in the ash. He then puts a hook on a "skewer" and, instead of writing in the ash, uses it to steal someone's cloak at the wrestling school. Cloak-stealing was a common crime in ancient Athens.

210   *the famous Thales*: Thales, an early scientist and astronomer, was celebrated in folklore as a sage.

216   *Pylos*: The Spartans who were taken as prisoners of war on the island of Sphacteria, off Pylos, in the summer of 425 BCE remained imprisoned in Athens until the spring of 421 BCE. Apparently they were kept in an emaciated state.

244–245   *And here's Euboea ... beside it*: In 446 BCE the cities of Euboea revolted from Athenian control, and Pericles led a campaign that forced them to submit. We are to believe that Strepsiades (or at least his generation) served in that campaign.

288   *Iron coins like in Byzantium*: Byzantium used a system of iron coinage, unlike the other Greek states.

296   *I don't want to play Athamas*: Strepsiades is alluding to one of Sophocles's (non-extant) two plays called *Athamas*, in which the namesake Boeotian king is portrayed as about to be offered as a human sacrifice.

316   *Lake Maeotis ... Mimas*: Lake Maeotis is the contemporary Sea of Azov in Eastern Europe. It is connected by the Straight of Kerch to the Black Sea. Mimas is a mountain on the peninsula of Erythrae in modern Turkey.

338–339   *the fruitful country ... Cecrops*: This country is Athens, of which the goddess Pallas Athena was patroness and Cecrops was an autochthonous early king.

346   *the Bacchic rites*: This phrase refers to the City Dionysia, a festival in honor of Dionysus held in the spring (days 8–13 of the Athenian month Elaphebolium). Competitions for tragedy and comedy were part of the festival, so it is appropriate that it be mentioned here.

371   *Thurii prophets*: The Athenian colony of Thurii was founded in Magna Graecia (southern Italy) in 446 BCE. The foundation of cities was, it seems, the occasion of much divination. See the Oracle Collector with whom Peisthetaerus has to deal in *Birds*, lines 970–1003.

375–379   *the poets sing ... "thrush-bird cutlets"*: Strepsiades cites examples from dithyramb, a wild and ecstatic form of hymn dedicated to Dionysus. None of these quotations can be attributed to a poet with any certainty.

390   *the son of Xenophantes*: The "son of Xenophantes" is a certain Hieronymous, ridiculed elsewhere in Aristophanes for his hairiness. Hairiness may have been regarded as an indicator of pederastic tendencies.

391   *Simon*: Nothing more is known about this Simon.

395   *Cleonymus*: Cleonymus allegedly dropped his shield in battle and fled; see *Birds*, lines 310–311.

396   *Cleisthenes*: Cleisthenes is often ridiculed as an effeminate by Aristophanes.

402   *Prodicus*: The most famous intellectual of his day in Athens; see *Birds*, line 705.

429   *Panathenaea*: An annual festival celebrating the glory of Athens, held in mid-August. Every fourth year it was celebrated on a larger scale and involved athletic competitions.

443   *Simon, Theorus and Cleonymus*: For Simon and Cleonymus, see notes above, lines 391 and 395. Theorus is mocked as a parasite and flatterer in Aristophanic comedy.

445   *sacred Cape Sunium*: Cape Sunium, modern Sounion, is a headland at the southeastern tip of the Attic peninsula. It was considered sacred as the location of the Temple of Poseidon.

452   *Diasia*: An important festival in Athens held on the twenty-third of the month Anthesterion (during harvesttime for figs, grain, grapevines, and olives). In it offerings of placation and purification were given to Zeus Meilichios ("the Easily Entreated").

494   *a wiener*: "Wiener" here translates the word *chorde*, a sausage consisting of meat stuffed into intestine.

542   *Chaerephon*: See note on "Chaerephon," *Clouds*, line 123.

547   *Trophonius's cave*: After comparing Chaerephon to the living dead, Strepsiades goes on to compare the entrance to the Thinkery to a famous entrance to the underworld. Near Lebadeia in Boeotia was a cave where visitors would seek oracular responses from the hero Trophonius. These visitors would customarily placate the snakes in the cave with an offering of honey cake.

561   *Though I deserved . . . the contest*: Aristophanes is referring to the first version of *Clouds* presented in 423 BCE. This *parabasis* (address to the audience) belongs to the later, second version.

565   *the Nice Boy and the Faggot*: Characters in Aristophanes's first play *Banqueters*. Produced in 427 BCE, most likely at the Lenaea, it won second prize.

571   *Electra*: In Aeschylus's tragedy *Choephoroi* (first produced in 458 BCE), Electra goes to her father Agamemnon's tomb and finds corroboration that her brother Orestes has returned in a lock of hair like hers left at the tomb. In the same way, Aristophanes's play *Clouds* (the second version) goes in search of audience approval and finds it in their favorable reaction.

576   *a sleazy cordax*: A salacious dance associated with drunkenness and the comic chorus.

581–582   *I'd never try . . . or three times*: Aristophanes accuses his rivals of presenting the same material under different titles. Though he has revised *Clouds*, Aristophanes prides himself on presenting new ideas in each play.

584   *Cleon's paunch*: Aristophanes leveled a sustained and vicious attack on Cleon in his play *The Knights* (424 BCE).

586   *Hyperbolus*: Aristophanes attacks Hyperbolus, an influential speaker in the Assembly, frequently in his comedies. Hyperbolus was ostracized from Athens in 417 BCE and murdered at Samos in 411 BCE.

588   *Eupolis put his* Maricas *before you*: A contemporary of Aristophanes and fellow writer of comedies, Eupolis died at sea sometime before the end of the Peloponnesian War. Debuted in 421 BCE, his play *Maricas* included Hyperbolus as a character.

591   *Phrynichus*: An older contemporary of Aristophanes, Phrynichus apparently wrote a play in which he included a burlesque, from myth, of the sea beast coming to eat Andromeda.

592   *Hermippus*: Another older contemporary of Aristophanes, Hermippus wrote a play called *The Bread-Makers* in which he included a character representing Hyperbolus's mother.

595   *the similes I wrote about the eels*: In the play *The Knights* (424 BCE), Aristophanes compares Cleon to an eel-fisherman stirring up the mud.

600   *The potent trident-wielder*: Poseidon is the god meant here, identified by his attribute the trident.

606 *the charioteer*: The sun god Helios was regarded as driving his chariot across the sky from east to west each day.

613–614 *that god-detested . . . Cleon as a general*: In classical Athens, citizens tended to elect wealthy aristocrats to public offices. Aristophanes here is mocking Cleon's pedigree (by claiming he is a foreigner from Paphlagonia) and his means of income (tanneries).

627–628 *blessed goddess of / Ephesus's golden temple*: There was a large temple to Artemis in Ephesus, and it was the center of both Greek and Lydian worship.

647 *to mourn the loss of Sarpedon or Memnon*: The gods mourn the loss of Sarpedon, killed by Patroclus in the Trojan War, because he was Zeus's son, and the loss of Memnon, also killed at Troy, because he was the son of Dawn.

649 *Sacred Signatory*: The holder of this office represented Athens in the Amphictyonic Council at Delphi.

664 *Measures*: Whereas Socrates intends *ta metra* ("measures") to mean poetic meters, Strepsiades understands units of physical measurement.

714–715 *how would you call . . . met him*: In the vocative case, this name is "Amynia," which, with its letter *a* ending (alpha in Greek), resembles a feminine nominative ending.

780 *to buy a witch from Thessaly*: The women of Thessaly had the reputation of being witches and were said to be able to remove the moon from the sky.

848–849 *your uncle / Megacles's fancy portico*: Strepsiades has mentioned that his wife is the niece of a Megacles the son of Megacles. Her brother, it seems, is named Megacles as well.

893–894 *I spent them on . . . like Pericles once said*: After paying ten talents to the Spartan king to lead his army out of Attica in 445 BCE, Pericles repressed the Euboean revolt. This bribe was entered in his accounts as the cost of "necessities."

901 *Diasia*: See note on "Diasia," *Clouds*, line 452.

950–951 *for chaining up / his father Cronus*: Victorious in the Titanomachy (the battle between his father Cronus's generation, the Titans, and his generation, the Olympians), Zeus chains Cronus and imprisons him in Tartarus in the underworld.

969–971 *Mysian Telephus . . . of Pandeletus*: This is an allusion to Euripides's play *Telephus* (produced in 438 BCE), in which the namesake Mysian king appeared in beggar's rags at the court of Agamemnon. Right Argument implies that, in former times, Wrong Argument had to live off scraps handed out to him for uttering clever talk like that of the politician Pandeletus, about whom nothing certain is known.

976 *You Cronus!*: The father of Zeus, Cronus here represents the superannuated.

1010 *their music teacher's*: Along with the gymnastics teacher (*paidotribes*) and reading and writing teacher (*grammatistes*), the "music teacher" (*kitharistes*) was entrusted with providing the traditional sort of education to Athenian youth.

1013–1014 *"Some Far-off Shout" / or "Queen Athena City-Leveler"*: We do not know to which songs Right Argument is referring here.

1018 *Phrynis*: Phrynis was a Mytilenean citharode (lyre player and songwriter) who won first prize at the Panathenaea circa 455 BCE. Right Argument accuses Phrynis of initiating innovations three decades before which have had a pernicious influence at the time of the first production of *Clouds*.

1032 *Dipolia*: The Dipolia was an ancient annual festival held on the fourteenth of the summer month Skirophorion. During this festival, barley mixed with wheat was placed on the altar of Zeus Polieus, the Protector of the City, and the Buphonia (see subsequent note) was performed.

1033   *Buphonia festival*: The Buphonia ("ox-slaying") refers to a sacrifice performed during the Dipolia. Oxen were driven to an altar on the Acropolis where grain had been spread, and the ox who first ate the grain was offered to Zeus Polieus.

1034–1035   *the men / who fought at Marathon*: Right Argument boasts that it was the traditional education that reared the soldiers who defeated the Persians at the Battle of Marathon in 490 BCE.

1037–1039   *when I see some youth . . . he should be dancing*: Right Argument is referring to one of the *pyrrichistai* who danced naked with large shields as part of the Panathenaea, an annual festival celebrating the city of Athens. This goddess is Athena, patroness of Athens. The title "Tritogeneia" refers to her supposed birth near the mythic Lake Tritonis, said to be in Libya.

1051   *a graybeard geezer Iapetus*: Iapetus, along with his brother Cronus, belongs, in myth, to the generation of the Titans, which precedes that of the Olympians. Calling a person a "Iapetus" or "Cronus" means that he is archaic.

1054   *Hippocrates's sons*: It is likely that the Hippocrates named here was the son of Ariphron and the general killed in battle at Delion in 424 BCE. His sons, orphaned by his death, had a reputation for unintelligence.

1084   *Antimachus's anal sex*: This Antimachus, ridiculed elsewhere by Aristophanes (*Acharnians* 1150), preferred, it seems, anal sex.

1094   *ten thousand staters*: Ten thousand staters equals forty thousand drachmas, an exorbitant sum.

1104   *"Baths of Heracles"*: In myth, hot springs were Hephaestus's gift to Heracles.

1110   *"market orators"*: Wrong Argument is quibbling on a shift in the meaning of the word *agora* in the word *agoretes*. Whereas *agora* means "meeting place" in Homer, it means "city center" or "market" in later authors.

1116   *The hero Peleus acquired a knife because of it*: In myth the hero Peleus resists the advances of his host Acastus's wife Hippolyte. Spurned, she accuses him of attempting to rape her. In punishment, Acastus has Peleus left without a weapon in a region full of wild beasts. The god Hephaestus provides Peleus with a knife.

1118   *Hyperbolus who sells the lamps*: Like Cleon the "tanner," Hyperbolus is derisively associated with trade.

1120   *Peleus's virtue got him Thetis as a bride*: In myth Thetis is fated to give birth to a son who is mightier than his father. Both Zeus and Poseidon desired Thetis but, fearing the prophecy, abstain. Zeus hands Thetis over to the hero Peleus partly because of the latter's "virtue" and partly to avoid a potential threat against his supremacy.

1137   *the hot-ash-on-the-pubes and radish-up-the-asshole treatment*: This "treatment" refers to the punishment imposed on an adulterer who was caught in the act: his pubic hair was removed with hot ash and a radish was forced up his anus.

1162–1163   *We want to tell you . . . who deserve to win*: The chorus again speaks directly to the judges, asking them to award first prize to *Clouds*.

1178   *the day called "Old and New"*: The last day of the month, when interest came due, was referred to as the "Old and New Day" in Athens.

1235   *Solon*: Solon the lawgiver (ca. 630–ca. 560 BC) came up with a code of laws for Athens in 594 BCE.

1320   *Carcinus*: An Athenian tragedian of the fifth century BCE.

1326   *Tlepolemus*: The preceding line by the Second Creditor contains, it seems, an allusion to a tragedy by a certain Xenocles, *Tlepolemus* or *Licymnius*. These words are spoken by Licymnius's half sister Alcmene after he has been killed by Tlepolemus.

1418 *Simonides, "The Shearing of the Ram"*: Simonides of Ceos (556–468 BCE) was a Greek lyric poet later included, by Alexandrian scholars, on the list of nine canonical lyric poets. This song likely contains a pun in which a ram is shorn and a man named Crios ("the Ram") of Aegina is "fleeced," so to speak.

1426–1427 *speak a speech / from Aeschylus*: A veteran of the Battle of Marathon, Aeschylus was a prominent tragedian in the first half of the fifth century BCE.

1434–1435 *a brother who . . . his half sister*: Pheidippides quotes from Euripides's tragedy *Aeolus*. Aeolus has two children by different mothers, Macareus and Canace. Marriage between children of the same father but different mothers was legal in Athens at the time of *Clouds*.

1478–1479 *Children cry . . . cry as well?*: Aristophanes here has Pheidippides mockingly adapt a quote from Euripides's *Alcestis*, line 691, in which Pheres refuses to die for his son Admetus.

Birds

13 *Execestides*: Execestides is taunted three times in *Birds* for being, allegedly, the foreign-born son of a slave.

15 *the mad Philocrates*: Philocrates the bird seller apparently made exaggerated claims about the abilities of his birds.

21 *a son of Tharrelides*: We do not know in what respect this "son of Tharrelides" is similar to a jay.

36–37 *the opposite of the disease / that Sacas has*: "Sacas" (the Scythian) was the nickname of the foreign-born tragedian Acestor, who apparently sought to become an Athenian citizen.

63 *Boy! Boy!*: An Athenian like Euelpides expects the door to be opened by a doorkeeper. This cry (*pai, pai* in ancient Greek) introduces a pun on the word "hoopoe" (*epopoi*).

72–73 *a scaredy-bird, / native to Libya*: This fictional bird is given an origin in Africa, which was, for Greeks, the land of fantastical creatures.

76 *a shit-bird from the Land of Pheasants*: The pheasant (*phasianos* in ancient Greek) was said to have originated at the river Phasis (now the Rioni in Georgia), another likely native land for an exotic bird. Part of the joke may turn on the pheasant's golden-brown tail.

85–86 *sardines / from Phalerum*: Fry like sardines were a favorite Athenian food, and Phalerum is the nearest coast to the city of Athens.

106 *The twelve great gods*: Traditionally, the twelve major Olympian gods were Zeus, Hera, Athena, Ares, Apollo, Artemis, Hephaestus, Aphrodite, Hermes, Poseidon, Hades, and Hestia.

111–112 *It's Sophocles that makes me, / Tereus, shameful in his tragedies*: The tragedian Sophocles, it seems, wrote more than one tragedy in which Tereus appeared as a character.

119 *the country of attractive warships*: Athens had been renowned for its warships since the Second Persian War (480–479 BCE).

120 *are you jurors?*: Athens was infamous for the number of its law courts, each of which sat a large number of jurors.

137 *an aristocracy*: Since the wellborn and wealthy in Athens regarded themselves as the *aristoi*, the aristocracy mentioned here would suggest an oligarchy.

138–139 *the son of Skellias . . . Aristocrates*: This son of Skellias (chosen here for his name "Aristocrates") signed the Peace of Nicias in 421 BCE and served as a general in 413–412 BCE, after *Birds* was produced. He was eventually a member of the oligarchic coup of 411 BCE.

162   *the Red Sea*: To the Greeks "the Red Sea" suggests not only the modern Red Sea but the Persian Gulf as well. Thus, the city described would be somewhere on the edge of the Persian Empire.

164   *the* Salaminia: Mention of the sea evokes, in Euelpides's mind, the Athenian official galley the *Salaminia*.

167   *Lepreus, in Elis*: This city, a few miles inland in Elis in the western Peloponnese, may have seemed a city open to settlers, since it had recently been declared independent by the Spartans, who settled helots (serfs) there as a reward for their service in the Thracian campaign.

168–170   *the city of Lepreus . . . Melanthius is a leper*: This line contains a pun on the name of the city and *lepreos* ("man with bad skin"). Melanthius was a tragedian attacked here and in Aristophanes's *Peace* for the sound of his voice, eating habits, and allegedly unwatchable tragedies.

171   *in Locris, the Opuntians*: Opuntians are inhabitants of the city Opus in Locris, on the eastern coast of central Greece. The mention of "Opuntians" sets up an insult against a man named Opuntius, said to be one-eyed and an informer.

178–180   *The gardens give us   mint to eat*: These items were standard at Athenian festivals.

189   *Teleas*: This Teleas is likely the one who was Secretary of the Treasurers of Athens in 415–414 BCE. He necessarily belonged to the wealthiest class of Athenian citizen and is mocked elsewhere in Aristophanes for gluttony and graft.

209   *Melian famine*: Athens besieged the island of Melos in 416 BCE, and famine there was one of the consequences.

211–213   *when we want to go . . . Boeotia for a visa*: An overland Athenian embassy to Delphi had to pass through Boeotian territory and needed, therefore, permission to do so.

227   *my darling Procne*: The elder daughter of King Pandion of Athens and the wife of Tereus, Procne kills her son Itys upon learning that Tereus had raped her sister Philomela. When he discovers that the dead Itys has been served to him in a meal, he chases the sisters with an ax. The sisters ask the gods to save them by transforming them into birds.

244–245   *Phoebus, with his golden hair, / listening to your elegies*: "Golden hair," though a particularly common attribute of Apollo, is only used of gods. It may be an expression of gilding on the hair of cult statues. Elegies were originally sung laments for the dead, and that is the meaning here.

256–257   *Epopopoi . . . ee-to*: This is the first example of Aristophanes's bird-language, a striking feature of this play.

299   *His name is Persian*: The "Persian bird" in ancient Greek is the cock, possibly represented here with an elaborate crest suggestive of the Persian king's tiara.

300   *how did he fly in here without a camel?*: Greeks associated Persians with camels.

303   *the son of Philocles*: That this Philocles is mocked here and later in the play for looking like a bird, the hoopoe and lark, respectively, suggests there was something bird-like about his appearance.

305–306   *This bird / is Callias! He sure has lost a lot of feathers!*: Dissolute and preyed on by parasites, Callias had reduced his fortune from two hundred talents to two.

309   *Cleonymus*: A pro-Cleon politician, Cleonymus is frequently referred to in Aristophanes's comedies as gluttonous, grotesquely large, effeminate, and cowardly.

313   *They are like Carians*: The native inhabitants of Caria in southwest Asia Minor lived in hilltop fortresses.

318 *Sporgilus*: Sporgilus (whose name means "sparrow") was a barber in Athens.

319 *Who has brought an owl to Athens?*: The owl was prevalent in Athens and featured on its coinage. Euelpides breaks dramatic illusion here by calling attention to the fact that the play was produced in Athens. "To bring an owl to Athens" is a saying that means to bring something of which there is enough already.

362 *The owl won't get us then*: Scholars have been unable to determine the significance of this line: Why would a kettle be a defense against an owl in particular?

366 *Nicias*: Nicias the son of Niceratus was, at the time *Birds* was produced, in Sicily as one of the generals sent to lead the Athenian expedition. He was killed there in 413 BCE.

371 *the relatives and fellow tribesmen of my wife*: Tereus's wife Procne is, in myth, native to Athens.

399 *Finchburg*: "Finchburg" is an attempt to translate a pun on Orneai, the name of a town in the Argolid, and *ornea* (birds). In the winter of 416–415 BCE the Athenians and their allies among the Argives laid siege to the town of Orneai, where the Spartans had settled a group of oligarchic exiles from Argos. The irony is that no lives were lost in that campaign, since the Argive exiles escaped from the siege during the night.

401 *hoplites*: Citizen-soldiers of Athens, who marched on foot carrying a spear and a shield.

442–443 *the knife-maker / (who was an ape)*: Scholars have not been able to identify the story to which Aristophanes is alluding here.

447 *the judges*: The Chorus Leader here breaks the fourth wall by referring to the ten judges, each chosen by lot from one of the ten tribes of Athens to rank the dramatic competitors in order of merit. The archon (an annually elected official), then, chose five of these rankings to decide the victor.

453–454 *keep an eye out / for future orders posted on the boards*: Peisthetaerus here uses the mock-military language in telling his companions to demobilize. He also refers to the practice of posting mobilization notices in public.

474 *long, long before the Titans, Cronus, even Earth*: Peisthetaerus here alludes to Hesiod's *Theogony*, in which Earth belongs to the earliest generation, followed by her children the Titans, led by Cronus.

477 *Aesop*: Aesop, the author of fables, is believed to have lived as a slave on Samos in the early sixth century BCE. This story of the Lark burying her father is not attested elsewhere.

483 *Headley Park*: "Headley Park" is an attempt to translate a pun on the deme Kephale, where there was a cemetery, and the word for head (*kephale*).

490 *Dariuses and Megabazuses*: Peisthetaerus has pluralized the names for King Darius of Persia and his cousin and general Megabazus, both active in the late sixth and early fifth centuries BCE.

501 *name-day party*: According to Greek custom, it was during this party, held on the tenth day after birth, that the father formally named the child and thereby acknowledged it as his own.

509–510 *the bird / they call the "kite"*: This bird is the black kite (*Milvus migrans*). It seems it was a custom to roll on the ground before this bird upon its arrival in spring as an acknowledgment of the end of winter.

514 *an obol that was in my mouth*: Greeks regularly stored spare change in their mouths.

515–516 *the cuckoo once / was king of Egypt and Phoenicia*: Peisthetaerus claims that the cuckoo "held sway" in grain-rich Egypt and Phoenicia because his call was a sign of harvesttime. The reference to barleycorn, regarded as a phallic symbol, sets up the joke in the next line.

518 *Dicks up. Hit the field*: The "fields" here are a double entendre for female pubic regions.

519–520 *some Agamemnon / or Menelaus*: Apulian vases from the late fifth and early fourth centuries BCE depict kings in tragedy with bird-topped scepters. See Trendall and Webster's *Illustrations of Greek Drama* (Phaedon, 1971). Apparently this practice was already in vogue at the time of the production of *Birds*.

523 *Priam*: Euelpides may be alluding to a production of Euripides's *Alexandros* in 415 BCE, in which Priam appeared as a character.

525 *the offerings Lysicrates embezzled*: Lysicrates was a common name. Scholars have been unable to identify which Lysicrates is intended here. In Athens holders of public office were often accused of graft and embezzlement.

526–529 *Zeus, who is now in charge . . . Apollo, has a hawk*: Peisthetaerus here cites as evidence of avian importance the birds associated with major deities: Zeus's eagle, Athena's owl, and Apollo's hawk.

534 *Lampon*: A prominent Athenian interpreter of oracles and religious authority.

537 *Manes*: Peisthetaerus singles out his slave Manes as an example of idiocy.

546 *silphium*: Also known as laserwort, silphium was used in antiquity as a seasoning, perfume, an aphrodisiac, and a medicine.

562 *Babylon*: Aristophanes may here be recalling Herodotus's account of the construction of the great walls of Babylon (*Histories* 1.178–79).

563 *O Cebriones! O Porphyrion!*: Two mythic giants who waged an unsuccessful war on the Olympian gods on the plain of Phlegra. There is a pun on the bird porphyrion, which is the purple gallinule.

568 *to screw their Semeles, Alcmenas and Alopes*: In myth Zeus has sex with the mortal princesses Semele and Alcmena, and Poseidon rapes Alope.

576 *nuts to the penis-bird*: The "penis-bird" is very likely the coot (*Fulica atra*), which migrated to Greece in the winter and was caught for food.

581 *Zan*: Euelpides uses the name for Zeus at his major cult center at Olympia in Elis.

594 *Dr. Phoebus*: Phoebus Apollo, god of healing, is here portrayed as a medical doctor. The mention of a doctor immediately suggests a doctor's fee.

597 *the Principle of Life Itself*: Peisthetaerus imagines humankind accepting birds as *bios* (life).

630 *Delphi or Ammon*: Two major seats of divination known in the Greek world. The temple at Delphi is located in central Greece and was sacred to Apollo; the temple at Ammon (a ram-headed Egyptian god associated with Zeus) is located at an oasis now named Siwa in the Libyan Desert. Travel to either of them would have involved the expenses of the travel itself as well as the cost of sacrifices to consult the god.

652 *while away the time like Nicias*: Nicias the son of Niceratus at first had been reluctant to support sending an expedition to Sicily.

657 *Crioa*: An actual Attic deme, the name Crioa suggests a ram (*krios*), associated with exaggerated male sexuality.

666 *eagle*: In a fable by Aesop, the eagle breaks its treaty with the fox by feeding her cubs to its eaglets.

689 *I'll take her mask off*: Euelpides breaks dramatic illusion by pointing out that Procne's "beak" is part of a mask.

704–705 *the famous / intellectual Prodicus*: Prodicus was an intellectual authority in mid to late fifth-century BCE Athens. Though we do not have any of his work on the origin of the gods, it is clear here that the Chorus Leader is saying the birds know better than he.

718 *they have opened their thighs through the power of us birds*: In Athenian pederasty, birds (swallows and doves) are often a love gift from the *erastes* (adult male lover) to the *eromenos* (pre-adult male love-object). The "opening of the thighs" refers to intercrural sex.

723   *time for Orestes to weave new clothing*: "Orestes" appears as, likely, the nickname for an Athenian who engaged in cloak-robbing.

753   *bee-like Phrynichus*: Phrynichus the son of Polyphradmon was a tragic poet active in the late sixth and early fifth centuries BCE. The poet/bee comparison is common in ancient Greek literature.

764   *has his brow tattooed*: The foreheads of runaway slaves were, in fact, tattooed, both as a punishment and as a deterrent to future escapes.

766   *as much a Phrygian as Spintharus*: Most Phrygians in Athens were slaves; Phrygians in general had a reputation for being effeminate. We do not know who this Spintharus is.

767   *Philemon's dovecote*: This Philemon is unknown. *Execestides*: See note on "Execestides," *Birds*, line 13.

773   *the Hebrus River's banks*: The Hebrus, now the Maritsa, Meriç and Evros, is a large river in central Thrace. In myth, after the Maenads tear apart Orpheus, his head flows down the Hebrus to the sea.

790   *Patrocleides*: This Patrocleides is likely the politician who sponsored decrees concerning trade and citizen enfranchisement in the last quarter of the fifth century BCE. It seems he was known as "the Shitter" because of some embarrassing incident.

795   *Dieitrephes*: Though portrayed as ambitious and newly rich, Dieitrephes, in fact, belonged to a distinguished family.

798   *cock-horse*: The "cock-horse" (*hippalektruon*) is a mythical beast with the head and foreparts of a horse and the rear parts of a rooster. Aristophanes may have gotten this image from Aeschylus's tragedy *Myrmidons*, in which a cock-horse is mentioned as the figurehead on a ship's prow.

804–805   *the words / of Aeschylus*: Peisthetaerus alludes to a passage in Aeschylus's tragedy *Myrmidons* in which an eagle, shot by an arrow fletched with eagle feathers, claims to have caused his own undoing.

813–814   *esparto / twine*: Peisthetaerus puns on Sparta, the capital city of Lacedaemonia, and on *sparte* (twine).

820–822   *the city where . . . his whole estate*: Both these men, it seems, were infamous for bragging that they were wealthier than they actually were.

823–824   *the Plain of Phlegra . . . the Braggart War*: Peisthetaerus proposes the Plain of Phlegra, the mythic location of the gods' defeat of the giants in the Gigantomachy, as a more suitable depository for imaginary wealth.

827   *Sacred Robe*: The Chorus Leader is referring to Athena Parthenos's role as keeper of the Acropolis and to her sacred *peplos* (robe).

828   *Athena Polias*: Athena Polias is the cult title for the Athena on the Athenian Acropolis.

831–832   *where Cleisthenes sits spinning / yarn from wool*: Cleisthenes is often mocked for being effeminate in Aristophanes's comedies.

859   *a Pythian cry*: The Pythian cry most likely refers to the shout *ie Paian* for good luck.

860   *Chaeris*: This Chaeris is most likely the bad flute player ridiculed elsewhere in Aristophanes.

867–868   *Pray to the avian . . . filches from altars*: Hestia was traditionally honored first with offerings and named first in prayers. The kite is named second here, known to be rapacious enough to steal meat from the sacrificial altar.

877 *Cleocritus's mom*: In *Frogs*, Aristophanes claims that Cleocritus has a large, unwieldy body like that of an ostrich.

908–911 *"The Muses' willing slave . . . a honey-tongue"*: Likely a cliché, "the Muses' slave" appears in the *Homeric Hymn to Selene* and the *Margites*, attributed to Homer in ancient times.

913 *A longhair slave*: In Athens wealthy young men, like Pheidippides in *Clouds*, wore long hair, as did those, like the impoverished poet here, who did not concern themselves with their appearance.

922–923 *a hundred gorgeous . . . Simonidean ditties*: Dithyrambs are songs sung usually in honor of Dionysus and danced in circular formations. Foreign to Athens, maiden-songs were a ritualized performance in Doric Greek–speaking communities. The most famous of them are by the poet Alcman (seventh century BCE). Simonides of Ceos (ca. 556–468 BCE) composed in a variety of poetic genres.

928 *ten days old*: Athenians celebrated an official naming ceremony for an infant on the tenth day after its birth.

931–936 *Swift are the Muses' . . . willing to bestow*: These lines are apparently quoted from a hypochreme, a lively song accompanied by dancing, by Pindar.

946 *Pindar*: Pindar of Thebes (517–438 BCE) primarily composed victory odes for victors at the various Panhellenic athletic competitions.

948–952 *Among the Scythian . . . an animal hide*: The Poet here slightly alters for the occasion lines by Pindar himself (fragment 105b).

973 *Bacis*: Bacis is a name associated with a collection of prophecies about internal conflicts during the fifth century BCE.

980 *twixt Sicyon and Corinth . . .*: Animals of ambiguous significance cohabiting in an unlikely way with other animals is common in oracular style. Since Sicyon and Corinth are neighboring states, there is no space between them. The phrase means "nowhere."

994–995 *the one / Apollo gave me*: Peisthetaerus trumps the oracles by Bacis by claiming to have an oracle of Apollo from Delphi.

1001 *Lampon*: See note on "Lampon," *Birds*, line 534. *the lordly Diopeithes*: This Diopeithes was a politician who took an active interest in oracles and the divine.

1004 *Meton*: Meton, an Athenian citizen of the deme Leuconoeum, was a famous astronomer and geometrician who used a sundial to observe the summer solstice on June 27, 432 BCE.

1013 *all Colonus too*: Meton may well have set up a sundial in Colonus, a deme of Athens. This sundial may have been the one used to observe the solstice in 432 BCE.

1027 *a Thales*: The early philosopher Thales of Miletus (first half of the sixth century BCE) came to represent scientific genius, much like Albert Einstein in America in the twentieth century.

1030–1031 *they're driving out . . . throughout the city*: In his speeches in Thucydides's *History of the Peloponnesian War* (1.144.2, 2.39.1), the Athenian statesman Pericles contrasts Sparta's policy of the expulsion of foreigners with Athens's openness.

1041 *Sardanapallus*: Sardanapallus is the Greek form of the name of the king of Assyria (reigned 668–ca. 627 BCE) Ashurbanipal. In the Greek tradition this king was an effeminate pleasure-seeker who dressed and behaved like a woman and wore makeup.

1043 *Teleas*: See note on "Teleas," *Birds*, line 189.

1049 *Pharnaces*: At the time of the production, this Pharnaces was the Persian satrap of Dascylium in northwest Asia Minor.

1064 *the Olophyxians*: This seems to be a reference to the Coinage Decree (passed in the 420s BCE), which imposed the use of Athenian silver coinage on "allied" states like Olophyxus, a small, semi-civilized town on the Acte (Athos) peninsula.

1069 *hubris in the month Munychium*: Hubris (aggravated arrogance) was a punishable and serious crime in ancient Athens. Since the month Munychium follows the month Elaphebolium (in which *Birds* was produced at the City Dionysia), it likely means "next month" here.

1076–1077 *to shit / on law codes in the evening*: The Decree Seller threatens to accuse Peisthetaerus of desecrating stone decree-steles.

1094 *Diagoras of Melos*: Diagoras of Melos was outlawed from Athens for impiety in 415–414 BCE. He allegedly divulged and mocked the Eleusinian mysteries.

1097 *Philocrates of Sparrowtown*: See note on "the mad Philocrates," *Birds*, line 15.

1119 *judges*: The Chorus Leader breaks dramatic illusion by addressing the ten judges in the audience; see notes on "the judges," *Birds*, line 447, and on "Let the wiser ones remember . . . vote for me," *Women of the Assembly*, lines 1301–1303.

1120–1121 *more gifts by far upon them / than Paris took in*: The Trojan prince Paris received lavish gifts upon visiting Menelaus in Sparta. *Laurium*: Athens stamped owls on its silver coinage. The silver came from mines from Laurium, located thirty-seven miles southeast of Athens on the coast of Attica.

1129 *fitted for copper coverings, like statues*: Copper discs were attached to the heads of statues to protect them from bird droppings.

1141–1142 *Proxenides of Blusterburg / and Theogenes*: Aristophanes uses these two notorious boasters to underscore the insubstantiality of this bird-wall built in the air.

1144 *the Trojan one*: Toward the end of the Trojan War, the Greeks build a colossal horse out of wood and fill it with men so that, when brought inside the walls of Troy, they might emerge and let other Greek soldiers in.

1183 *a battle dancer*: In the battle dance at the Panathenaea festival, citizens carrying, each, a large and heavy shield, danced in a lively manner.

1206 *Erebus's son, the Air*: Air is the son of Erebus in no known cosmology, though in Hesiod's *Theogony* Night and Erebus mate to produce Aether.

1215–1216 *The* Salaminia? / *The* Paralus?: These are the two official galleys of Athens, dispatched on government business.

1260 *Licymnian force*: In myth, Licymnius, the uncle of Heracles, is killed when his great-nephew Tlepolemus, the son of Heracles, throws a staff at a servant, misses, and inadvertently hits him.

1264 *some Lydian or Phrygian*: It was a Greek stereotype that the peoples of Asia Minor were cowardly.

1268 *Amphion's, too*: In this mock-tragic tirade, Peisthetaerus may be quoting from Aeschylus's lost play *Niobe*, in which the house of Amphion and Niobe is left desolate when Apollo and Artemis kill their twelve children.

1272 *Porphyrion*: See note on "O Cebriones! Oh Porphyrion!," *Birds*, line 563.

1302 *mad for all things Spartan*: Some Athenian aristocrats affected Spartan behaviors such as antidemocratic views and a comparative disregard for grooming and cleanliness.

1304–1305 *behaved like Socrates . . . with walking sticks*: Socrates was notoriously barefoot and unkempt. It seems some Athenians also carried, as an affectation, something like the *skutalon* or Spartan ambassadorial staff.

1315 *Menippus*: This Menippus is otherwise unknown.

1316 *Opuntius*: See note on "in Locris, the Opuntians," *Birds*, line 171.

1317 *Philocles*: See note on "the son of Philocles," *Birds*, line 301.

1318 *Theogenes*: This may be the same boastful Theogenes mentioned above (line 1143). *Lycurgus*: Likely Lycurgus the son of Lycomedes, he belonged to a family that held the priesthood of Poseidon Erechteus (of the Erechtheum on the Acropolis). That he has the nickname "Ibis" suggests some Egyptian connection.

1319 *Chaerephon*: The Greeks classified bats as birds. Chaerephon earned his nickname "the Bat" presumably because of his unhealthy complexion; see note on "Chaerephon," *Clouds*, line 123, above.

1320 *Syracosius*: The politician Syracosius probably earned the nickname "Magpie" because of his grating oratorical style.

1321 *Midias*: Elsewhere in comedy, this Midias is called out for stealing public funds and for being fond of cock- and quail-fighting.

1322 *a quail hit on the noggin by a finger*: The herald is referring to the popular game of "quail-tapping" (*ortugokopia*), in which a player set a quail on a game board, and his opponent, by "tapping" the quail on the head, tried to force it out of bounds.

1400 *Cinesias*: Son of Meles the lyre player, Cinesias was a successful dithyrambic poet. Aristophanes here mocks him for being tall and slender and for his "new music" compositions.

1436 *Leotrophides*: Teased elsewhere for being skinny.

1446 *a couple swallows*: Peisthetaerus is referring to the proverb "one swallow does not make a summer."

1451 *Pellene*: Pellene, a city in Achaia, hosted chariot races for which the prize was a warm woolen cloak.

1499 *Corcyrean wings*: Whips from Corcyra (contemporary Corfu) were well known in ancient Greece. Wings come in pairs and whips were often double-thonged. In Athens, one whips a slave, so Peisthetaerus is treating the Informer as such.

1509–1510 *near Cowardtown, / a strange tree called Cleonymus*: See note on "Cleonymus," *Clouds*, line 395.

1521 *Orestes*: See note on "time for Orestes to weave new clothing," *Birds*, line 723.

1548 *fasting at the Thesmophoria*: An important festival held in honor of Demeter and Persephone in September–October in Athens, the Thesmophoria required fasting in the middle of its three-day celebration.

1550 *Illyrians*: Indo-European-speaking Balkan tribes located in what is now Albania and the former Yugoslav Republic of Macedonia, the warlike Illyrians, by their famous shrieking, are here expressing hunger.

1556 *Execestides's forebears*: See note on "Execestides," *Birds*, line 13.

1559–1560 *"Triballian" must be the word / that "tribbing" comes from*: In the original, Peisthetaerus makes a ridiculous etymological connection between Triballians and *epitribeies* ("May you be smashed!"). To preserve the pun, I have imported tribadism.

1575–1576 *it's because of you and you alone / that we get barbecues*: In Hesiod's *Theogony*, Prometheus tricks Zeus into choosing a pile of sacrificial meat consisting mostly of tripe and bone, so that humans are able to enjoy the meat and fat.

1578 *Timon*: Timon of Athens, frequently mentioned in comedy, was a notorious misanthrope who withdrew into a hermit's life. We do not know whether he is mythic or historical.

1581 *a butler for a basket-bearer*: Aristocratic girls served as basket-bearers at the head of religious processions. Sometime an attendant would accompany them.

1585 *Pisander*: This Pisander, the son of Glaucetes of Acharnae, was an army officer in 422–421 BCE and served on the board that investigated the mutilation of the Herms in 415 BCE.

1588 *Odysseus*: The chorus here alludes to the beginning of the *Nekuia*, book 11 of Homer's *Odyssey*, in which, as part of a necromantic rite, Odysseus digs a pit for liquid sacrifices and takes a step back from it.

1589 *Chaerephon*: Rather than the expected risen ghost, the "living dead" Chaerephon emerges.

1596 *Laespodias*: This Laespodias, a candidate for a generalship in 414 BCE, apparently draped his cloak in an irregular way to conceal something unbecoming about his calves.

1608 *silphium*: An item for trade from the North African city of Cyrene, silphium was used as a seasoning, perfume, and aphrodisiac.

1683 *The law says you don't get a single straw*: Peisthetaerus is here applying the laws of Athens to the gods.

1689 *"Heiress"*: Athena may have won this cult title either because she defeated Poseidon in the contest of patronage of Athens or because she was the patron goddess of heiresses.

1696 *this law of Solon's*: See note on *Clouds*, line 1235; Peisthetaerus may well be quoting his law on intestate succession.

1703 *inducted you into his phratry*: In Athens, an infant was registered at his father's "phratry" (district), and this registration could later be attested as evidence of his legitimacy.

1734 *like Gorgias and Philippus*: Gorgias is the famous teacher of rhetoric from Leontini in Sicily. We do not know whether Philippus was Gorgias's actual son or a disciple. He may well have been, unlike Gorgias, an Athenian citizen.

1768 *O Hymen! O Hymenaeus!*: A version of the ritual cry uttered at ancient Greek weddings.

Lysistrata

2–3 *the Goddesses of Sex / at Colias*: Lysistrata feels that if the women had been called to celebrate a raucous religious festival, they would already be present. The three festivals she lists as examples are in honor of Dionysus (Bacchus), Pan, and, lastly, the Genetyllides (Goddesses of Sex, including Aphrodite) at a temple on a cape "Colias," the location of which is unknown.

39 *their precious eels*: The eels of Lake Copais in Boeotia were regarded as a great delicacy in Athens.

54 *by Demeter and Persephone*: Calonice swears a mild oath by the two goddesses Demeter and Kore (Persephone). This is a specifically woman's oath.

61 *always later than they should be*: Athenians were stereotypically tardy.

63 *over from Salamis and the Paralia*: Salamis is a large island in the Saronic Gulf, and the Paralia is coastal Attica. These seafaring sections of greater Athens serve as a feed for the subsequent double entendre about females "riding" on a boat/having sex mounted on the male.

65 *the Acharnian women*: The Acharnians (people of the deme Acharnae) were supposedly especially anti-Spartan. Their lands had suffered great destruction as a consequence of the Spartan incursions into Attica during the Peloponnesian War.

67–68 *Theogenes's wife . . . high to get here*: Mention of Acharnae prompts a joke about the wife of presumably Acharnian Theogenes. Theogenes was a fairly common name, and it is impossible to pin down a historical figure. The joke seems to be that Theogenes's wife is a drunk, as there is a double entendre on *akateion* (sail/wine cup) in the original.

71 *Stinkydale*: "Stinkydale" translates the geographical region of Anagyrous, a swampy region named for the malodorous plant *anagyros*.

107-108 *in Thrace fighting to save Eucrates / the general*: Thrace (now split between Bulgaria, Greece, and Turkey) was strategically important to the Athenians throughout the Peloponnesian War. Nothing more is known about this general Eucrates.

109 *Pylos*: The Athenians had captured (in 425 BCE) and still held (in 411 BCE) the peninsula of Pylos at the southwestern end of the Peloponnesus.

115 *those five-inch dildos*: The Ionian city of Miletus had defected to the Spartan side in 412 BCE. As Miletus was the major producer of dildos, the Athenians would have had difficulty importing them.

125 *Mount Tayeegety*: Mount Taygetus (southwest of Sparta) is, at 7,887 feet, the tallest mountain in Laconia.

147 *hump and dump*: The original reads, in translation, "Poseidon and a tub." The tragedian Sophocles twice portrayed Poseidon's seduction of Tyro and her subsequent exposure of their twin sons in a tub beside a river.

166 *lickety-split he threw his sword aside*: In myth, Menelaus, though he intends to kill Helen of Troy, drops his sword when she exposes her breasts to him.

168-169 *Well, like a poet . . . dildo away*: The "poet" referred to here is the comic playwright Pherecrates, an older contemporary of Aristophanes. The joke turns on the fact that dildos were often covered in dog skin.

187 *and tons a' money in Athena's temple*: The treasuries of Athena on the Acropolis were Athens's main financial reserve in 411 BCE.

189-190 *to occupy the hilltop fortress / of the Acropolis this very morning*: Lysistrata reveals that she has sent another group of women to seize the Acropolis (and thus secure the treasury for the Delian League and the treasuries of Athena).

207 *they slit a victim's throat above a shield*: Lysistrata here mentions a scene in Aeschylus's tragedy *Seven Against Thebes*, first produced in 469 BCE. In it seven allied leaders swear an oath with their hands dipped in the blood of a horse.

210-211 *What if we got / a pure-white steed somewhere and cut it up?*: Horse sacrifice is highly exceptional in ancient Greek culture. Calonice's proposal is ridiculous.

216 *never to add a drop of water*: The ancient Greeks controlled the potency of wine by "cutting" it with a greater or lesser amount of water. The joke here is that the women will drink wine from the island of Thasos, a particularly dark and aromatic wine, uncut.

276 *Draces*: Aristophanes includes names of members of both choruses. I have retained the names only of Draces for the men's chorus leader and Stratyllis for the women's chorus leader.

289 *Lycon's drunken wife*: Lycon's wife had a reputation for promiscuous behavior. The old men here suspect that she has instigated the female uprising.

291 *Cleomenes*: In 508 BCE, the Spartan general Cleomenes came to Athens with Spartan troops at the invitation of the Athenian Isagoras and seized the Acropolis. His intention was to help Isagoras establish in Athens an oligarchic government sympathetic to Sparta. After a two-day occupation of the Acropolis, he was allowed to depart with troops as part of a truce. These lines are humorous because of the hyperbole—they claim that they received the spear of Cleomenes (even though his surrender took place ninety-seven years

prior to 411 BCE), in which case they would be well over a hundred years old. They also exaggerate the two-day occupation to "six years."

300 *Euripides as well*: In fifth-century comedy, Euripides is famous for misogyny.

301 *May Marathon no longer feature my memorial*: The chorus members claim to have been *Marathonomachoi* (veterans of the Battle of Marathon). In 490 BCE a vastly outnumbered army consisting of Athenians and Plataeans defeated the Persian army camped at Marathon in southeast Attica. A monument at the battle site commemorated the victory.

312 *Great Lord Heracles!*: An oath uttered by males to express shock. Heracles is appropriate in relation to fire in that he immolates himself on Mount Oeta.

315 *the Lemnian sort of fire*: The island of Lemnos is associated with fire because of the volcano on it. Here there is an untranslatable pun on Lemnos and the word *lēmē* ("eyesore" or "mote in the eye").

328–329 *generals at the naval base / in Samos, do you want to help us stack this lumber?*: Samos was the Athenian naval headquarters for northern Greece, with seventy-three ships. The old men of the chorus, elsewhere self-identified as proud infantrymen, ask whether the members of the navy might want to help them drive the women off the Acropolis.

332 *Victory Goddess Nike*: Nike, goddess of victory, is in the retinue of Athena, goddess of wisdom and warcraft. It is likely that the men are represented as praying to Nike in her temple on a bastion overlooking the Propylaea of the Acropolis.

361 *Golden-Crested Fortress Guardian*: "Golden-Crested" refers to the tiara worn by the image of Athena Polias in the Parthenon. Among Athena's prerogatives was the protection of hilltop fortresses in general and of the Acropolis in Athens in particular.

363 *Tritogeneia*: This epithet for Athena first appears in Hesiod and is commonly interpreted as referring to her birthplace in Lake Tritonis in Libya.

377 *Bupe-Bupe-Bupalus*: The sixth-century poet of invective Hipponax threatens to punch his enemy, Bupalus, in fragment 120 of *Iambi et Elegi Graeci: Ante Alexandrum Cantati*, Vol I: *Archilochus, Hipponax Theognidea*, ed. Martin L. West (Oxford, UK: Oxford University Press, 2nd ed. 1989): "Take my cloak, I'll hit Bupalus in the eye! For I have two right hands and I don't miss with my punches" (translated by Douglas Gerber). According to one ancient source, Hipponax so viciously attacked Bupalus with invective verse that Bupalus hanged himself (Pseudo-Acron on Horace, *Epodes*, cited by Douglas Gerber in *Greek Iambic Poetry*, Loeb Classical Library No. 259 [Cambridge, MA: Harvard University Press, 1999], 351).

396 *You aren't on a jury now!*: Older men in Athens tended to make an income by serving on juries.

405 *that exotic god Sabezius*: Sabezius was an ecstatic Phrygian deity who arrived in Athens in the 430s BCE. As his worship involved drinking to excess, he was associated with Dionysus.

406 *Adonis*: The worship of Adonis in Greece, similar to that of Dumuzi (Tammuz) in Egypt, was exclusive to women and involved ritual lamentation over the annual death of Adonis and the cultivation of "Adonis gardens" on rooftops.

413 *Zacynthus*: The Commissioner is recounting speeches given by the politician Demostratus in the months leading up to the disastrous Sicilian expedition, which began in 415 BCE. Demostratus pushed both for the expedition and for the recruitment of hoplites (foot soldiers) from the island of Zacynthus.

424 *By Poseidon*: The Commissioner aptly swears a mild oath by Poseidon, god of the sea, in response to the chorus's complaint of being drenched.

468 *a cup*: The Second Old Woman refers to the practice of "cupping" a black eye. Cupping therapy, now classified as a pseudoscience, was and is believed to have positive effects such as pain relief and wrinkle reduction.

485 *Don't wait to strip the corpses*: In the *Iliad*, Homeric heroes customarily stripped the armor from the soldiers they had killed.

548 *War is an affair for men*: The Trojan hero Hector utters these words in Homer's *Iliad* (6.492).

564–565 *get some beans / to chew on*: Both male and female Athenians chewed beans while doing repetitive tasks.

591 *a hoopoe*: "Hoopoe" refers to the Thracian hero Tereus, who was transformed into a hoopoe after raping his wife Procne's sister Philomel; see Ovid, *Metamorphoses* 6.671ff.

636–637 *the honey cake / for Cerberus*: The dead presumably used honey cakes to placate wardens of the underworld, such as Cerberus, in much the same way that visitors to underground shrines used them to placate sacred snakes.

641 *Charon is calling out your name*: Charon, the ferryman of the underworld, is here represented as summoning the "dead" Commissioner to embark and cross the river Styx.

650 *the third-day offerings at your grave*: Counting from either the *prosthesis* (setting forth of the body for viewing) or burial, offerings were given to the dead on the third, ninth, and thirteenth days and annually thereafter.

656 *Hippias's tyranny*: Hippias, the last tyrant of Athens, was driven out in 510 BCE.

658 *Cleisthenes's house*: Frequently mocked as an effeminate in the plays of Aristophanes, Cleisthenes is here accused of being sympathetic to the Spartans as well.

670 *Aristogeiton's statue in the market*: In 514 BCE two Athenians, Harmodius and Aristogeiton, assassinated Hipparchus, the brother of the tyrant Hippias. They were subsequently regarded as heroes of the democracy, and statues of them were set up in the *agora* (marketplace) of Athens.

679 *Weaver of Athena's Gown*: The chorus members cite their service in various female religious roles as evidence of their patriotism. First, at the age of seven, they served as *arrhephoroi*, weavers of the sacred *peplos* for the statue of Athena Polias.

681 *Artemis the Foundress*: Second, they served as grain-grinders for the sacred cakes of Artemis the Foundress.

682–683 *Bear / at Brauron*: Third, they served as *arktoi*, she-bears, in the Brauronia, a festival held every five years, in which girls performed ritual dances dressed as bears.

684–685 *Basket-Carrier / and wore dried figs around my neck*: Finally, when they were of marriageable age, females could serve as *kanephoroi* (basket-carriers) for the annual Panathenaea festival in Athens. Dried figs are associated with sexuality and fertility.

700 *"White Feet"*: "White Feet" is most likely an honorific address to foot soldiers.

701 *Leipsydrium*: In 514 BCE the family of the Alcmaeonidae and other exiles from Athens fortified the city of Leipsydrium on a slope of Mount Parnes near Athens in a failed attempt to procure their re-enfranchisement in the state; see Herodotus, *Histories* 5.62.

708 *Artemisia*: Artemisia, queen of Caria, fought on the side of Xerxes and the Persians in the naval battle of Salamis, 480 BCE; see Herodotus, *Histories* 7.99, 8.87–88.

711–712 *Micon's paintings of / the Amazons*: Amazons, warrior women, were believed to have invaded the area around the Acropolis in mythic times. In the middle of the fifth century BCE Micon painted an "Amazonomachy" (a battle between Theseus and the Amazons) in the Stoa Poikile to accompany other paintings by his teacher Polygnotus.

723–724 *like/the beetle... "crack"*: The Chorus of Old Women alludes here to Fable 3 of Aesop, in which a beetle, in retaliation for a wrong a done to it, breaks an eagle's eggs. The women are threatening, figuratively, to injure the men's testicles.

729–730 *when I was celebrating / Hecate with my friends*: Hecate is a popular deity, especially for women. For the eel of Lake Copais as a delicacy, see note above, line 39.

749 *Pan's Grotto*: This cave is located on the north face of the Acropolis in Athens.

753 *Orsilochus*: In addition to being associated with Aphrodite, the *strouthos* (sparrow) was a slang term for penis. Although this Orsilochus is unknown, the context suggests he was a gigolo or pimp.

764 *unscutched*: "Scutching" is the process by which impurities are removed from raw material. The Second Woman is referring to separating the straw and stems from flax.

770 *Queen Eileithyia*: Daughter of Zeus and Hera, Eileithyia is the goddess of childbirth, usually sent at Hera's behest. Giving birth, a ritually impure activity, was not permitted on hallowed ground.

781 *Sacred Helmet*: The cult image of Athena Parthenos wore a helmet that featured a sphinx flanked by two griffons.

879 *Harden, up from Dickersdale*: I have opted to translate the name Cinesias here as "Harden" to distinguish this character from the dithyrambic poet Cinesias who appears in *Birds*. The scholar Jeffrey Henderson hears a pun on Cinesias (*kinein*, "to fuck") and on the deme Paeonides (*paiein*, "to bang").

948 *the Clepsydra*: After sex, one could become ritually pure (so as to enter sacred space) by bathing in flowing water. The Clepsydra was a spring on the western side of the Acropolis.

965–967 *is my dick... his dinner now?*: In comedy Heracles is often portrayed as a glutton who is being cheated out of a feast.

996 *Foxhound*: "Foxhound" is the nickname of the pimp Philostratus; see Aristophanes's *Knights*, 1089.

1033 *Pellene*: The most easterly of the cities of mountainous Achaea, Pellene was on the coastal strip of Arcadia. The Spartan Messenger here talks about the city as if it were a female.

1072 *the swamps of Tricorysia*: Tricorysia was a forested, swampy area on the eastern coast of Attica. One could imagine insects growing to an impressive size there.

1095 *Carystus*: Carystus, an ally, had troops stationed in Athens.

1129 *mutilate your... Herms*: Herms were boundary-marking statues featuring a head of Hermes and an erect phallus. In 415 BCE, before the Sicilian expedition departed, Herms were famously "mutilated" (disfigured), allegedly by the aristocrat Alcibiades and his friends.

1175–1176 *at Olympia / at Pytho, at Thermopylae*: Lysistrata refers to several Panhellenic athletic sites in the Greek-speaking world: the Olympian and the Pythian games, and the Pylaea at Thermopylae. Competitors traveled to and participated in these games under the protection of a sacred truce, even during wartime.

1184 *Pericleidas*: In 464 BCE there was a major earthquake in Laconia. The helots, or serf population, there revolted. Pericleidas, a king of the Spartans, came to Athens and asked for assistance in suppressing the uprising. In response to his request, Cimon, an Athenian general, led four thousand Athenian troops to assist the Spartans.

1200–1202 *Spartans showed up... Hippias as well*: In 510 BCE Cleomenes the Spartan king led his troops against Hippias, the tyrant of Athens, his supporters, and his Thessalian cavalry and drove them out of the city.

1217 *Pylos*: See notes on "Pylos," *Clouds*, line 216, and *Lysistrata*, line 109.

1221–1223 *this, er, mound . . . out of Megara*: Geography represents anatomy here through double entendre. Echinous refers, on a literal level, to a city in Phthiotis (northern Greece) held by the Spartans since 426 BCE, and the Malian Gulf is the coastline in Phthiotis, in the western Aegean Sea. The scholar Jeffrey Henderson argues that they refer, through double entendre, to pubic hair and the vulva, respectively. *both these long legs* refers to the long walls connecting the city of Megara to its port Nisaea.

1289–1291 *singing / the* Telamon . . . *been singing /* Cleitagora: The *Telamon* and *Cleitagora* are both *skolia*, songs written to be sung at banquets. It was considered an important social grace to be able to sing *skolia* appropriately, but the guests at this banquet are so forgiving as to overlook an erroneous choice.

1306 *while Spartans under Leonidas fought on land*: The Spartan Ambassador sings of the simultaneous battles of Artemisium and Thermopylae in 480 BCE during the Second Persian Invasion. In the naval battle of Artemisium, the Greek fleet, led by the Athenians, defeated the "Medes" (Persians), while Leonidas famously died fighting to defend the pass of Thermopylae along with three hundred other Spartans.

1346 *Athena a' the Brazen House*: "Athena of the Brazen House" is the citadel-goddess for the Spartans, as Athena Polias is for the Athenians.

1349 *the Eurotas*: The Eurotas is the main river of Laconia. Starting near the border of Laconia and Arcadia, it flows south for fifty-one miles and empties into the Laconian Gulf.

1358 *Leda's daughter*: Leda's daughter is Helen of Troy. We should think, here, not of the adulterous wife of Menelaus but rather of the maiden-goddess of Spartan cult who was the patron deity of adolescent females.

Women of the Assembly

5 *your nostrils*: Praxagora compares the lamp, absurdly, to a fire-breathing monster.

20 *the Scira*: The Scira marked the end of the Athenian year in the spring. This festival included a procession involving the priestess of Athena and priest of Poseidon to a place called Skiron near Eleusis. The social order was inverted, and married females were permitted to leave their homes, band together, and revel. The females are here portrayed as having plotted to overthrow the government during the Scira.

25 *Pyromachus*: This Pyromachus apparently referred to the "men of the Assembly" (*hetairoi*) as *hetairai* (prostitutes).

71–72 *stand / all day out in the sun and get a tan*: Because they anoint themselves with oil and go out into the sun, males were tan in contrast to cloistered females.

83 *their Spartan boots*: An originally Spartan red and heavy sort of boot that contrasts with feminine "Persian slippers."

84 *Lamius's cane*: Lamius is apparently the woman's husband. His name suggests the Lamia, a mythic monster that Aristophanes in *Wasps* and *Peace* includes among examples of foul-smelling things.

87 *All-Eyes' goatskin jacket*: "All-Eyes" is Argus, the many-eyed shepherd of Io. He wears the goatskin jacket associated with rusticity.

106 *Phormisius*: This Phormisius was famous for his hairiness.

111 *Pronomus's beard*: Pronomus is a rare name; we know nothing more about this particular Pronomus.

112   *Agyrrhius*: Agyrrhius was a prominent politician at the time of the play. He had gotten a
       bill passed in the Assembly that raised the pay for serving in the Assembly from one obol
       to three.

118   *becalmed and rudderless*: Praxagora claims, through this nautical metaphor, that the city
       of Athens is not moving forward.

139   *the sacrificial cat*: The "purifier" who ritually cleansed the place of the Assembly before a
       meeting normally sacrificed a young pig, not a cat.

141   *Ariphrades*: This Ariphrades had a reputation, it seems, for garrulousness.

169   *water kegs*: The Second Woman proposes that wine in bars never be watered down. The
       humor here lies in Athenian women's alleged preference for strong drink.

170   *by Demeter and Persephone*: In Athens, Demeter and Persephone are "the two gods"
       invoked in oaths by women.

184   *Epigonus*: The Second Woman here insults a member of the original audience. This is a
       common practice in the plays of Aristophanes.

204   *There was a time when we had no Assemblies*: Praxagora seems to be referring to the rule
       of the Thirty (Tyrants), during which an oligarchy governed in Athens (404–403 BCE).

215   *our late alliance*: Praxagora is referring to the first anti-Spartan league, consisting of
       Thebes, Locris, and Athens.

222   *a new armada*: This is a hypothetical example, for the sake of argument.

224   *the Corinthians*: R. G. Ussher argues that this line refers to Corinthian disenchantment
       with its membership in the anti-Spartan league (*Aristophanes Ecclesiazusae* [Bristol Clas-
       sical Press, 1973]).

226–227 *Argives are dunces / and Hieronymus a mastermind*: It is not known to what histor-
       ical event Praxagora is referring here, though her purpose is to show the fickleness of
       Athenian policy-making. The implication is that the "Argives are dunces" because they
       opposed the peace.

229   *Thrasybulus*: In 404–403 BCE Thrasybulus led a group of exiles against the Spartan garri-
       son and the Thirty Tyrants in Athens and successfully restored democracy. In the fourth
       century BCE he worked to restore Athens to imperial power.

235   *Aesimus*: Aristophanes wants to use this Aesimus, it seems, as an example of an unsteady
       character.

253   *the Thesmophoria*: A fertility festival held in the spring in honor of the goddess Demeter
       and her daughter Persephone. It was exclusively celebrated by women, and men were for-
       bidden to witness or hear about the rites involved.

278   *the Pnyx*: The Pnyx is a hill in central Athens. It had been the site for Assemblies since 507
       BCE. Praxagora and her husband were most likely displaced during the rule of the Thirty
       (404–403 BCE).

284   *Cephalus*: This Cephalus was, as well as being a potter, a distinguished orator and advo-
       cate for democracy.

292   *Neocleides*: This Neocleides, an orator and informer, is here mocked for a physical defect,
       a common practice in Aristophanes.

332   *garlic pickles for his morning meal*: Dining on garlic is associated with rural Athenians in
       comedy.

333   *three obols*: In classical Athens, obols were made of silver, and six of them equaled a
       drachma. All male citizens could attend the Assembly. Originally they were unpaid, then

paid an obol. Agyrrhius had recently raised the payment to three obols, and since then a large crowd jostled for entry each morning.

334 *Smicythus, Draces, Charitimides*: The chorus addresses three of its members with common men's names.

377 *Cinesias the poet*: See note on "Cinesias," *Birds*, line 1400.

405–406 *the same pear . . . introduced to the Spartans*: It is unclear to what this line refers. Thrasybulus may have claimed an indisposition brought about by pears to avoid speaking in the Assembly. He may also have referred to some "blockade" against Spartans.

421 *Goddess of Childbirth*: The daughter of Zeus and Hera, Eileithyia is the goddess who presides over childbirth. Blepyrus prays to her to relieve him of his "burden."

448–449 *Antilochus, sing . . . All I had is lost*: Blepyrus here quotes from the tragedian Aeschylus's play *Myrmidons*, though he substitutes "three obols" for the "dead Patroclus."

465 *Euaeon*: Euaeon, a son of the tragedian Aeschylus, allegedly a poor speaker at the Assembly.

471 *four staters' worth*: Four staters equals sixteen drachmas, a substantial sum.

485 *Nausicydes*: This Nausicydes made his fortune as a dealer in grain and flour.

487 *the little Nicias*: Likely the grandson of the general Nicias who led the Sicilian expedition (415–413 BCE).

664 *"mine new veins of silver"*: This metaphor from mining means to "make innovations." The Athenian silver mines in Laurium had reopened in the early fourth century BCE after having been seized by the Spartans and shut down during the Peloponnesian War.

666–667 *The guiding principles in Athens . . . all that is traditional*: Blepyrus is voicing the conservative's view of Athenian politics.

714 *Lysicrates's nose*: This Lysicrates apparently has a malformed nose. He dyes his hair as well; see note below, line 819.

729 *Leucolophas and Epicurus*: We know nothing of these two men; the context suggests they are repulsive.

731 *Aristyllus*: Aristophanes elsewhere mocks Aristyllus as a coprophile.

732 *You'd reek of mint if he came up and kissed you*: This line contains a pun on mint and *minthos* (human feces) that is impossible to translate.

760 *I'll make them into dining rooms . . . podiums*: The word translated as "dining rooms" is *andrones*, which originally referred to dining halls exclusive to males. *the podiums*: Blepyrus is referring to the platforms in the law courts on which the litigants were seated.

819 *Lysicrates's hair*: The pot, made black from work in the kitchen, is compared to the dyed hair of a certain Lysicrates.

841 *Hieron the auctioneer*: Nothing is known about this Hieron.

901 *Antisthenes*: This Antisthenes apparently suffered from chronic constipation.

904–905 *Callimachus / the chorus master*: The point here seems to be that this Callimachus was a poor man, in contrast to the affluent Callias.

906 *Callias*: Dissolute and preyed on by parasites, Callias had reduced his fortune from two hundred talents to two.

910–911 *the mandate that they passed / regarding salt*: Salt was imported to Athens from Megara. The decree mentioned here, it seems, was intended to bring the price down.

912 *we voted out those copper coins*: There was a shortage of silver in Athens when the Spartans, on the advice of Alcibiades, captured the silver mines at Laurium. They were eventually reopened in the fourth century BCE.

921 *Heurippides*: This Heurippides had apparently gotten a tax passed in the Assembly that took 2.5 percent to raise five hundred talents. Subsequently, it seems, this tax proved unpopular.

944 *Smoeus*: This Smoeus, about whom nothing more is known, seems to have had a predilection for cunnilingus.

945 *Geron*: Geron, about whom nothing specific is known, seems to have, in old age, acted like a young man.

986–987 *Muses, come / into my lips*: The First Old Woman here parodies the invocation of a formal kletic hymn, or hymn to summon a deity.

988 *risqué Ionian tune*: Greek-colonial Ionia in Asia Minor evoked luxury and wantonness.

1025 *the Ionian tool*: Athens imported dildos from Miletus in Ionia; see note on "those five-inch dildos," *Lysistrata*, line 115.

1029–1030 *the way that all / the Methymnan women do*: The women of Lesbos had a reputation in antiquity not for lesbianism but for fellatio. To avoid confusion, I have translated "Lesbians" (people of Lesbos) with the adjective for the largest city on Lesbos: Methymnus.

1059 *Charixena's hour*: A musician and writer of erotica, Charixena is a legendary figure like Coesyra (see *Clouds*, line 57). The implication of this sentence seems to be "times have changed."

1111 *Right now we're trying cases under twenty*: Epigenes uses the language of the (infamously slow) law courts to try to defer his sexual obligation. He means "sixty" and "twenty" as ages, but the joke is that legal cases were determined to be more or less serious based on the amount of money involved.

1149 *Procrustes*: Procrustes, a sadistic highwayman of Eleusis, stretched his victims out to the full length of a bed.

1152–1153 *to transact / business of greater value than a bushel*: This law had previously applied to women. Praxagora has turned the tables.

1155 *a businessman's exemption*: Epigenes hopes to be exempt from his sexual obligations in the same way that merchants were exempt from military service.

1158 *the strength of Diomedes*: This is a proverbial phrase expressing ultimate compulsion.

1161–1163 *Drape the bed . . . a water jug*: Epigenes compares the First Old Woman's bed to a funeral bier. Marjoram was customarily spread out under the body, and the "four boughs" would eventually serve for its immolation. The ribbons would adorn the body, the flasks were for oil, and the water jug was for visitors to purify themselves upon leaving the house.

1175 *Oedipuses*: Oedipus, in addition to killing his father Laius, engenders children on his mother Jocasta.

1190 *Empusa*: An Empusa is a lustful female monster, an aspect of the goddess Hecate. Redness (from the blister) is associated with this sort of monster; see Aristophanes's *Frogs* 293.

1205 *Great Heracles! Great Pan! O Corybantes!*: On seeing the Third Old Woman, Epigenes invokes the hero Heracles, who fought monsters; Pan, who excites panic; and the Corybantes, who are ecstatic worshippers of Cybele.

1206 *O Dioscuri!*: The Dioscuri are Castor and Pollux, the twin sons of Leda and Zeus.

1227 *Cannonus's decree*: This decree insists that "all who harm the Athenian people be bound and face the charge in court" (Xenophon, *Hellenica* 1.7).

1232 *potent bulbs*: These bulbs, identified as *Muscari comosum*, were regarded as an aphrodisiac.

1301–1303 *Let the wiser ones remember . . . vote for me*: These lines are addressed to the judges of the dramatic competition. Five of their verdicts were chosen at random to decide the victorious production. Whether for humor or because the judges were actually susceptible to bias, Aristophanes here encourages them to favor his play.

ABOUT THE AUTHOR

Aristophanes was the most celebrated comic playwright in fifth-century BCE Athens. By his own account, he went bald at a young age.

ABOUT THE TRANSLATOR

Aaron Poochigian earned a PhD in classics from the University of Minnesota and an MFA in poetry from Columbia University. He is the translator of, among other classical works, Sappho's poetry (published under the title *Stung with Love*), Apollonius's *Jason and the Argonauts*, and Euripides's *Bacchae*, and has published two books of poetry—*The Cosmic Purr* and *Manhattanite*—and a novel-in-verse, *Mr. Either/Or*. His poems have appeared in such publications as *Best American Poetry*, the *Paris Review*, and *Poetry*. He lives in New York.